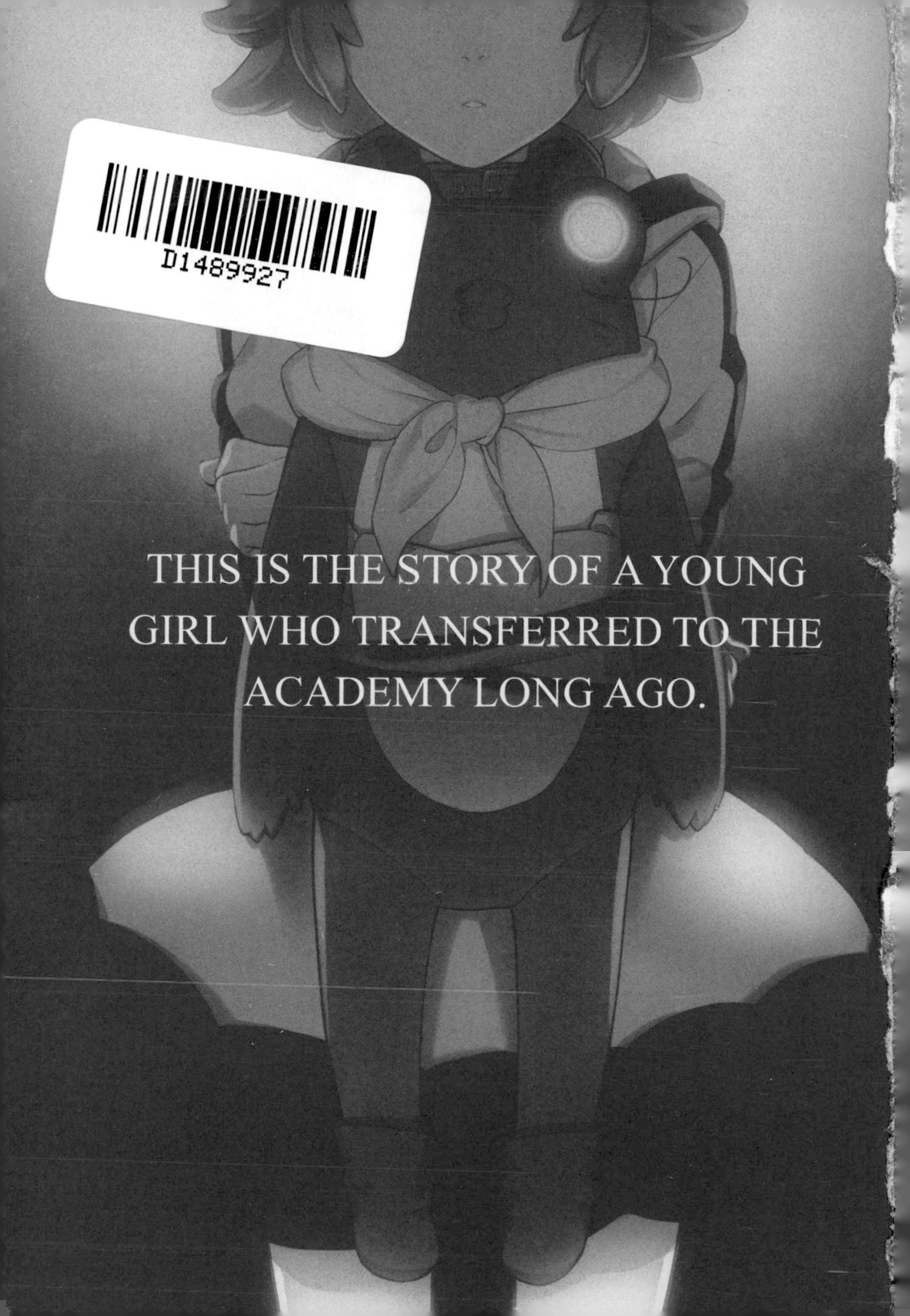
THIS IS THE STORY OF A YOUNG GIRL WHO TRANSFERRED TO THE ACADEMY LONG AGO.

#10 THE GIRL IN THE NIGHT

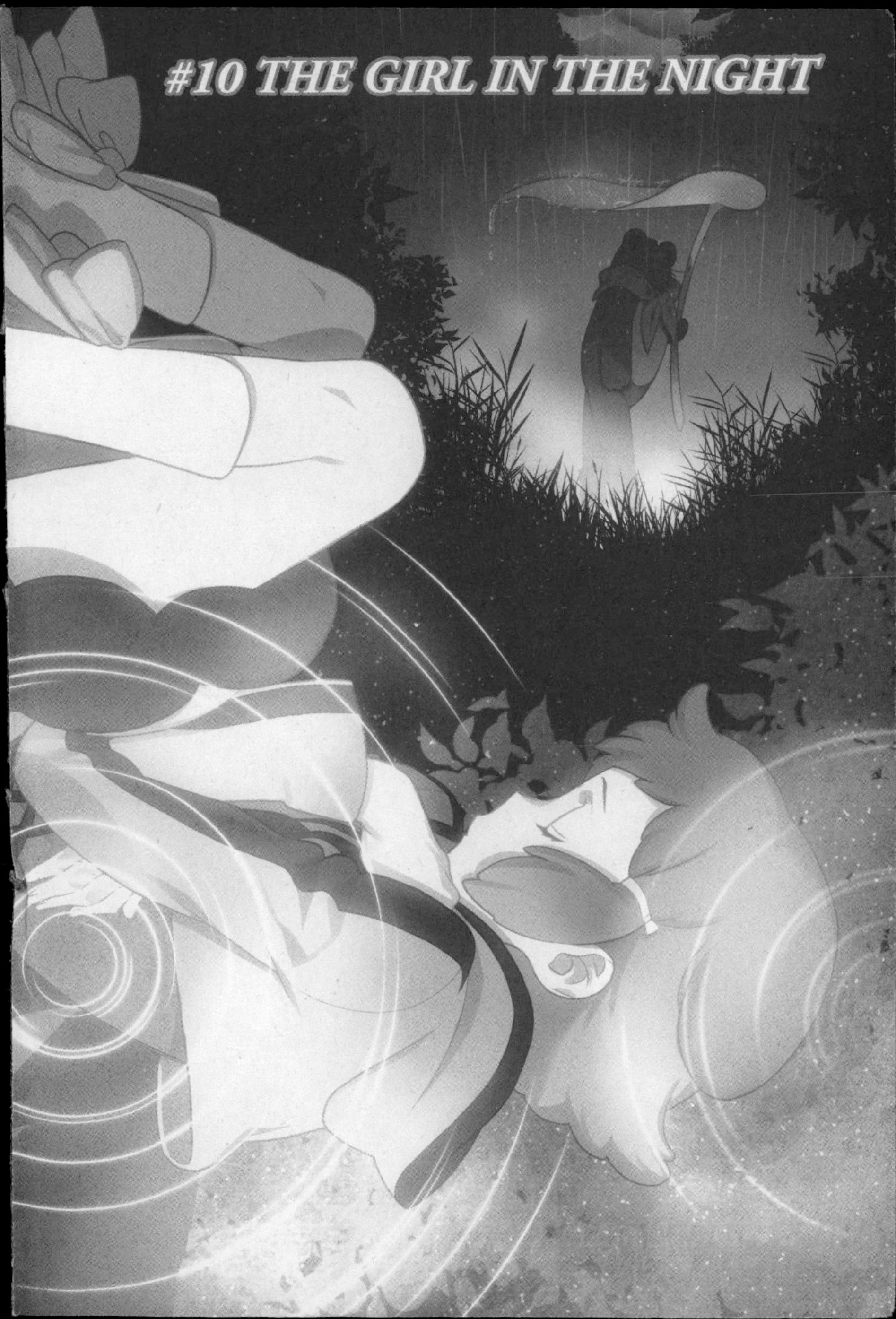

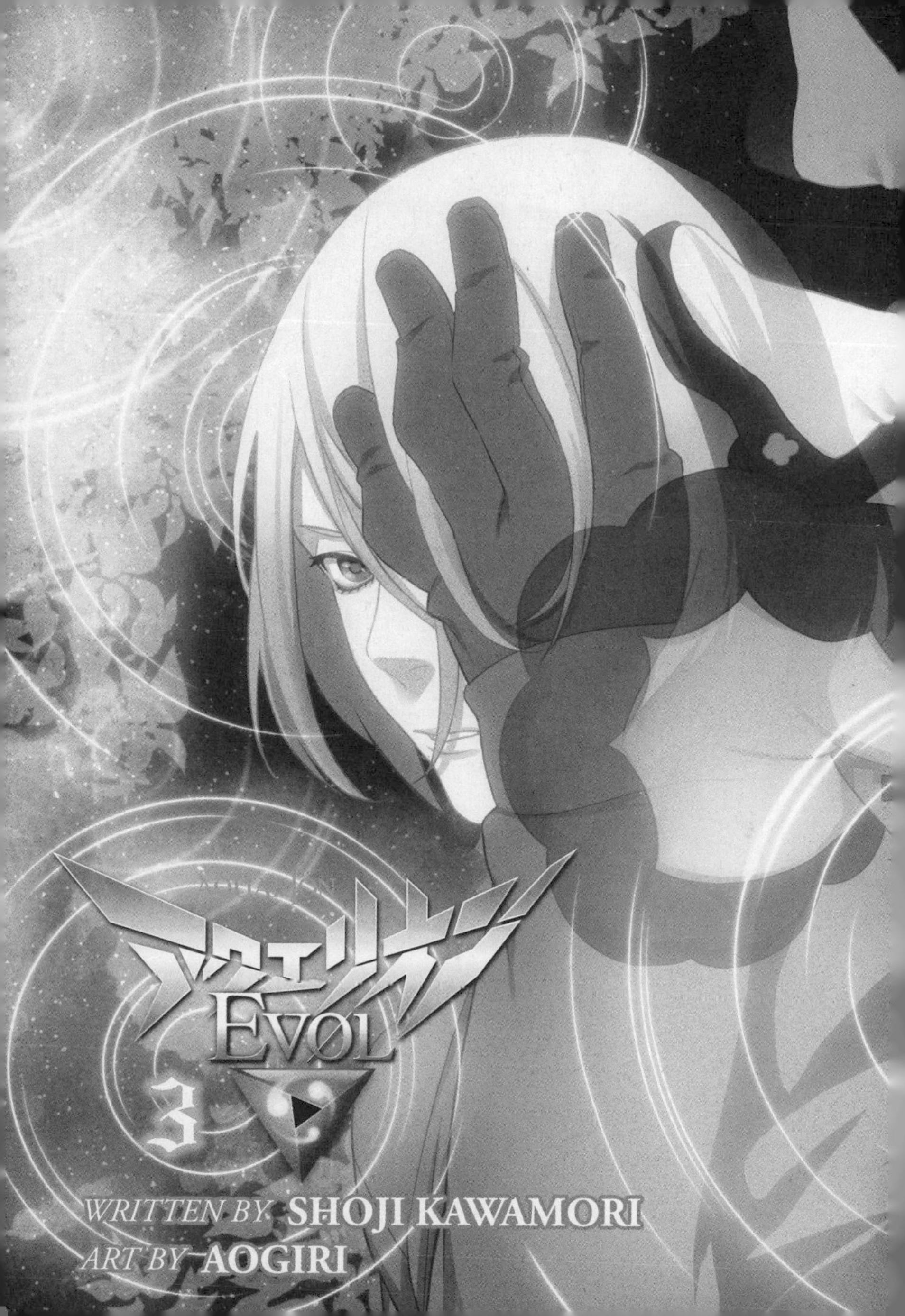
EVOL
3
WRITTEN BY: SHOJI KAWAMORI
ART BY AOGIRI

AQUARION

EVOL

3

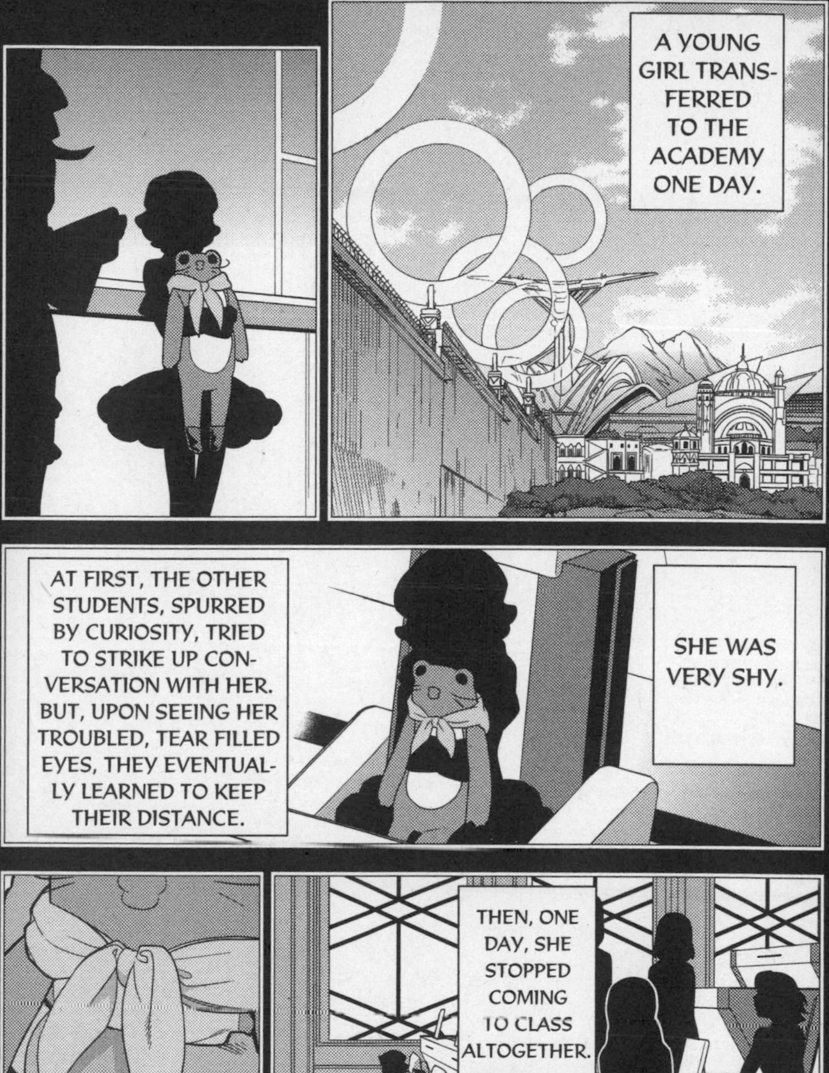
A YOUNG GIRL TRANSFERRED TO THE ACADEMY ONE DAY.
SHE WAS VERY SHY.
AT FIRST, THE OTHER STUDENTS, SPURRED BY CURIOSITY, TRIED TO STRIKE UP CONVERSATION WITH HER. BUT, UPON SEEING HER TROUBLED, TEAR FILLED EYES, THEY EVENTUALLY LEARNED TO KEEP THEIR DISTANCE.
THEN, ONE DAY, SHE STOPPED COMING TO CLASS ALTOGETHER.

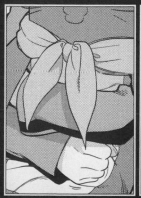

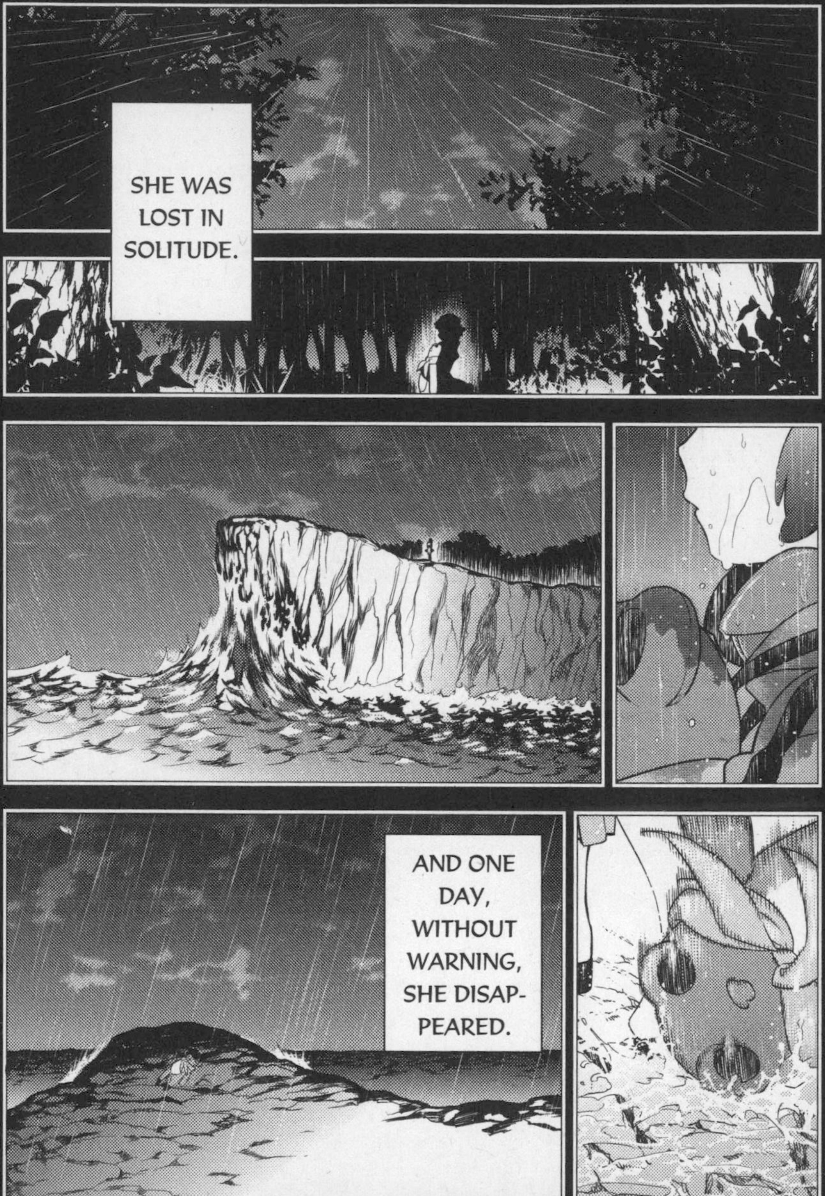
SHE WAS LOST IN SOLITUDE.
AND ONE DAY, WITHOUT WARNING, SHE DISAP-PEARED.

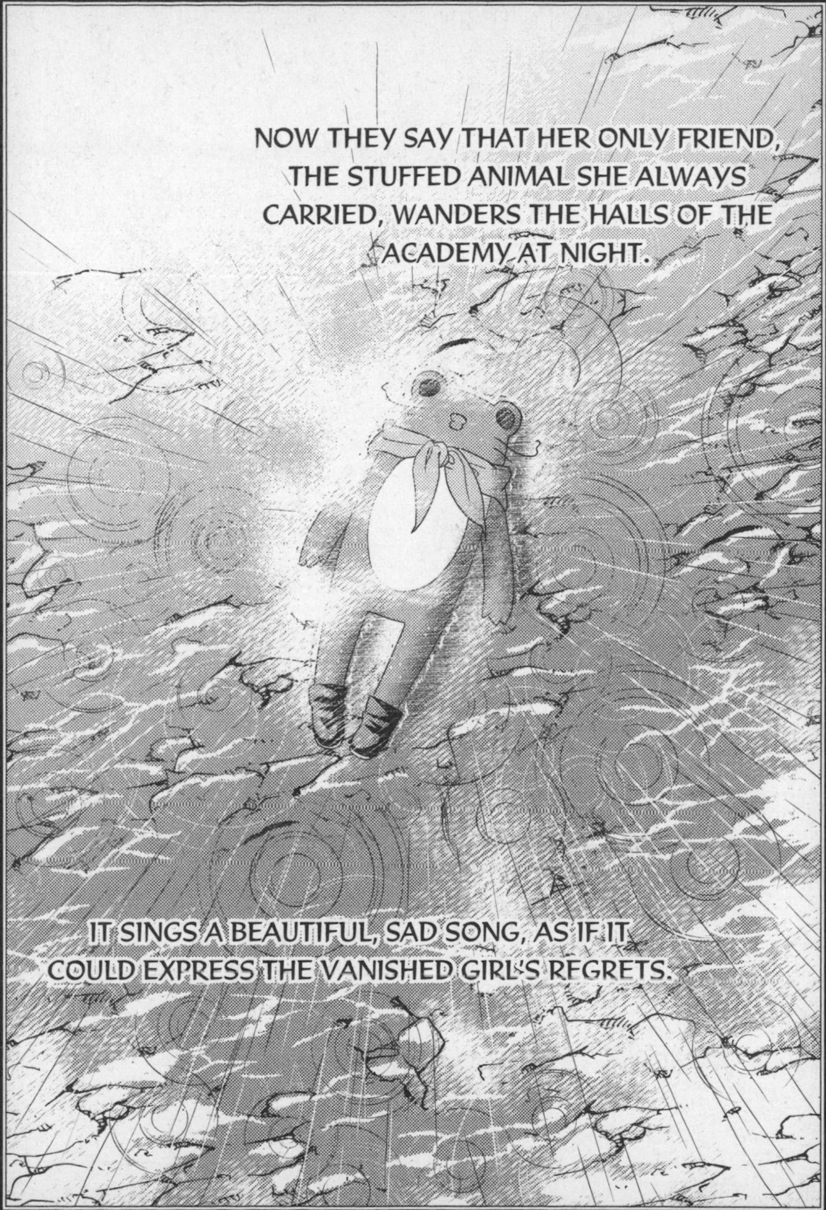
NOW THEY SAY THAT HER ONLY FRIEND, THE STUFFED ANIMAL SHE ALWAYS CARRIED, WANDERS THE HALLS OF THE ACADEMY AT NIGHT.
IT SINGS A BEAUTIFUL, SAD SONG, AS IF IT COULD EXPRESS THE VANISHED GIRL'S REGRETS.

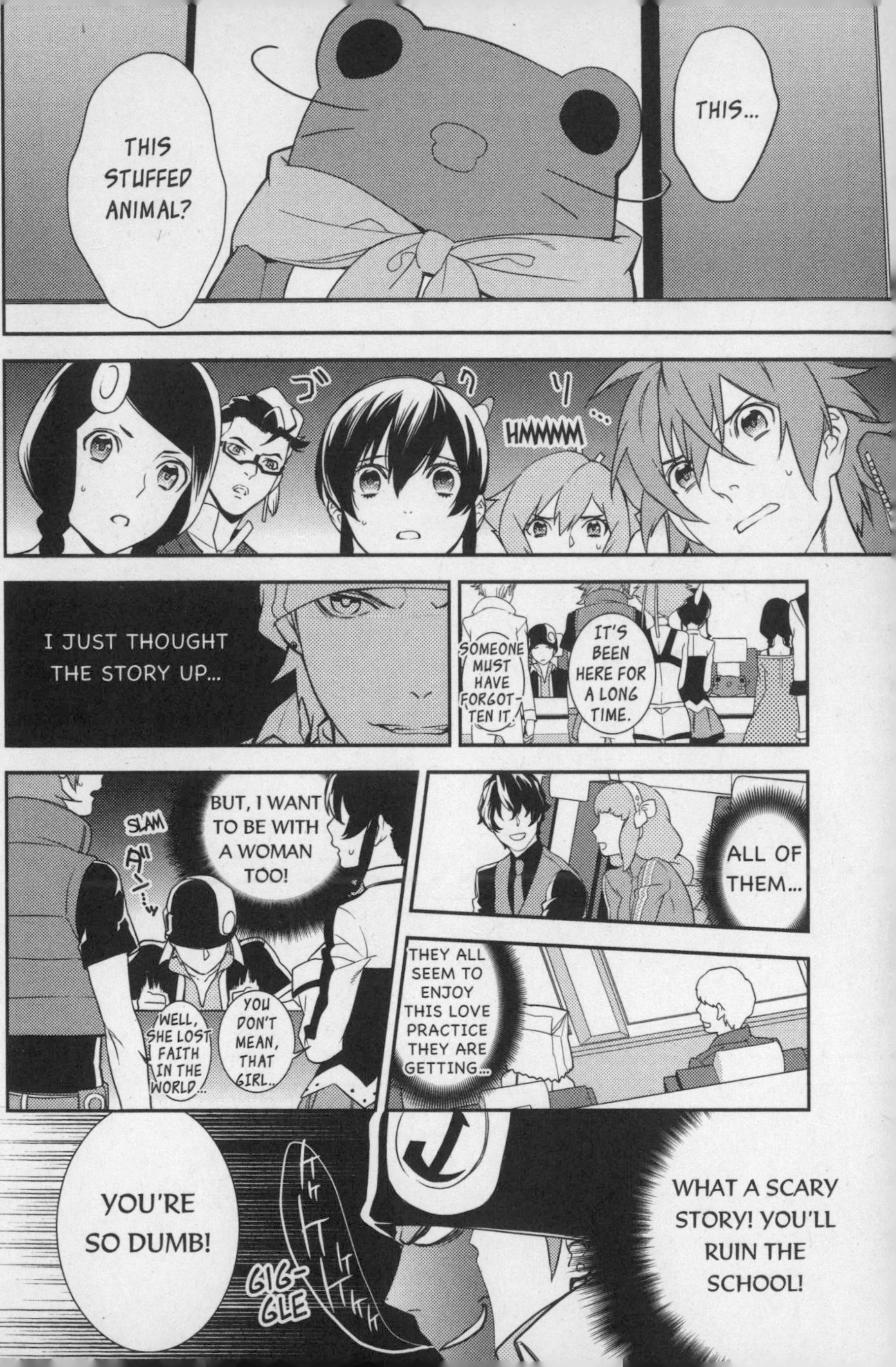
THIS...
THIS STUFFED ANIMAL?
HMMMM
IT'S BEEN HERE FOR A LONG TIME.
SOMEONE MUST HAVE FORGOT-TEN IT.
I JUST THOUGHT THE STORY UP...
ALL OF THEM...
THEY ALL SEEM TO ENJOY THIS LOVE PRACTICE THEY ARE GETTING...
BUT, I WANT TO BE WITH A WOMAN TOO!
SLAM
YOU DON'T MEAN, THAT GIRL...
WELL, SHE LOST FAITH IN THE WORLD...
WHAT A SCARY STORY! YOU'LL RUIN THE SCHOOL!
GIG-GLE
YOU'RE SO DUMB!

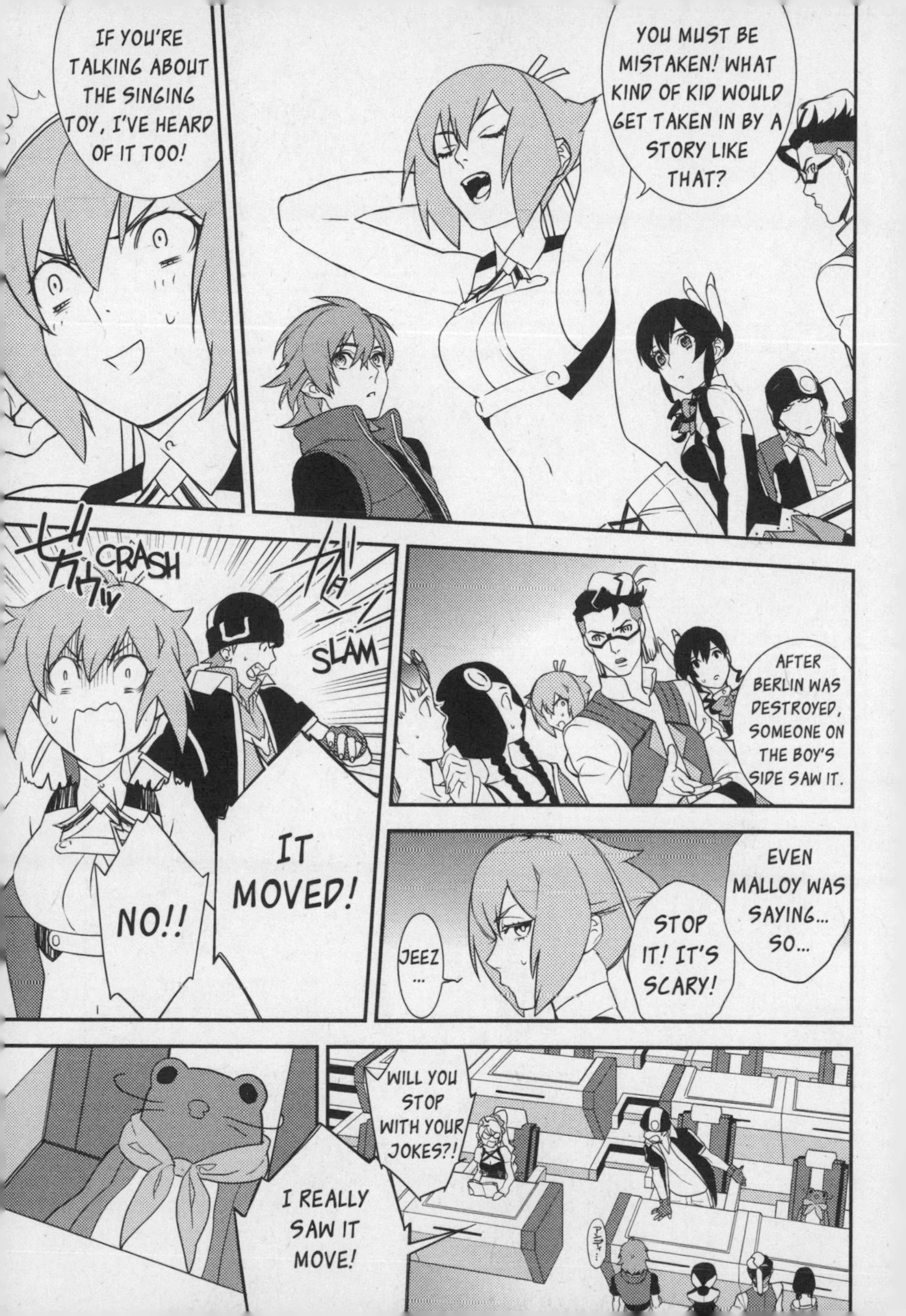
YOU MUST BE MISTAKEN! WHAT KIND OF KID WOULD GET TAKEN IN BY A STORY LIKE THAT?
IF YOU'RE TALKING ABOUT THE SINGING TOY, I'VE HEARD OF IT TOO!
AFTER BERLIN WAS DESTROYED, SOMEONE ON THE BOY'S SIDE SAW IT.
EVEN MALLOY WAS SAYING... SO...
STOP IT! IT'S SCARY!
JEEZ ...
SLAM
CRASH
IT MOVED!
NO!!
WILL YOU STOP WITH YOUR JOKES?!
I REALLY SAW IT MOVE!

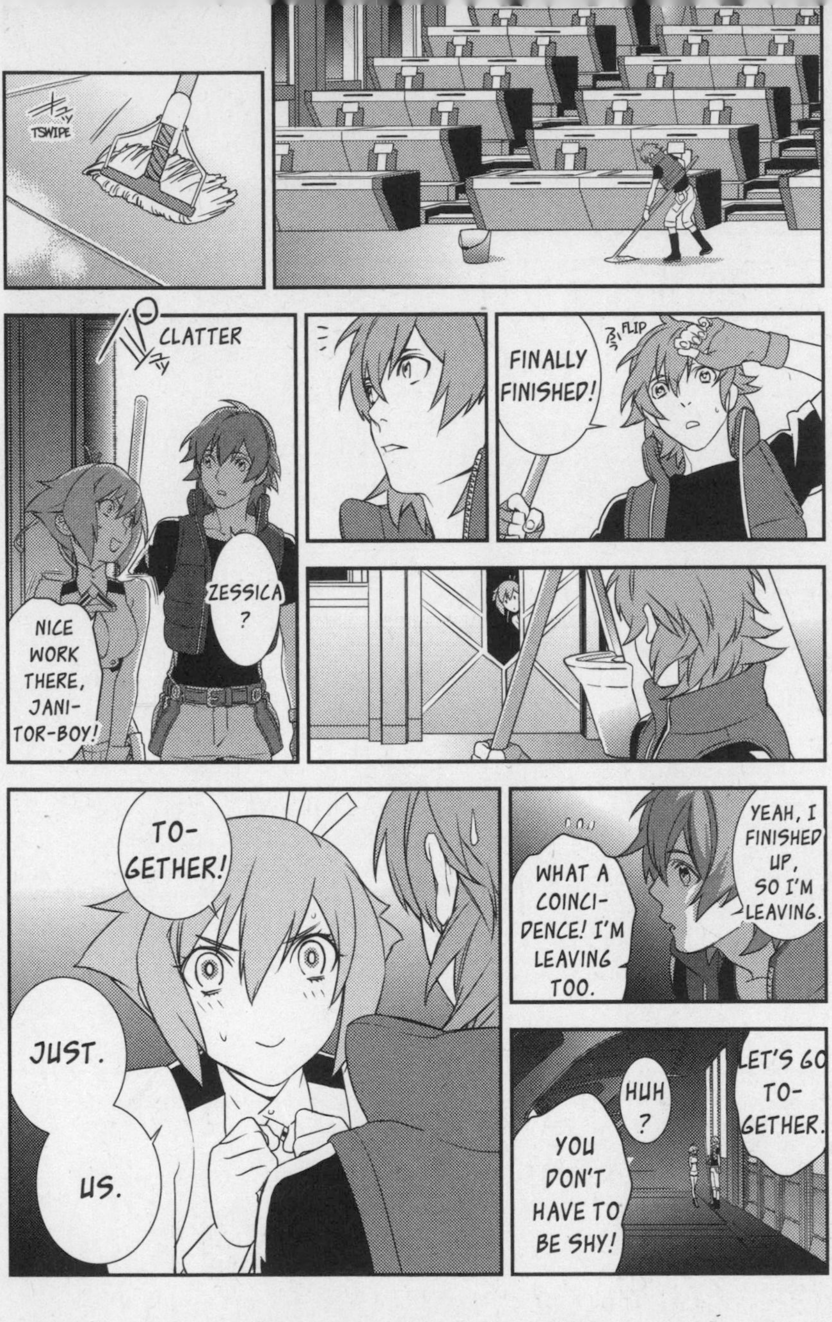
TSWIPE
FLIP
FINALLY FINISHED!
CLATTER
ZESSICA?
NICE WORK THERE, JANI-TOR-BOY!
YEAH, I FINISHED UP, SO I'M LEAVING.
WHAT A COINCI-DENCE! I'M LEAVING TOO.
LET'S GO TO-GETHER.
HUH?
YOU DON'T HAVE TO BE SHY!
TO-GETHER!
JUST.
US.

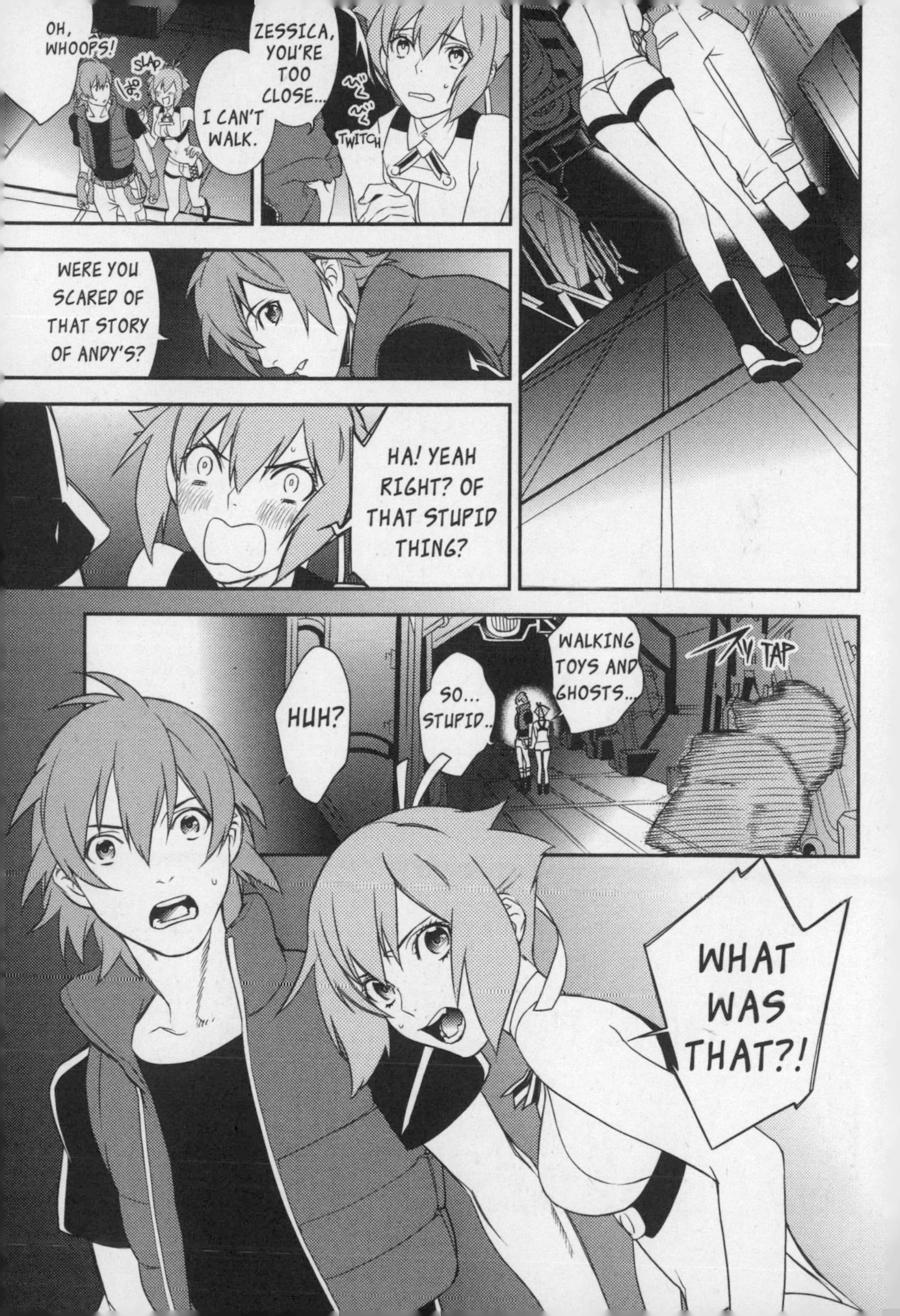
ZESSICA, YOU'RE TOO CLOSE...
I CAN'T WALK.
TWITCH
OH, WHOOPS!
SLAP
WERE YOU SCARED OF THAT STORY OF ANDY'S?
HA! YEAH RIGHT? OF THAT STUPID THING?
TAP
WALKING TOYS AND GHOSTS...
SO... STUPID..
HUH?
WHAT WAS THAT?!

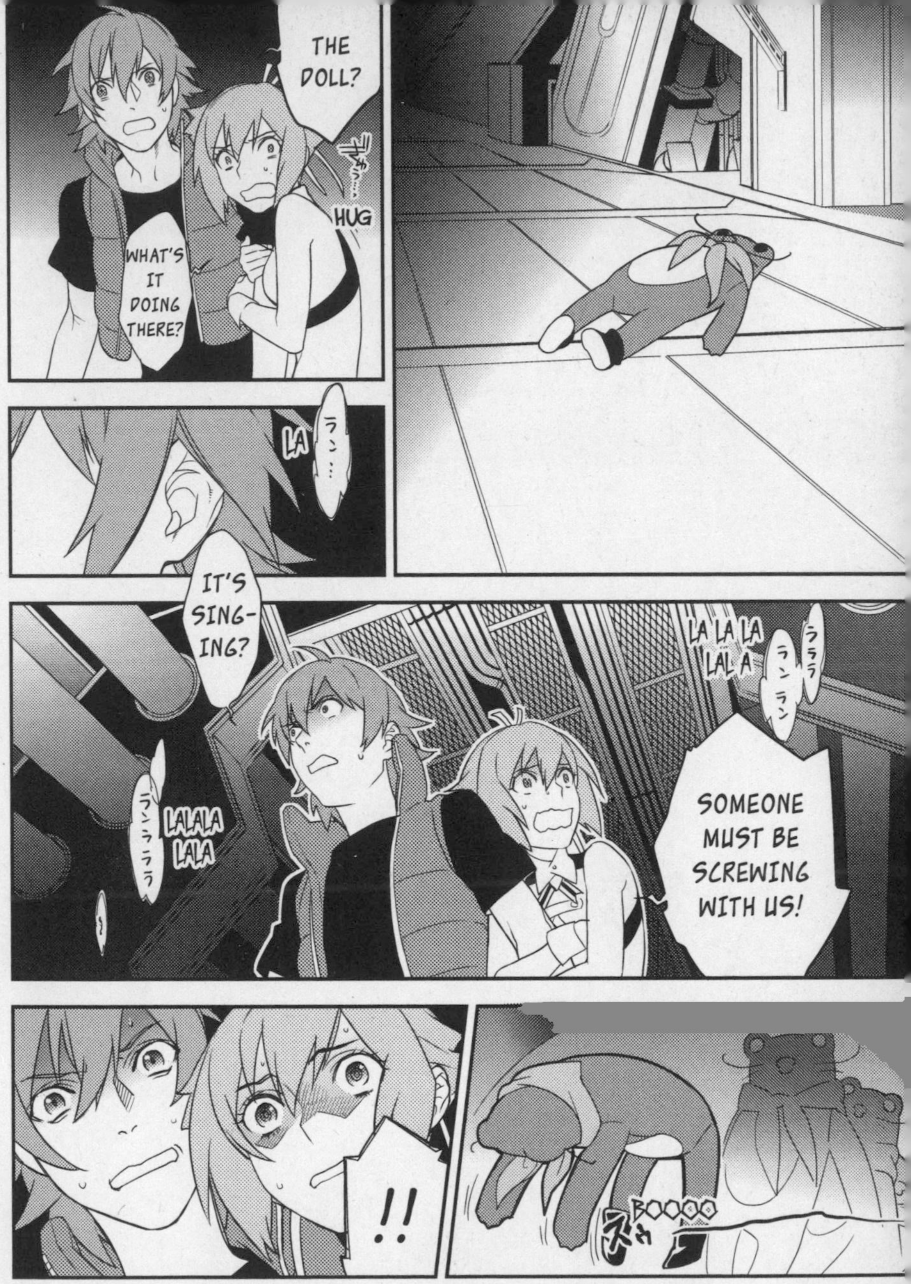
THE DOLL?
HUG
WHAT'S IT DOING THERE?
LA
ラン…
ラララ ランラン
LA LA LA LAL A
SOMEONE MUST BE SCREWING WITH US!
IT'S SINGING?
ランララ
LALALA LALA
BOOOO
!!

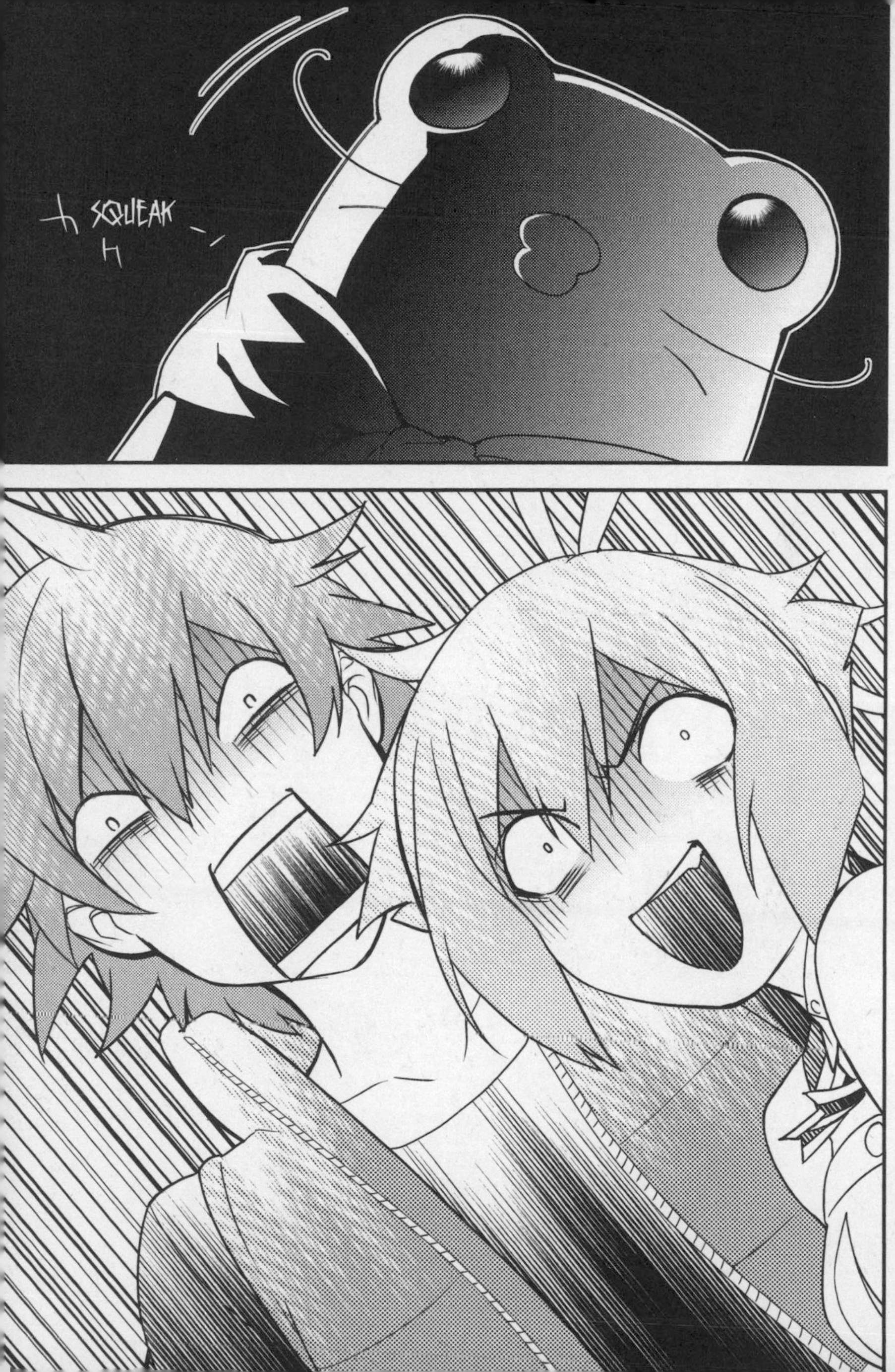
SQUEAK

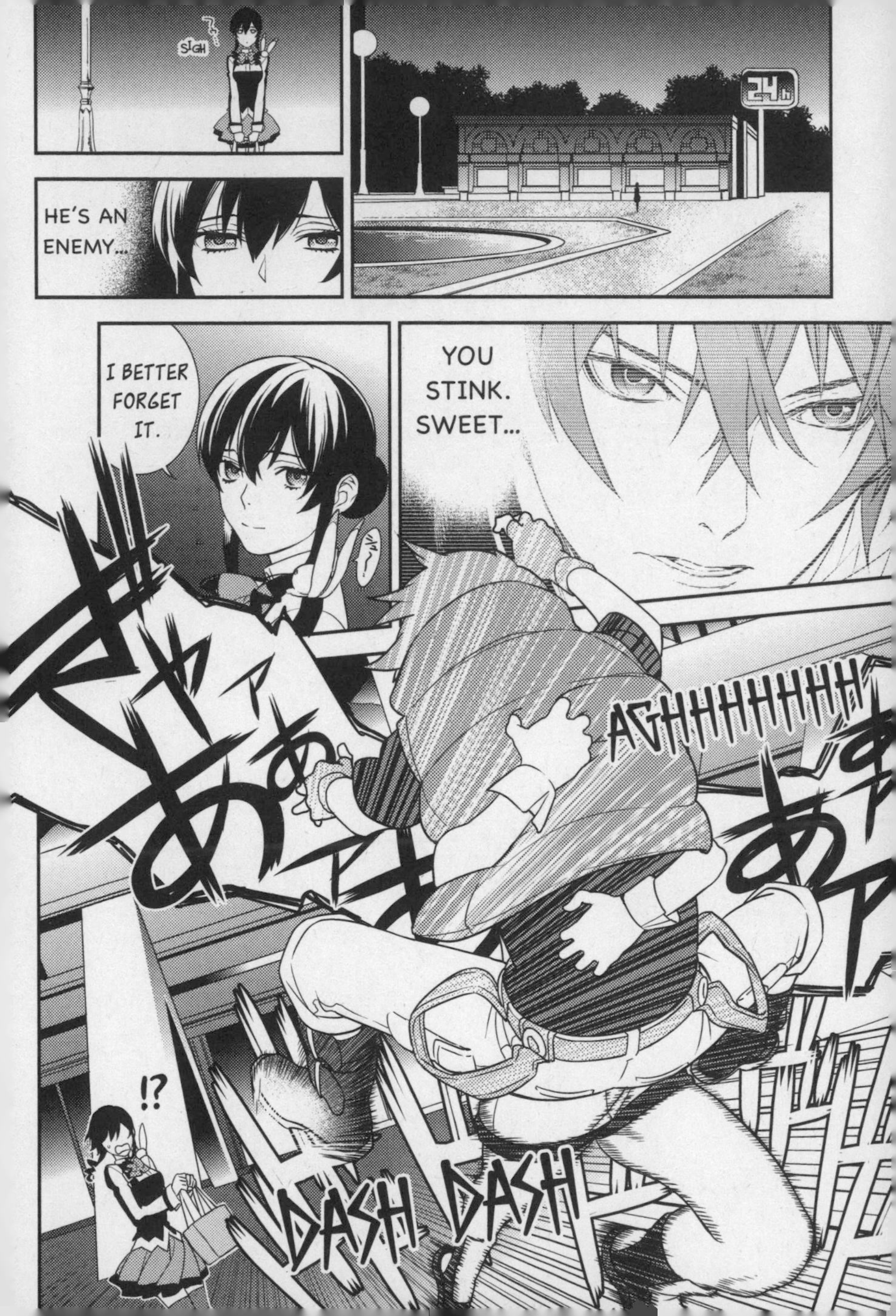
24h
SIGH
HE'S AN ENEMY...
YOU STINK. SWEET...
I BETTER FORGET IT.
AGHHHHHHHH
!?
DASH DASH

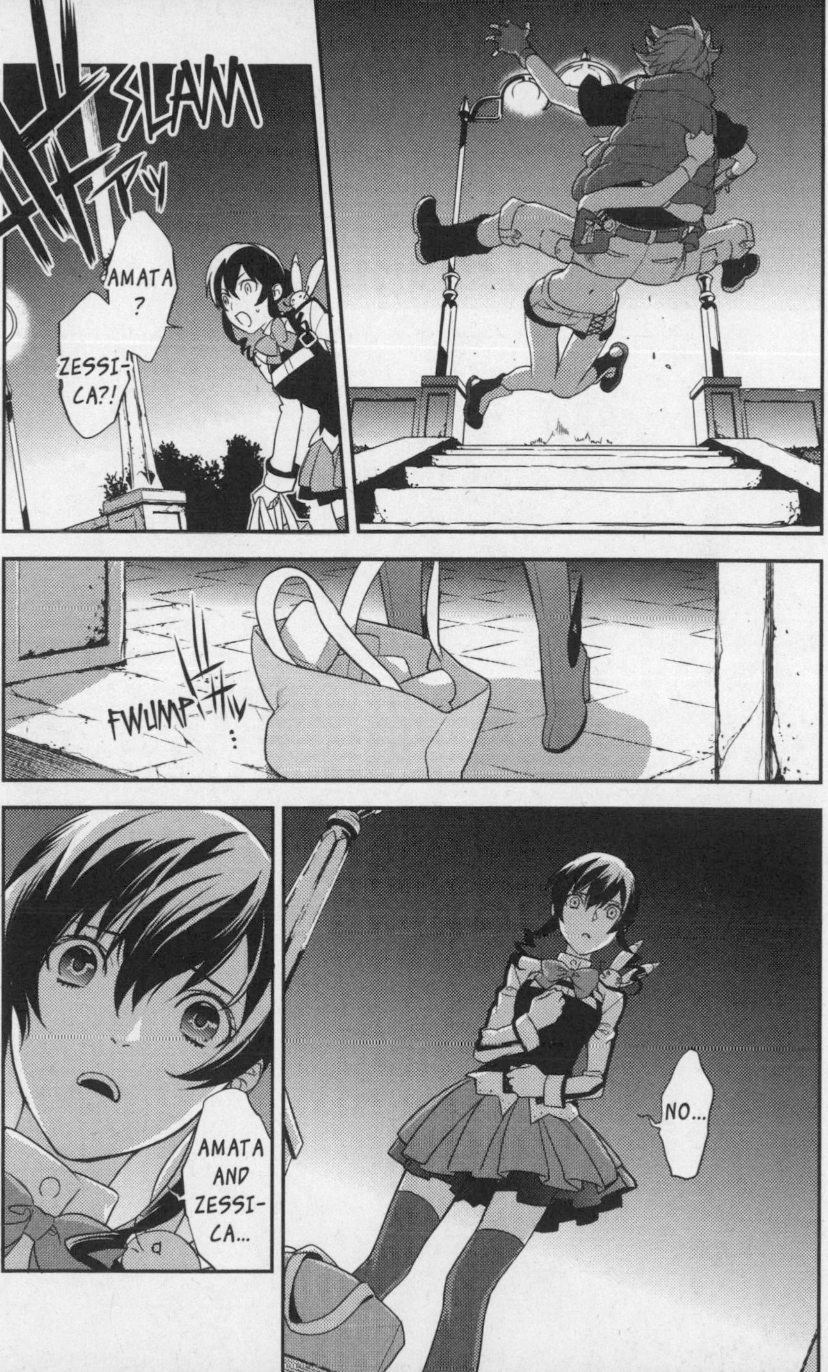
SLAM
AMATA?
ZESSICA?!
FWUMP
NO...
AMATA AND ZESSICA...

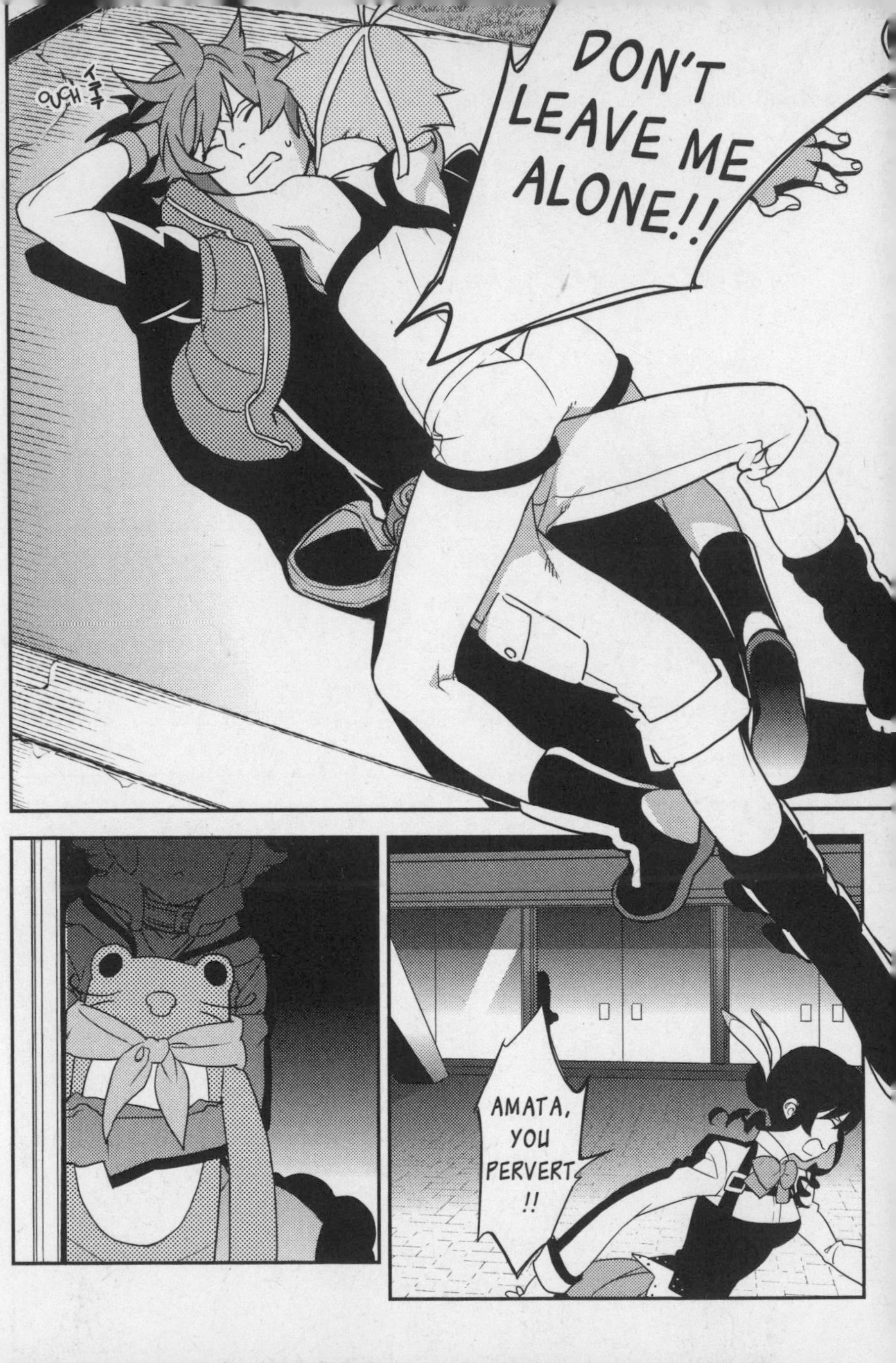
OUCH
イテテ
DON'T LEAVE ME ALONE!!
AMATA, YOU PERVERT!!

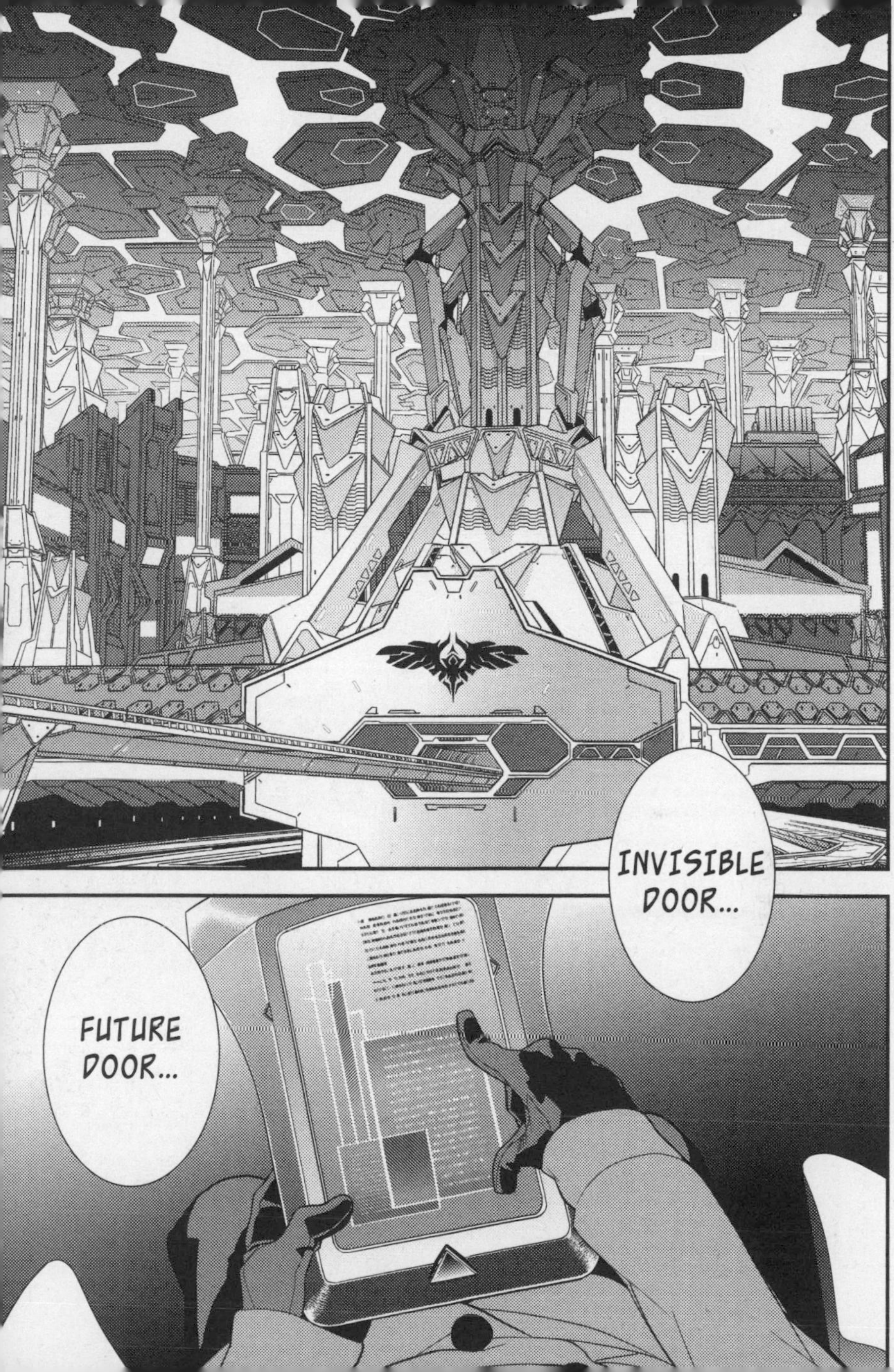
INVISIBLE DOOR...
FUTURE DOOR...

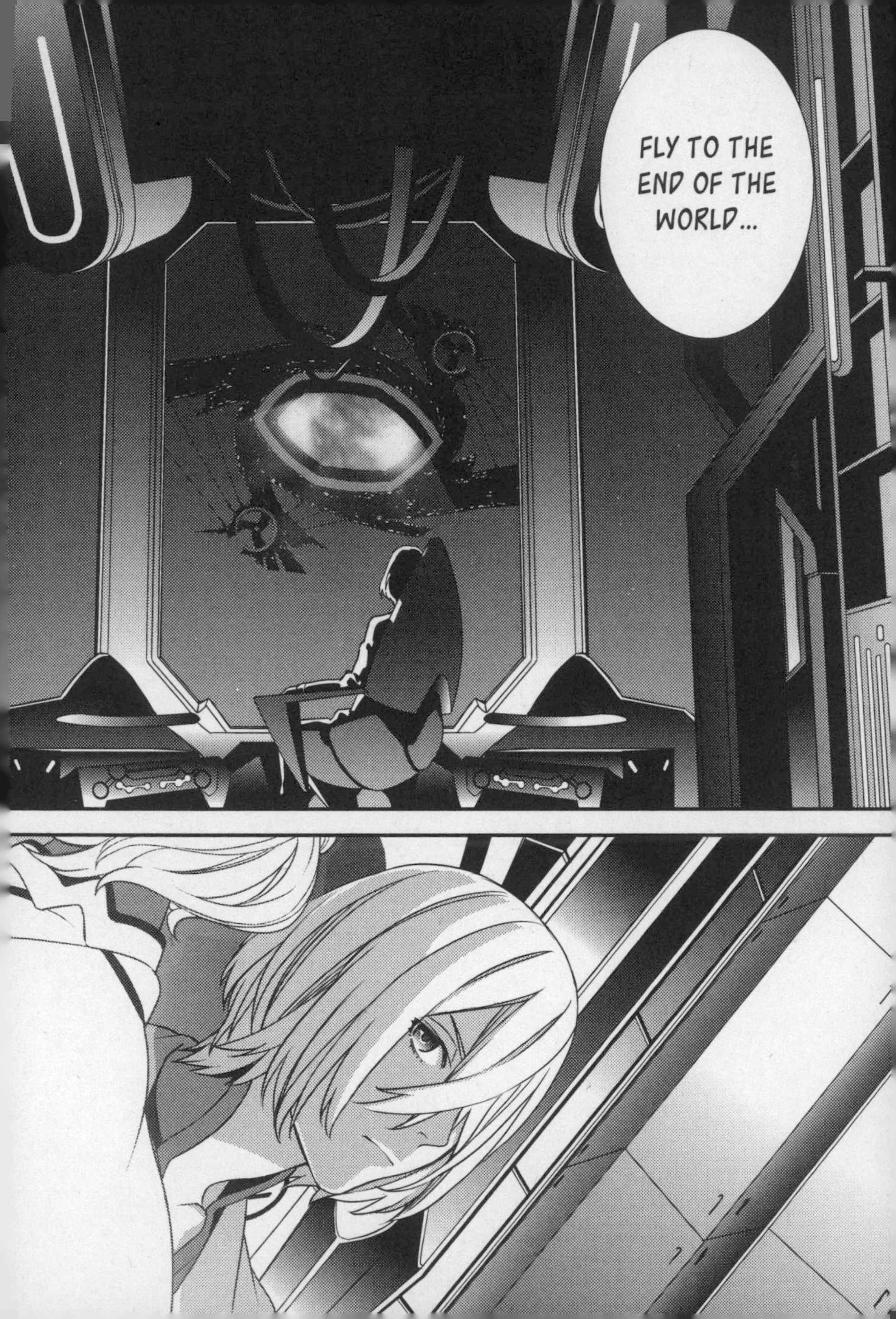
FLY TO THE END OF THE WORLD...

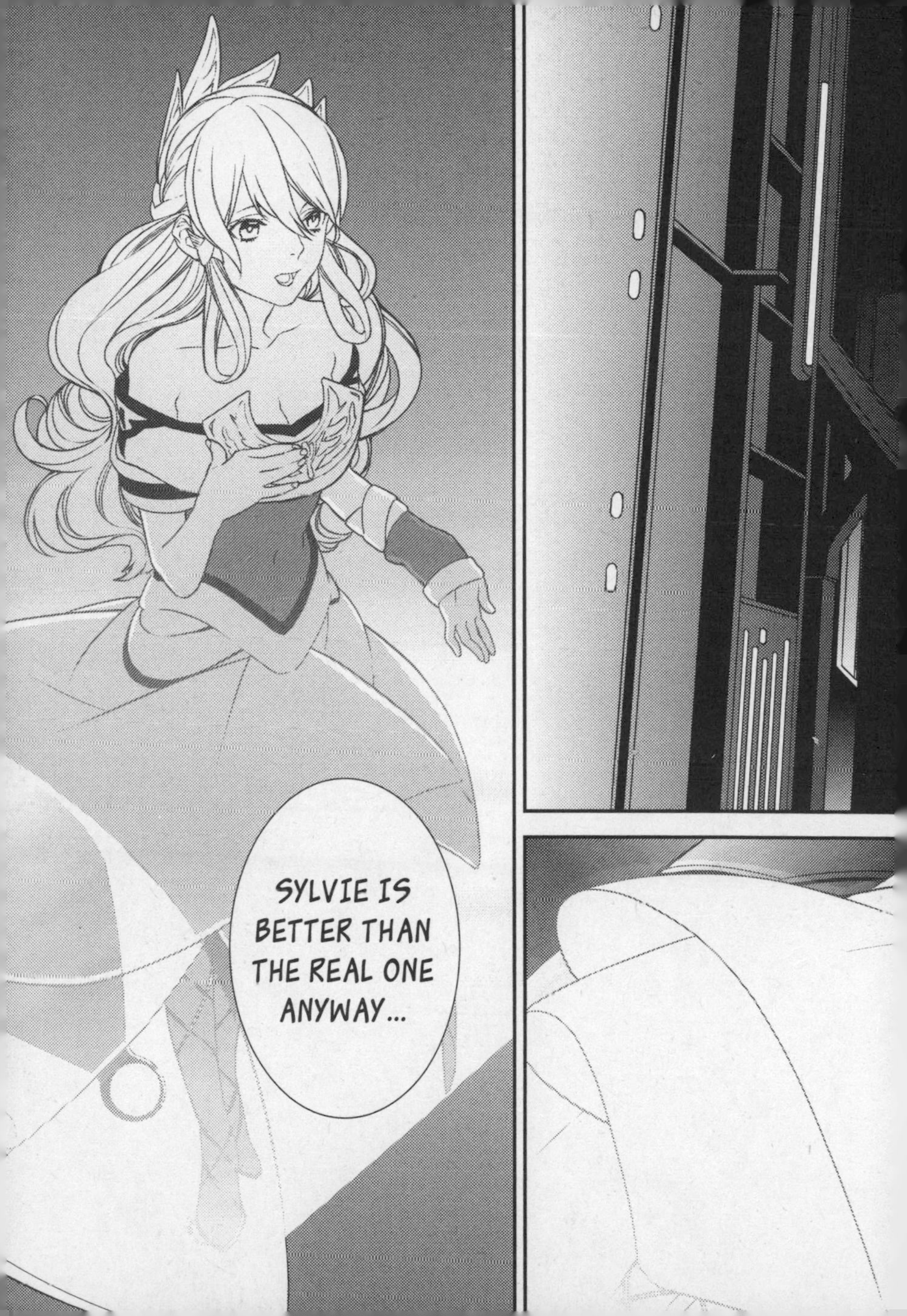
SYLVIE IS BETTER THAN THE REAL ONE ANYWAY...

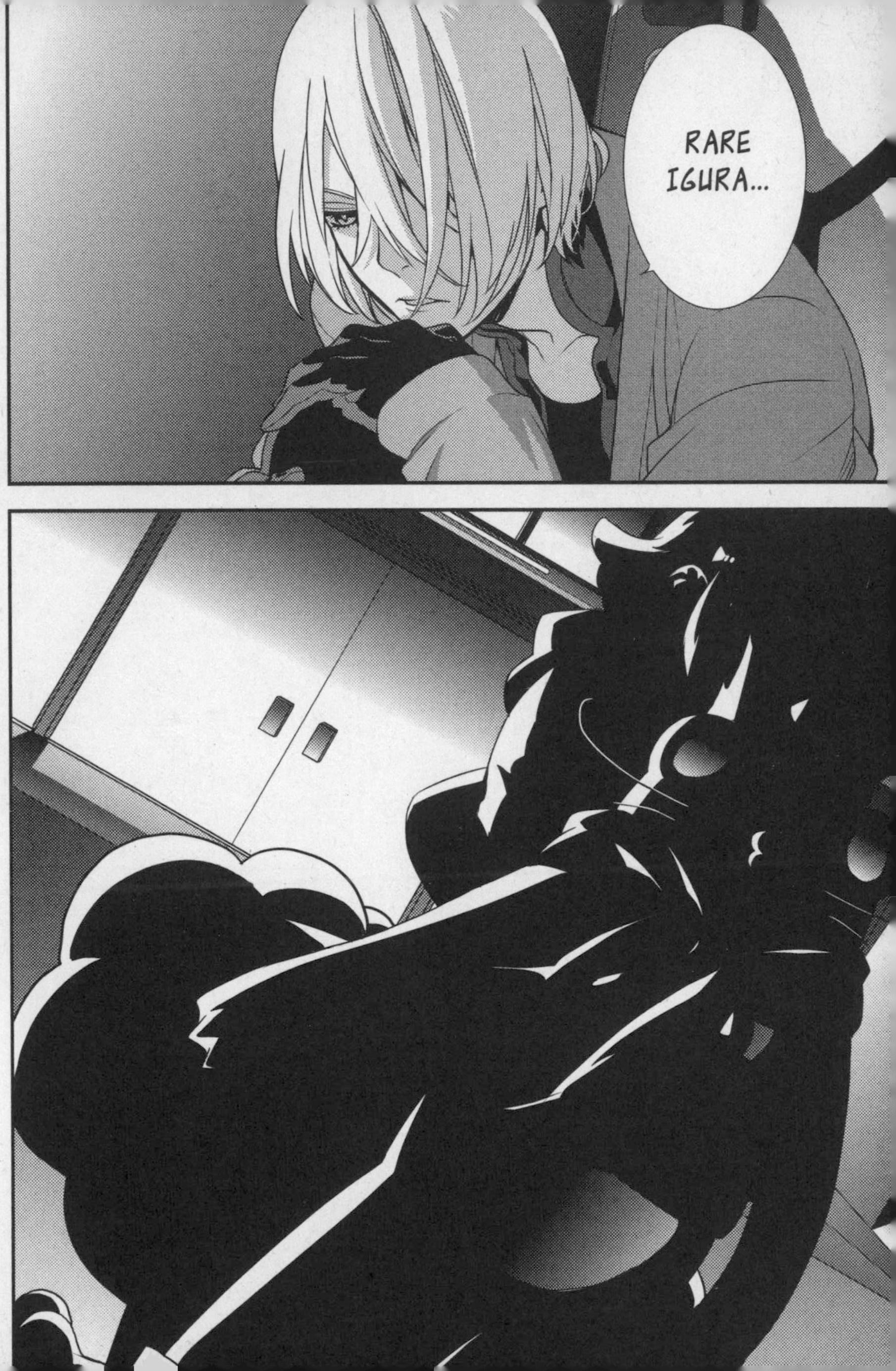
RARE IGURA...

#11 HIDDEN HEART

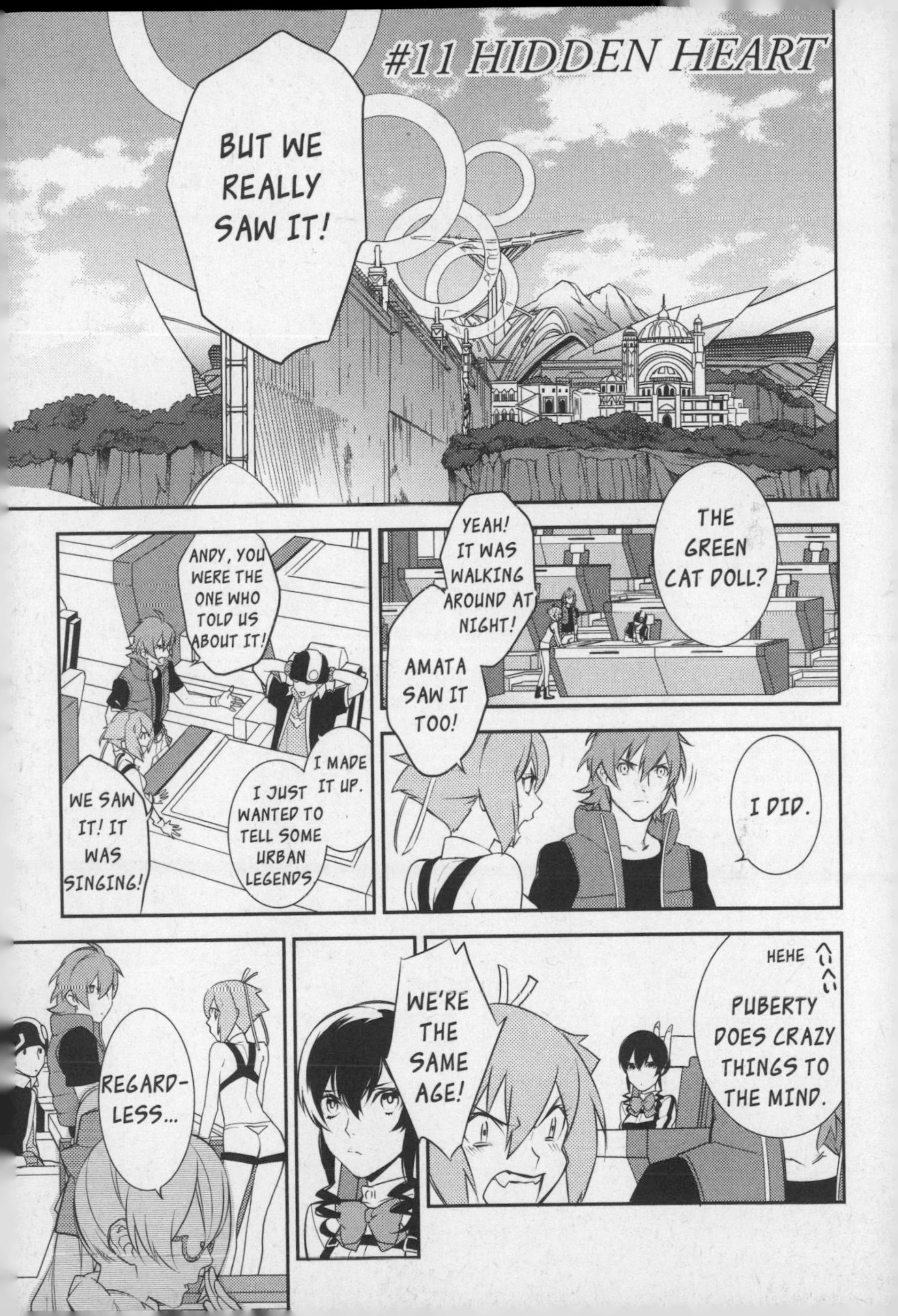
BUT WE REALLY SAW IT!
THE GREEN CAT DOLL?
YEAH! IT WAS WALKING AROUND AT NIGHT!
AMATA SAW IT TOO!
I DID.
ANDY, YOU WERE THE ONE WHO TOLD US ABOUT IT!
I MADE IT UP.
I JUST WANTED TO TELL SOME URBAN LEGENDS.
WE SAW IT! IT WAS SINGING!
HEHE
PUBERTY DOES CRAZY THINGS TO THE MIND.
WE'RE THE SAME AGE!
REGARD-LESS...

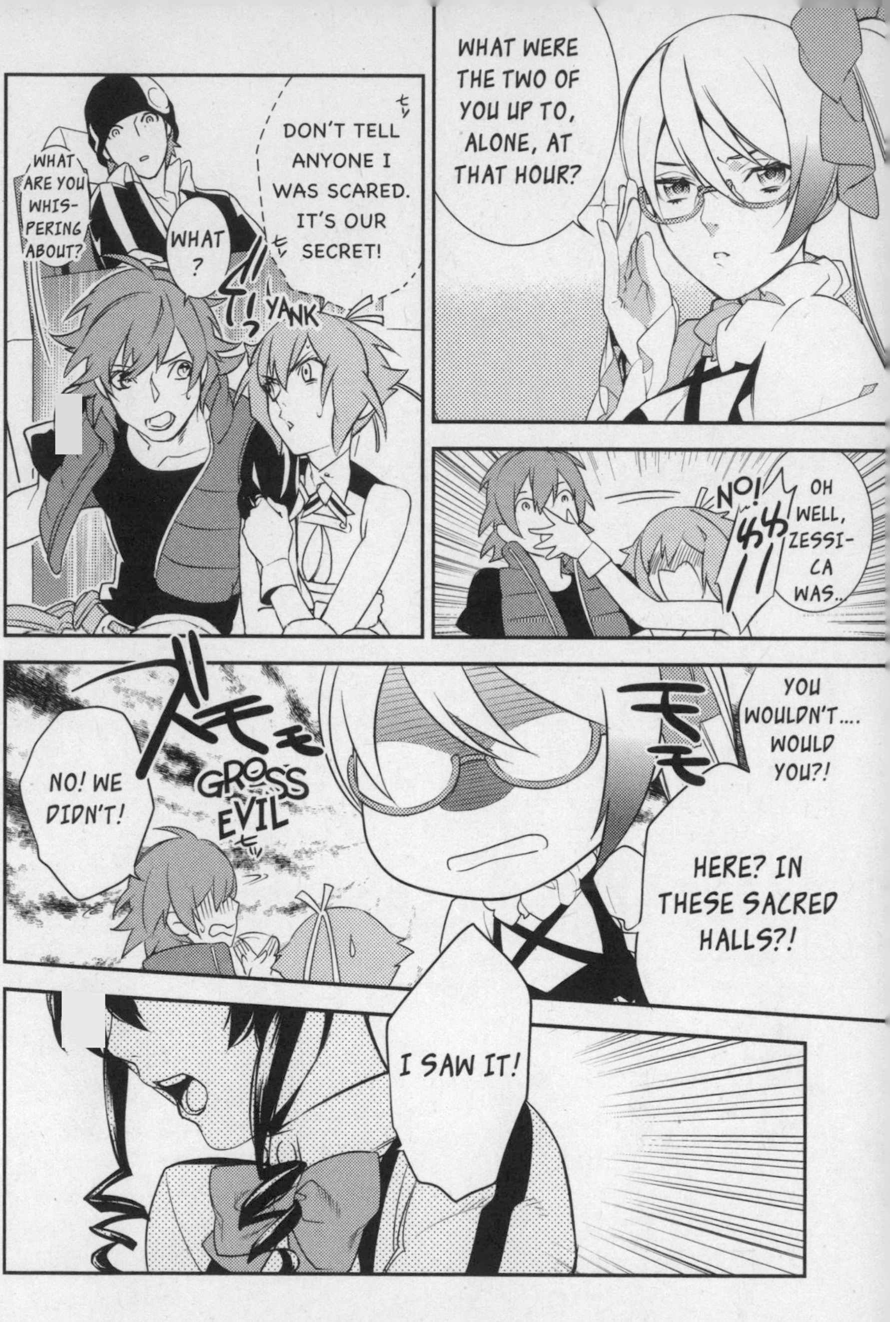
WHAT WERE THE TWO OF YOU UP TO, ALONE, AT THAT HOUR?
NO!
OH WELL, ZESSI- CA WAS..
DON'T TELL ANYONE I WAS SCARED. IT'S OUR SECRET!
WHAT ARE YOU WHIS- PERING ABOUT?
WHAT?
YANK
YOU WOULDN'T.... WOULD YOU?!
HERE? IN THESE SACRED HALLS?!
GROSS
EVIL
NO! WE DIDN'T!
I SAW IT!

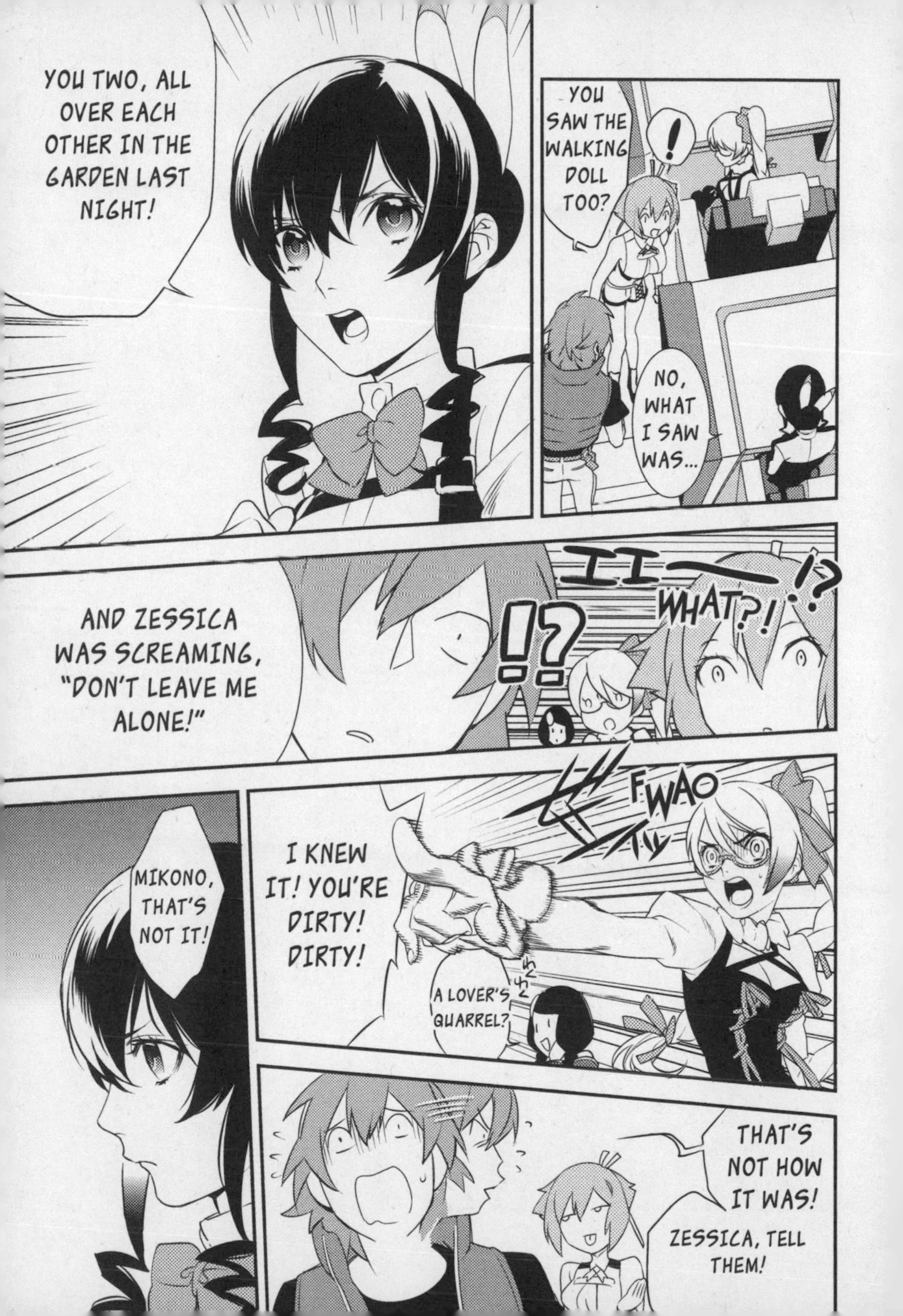

YOU SAW THE WALKING DOLL TOO?
!
NO, WHAT I SAW WAS...
YOU TWO, ALL OVER EACH OTHER IN THE GARDEN LAST NIGHT!
エエ―!?
WHAT?!
!?
AND ZESSICA WAS SCREAMING, "DON'T LEAVE ME ALONE!"
FWAO
I KNEW IT! YOU'RE DIRTY! DIRTY!
A LOVER'S QUARREL?
THAT'S NOT HOW IT WAS!
ZESSICA, TELL THEM!
MIKONO, THAT'S NOT IT!

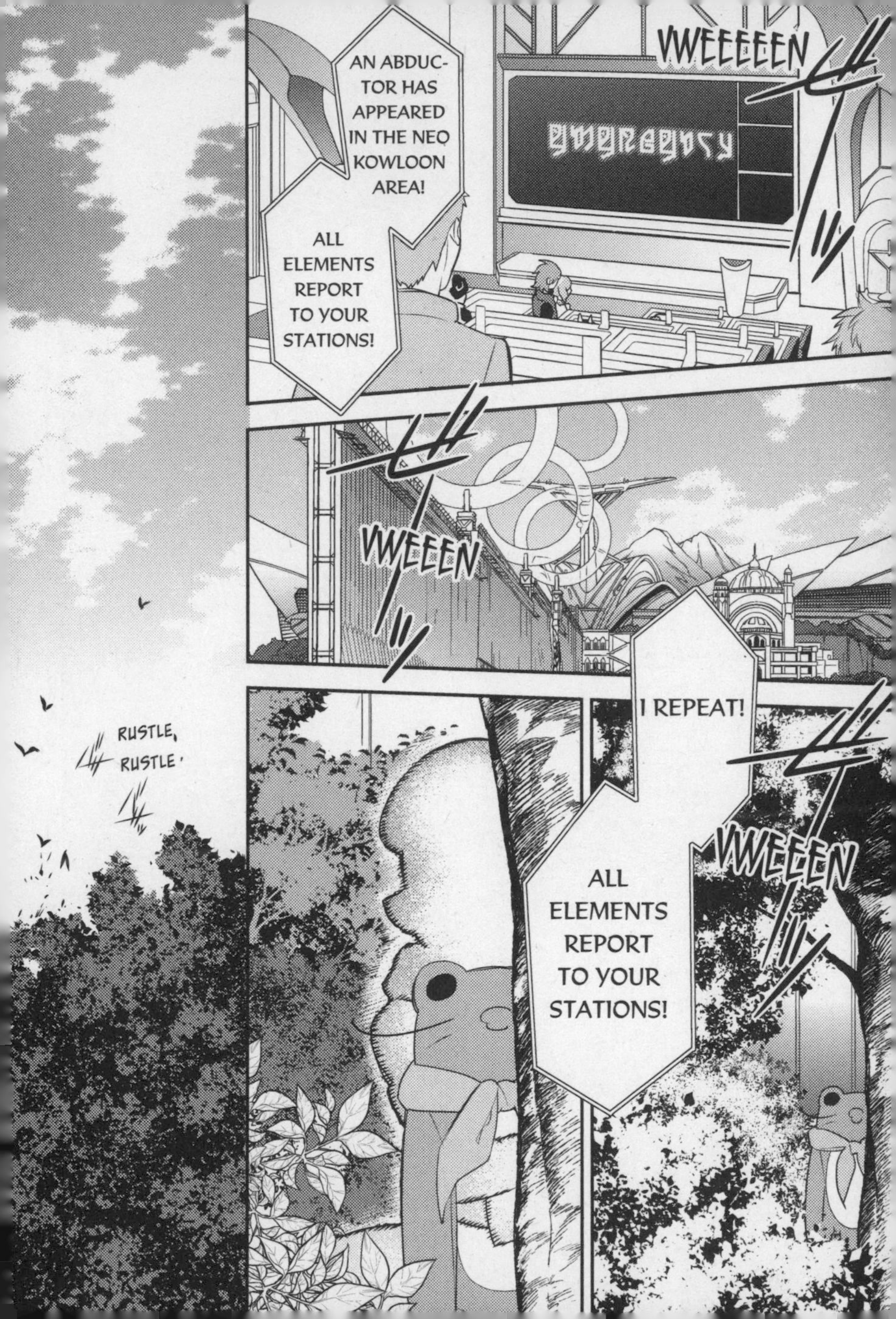
VWEEEEEN
AN ABDUC-TOR HAS APPEARED IN THE NEO KOWLOON AREA!
ALL ELEMENTS REPORT TO YOUR STATIONS!
VWEEEN
I REPEAT!
ALL ELEMENTS REPORT TO YOUR STATIONS!
VWEEEN
RUSTLE, RUSTLE

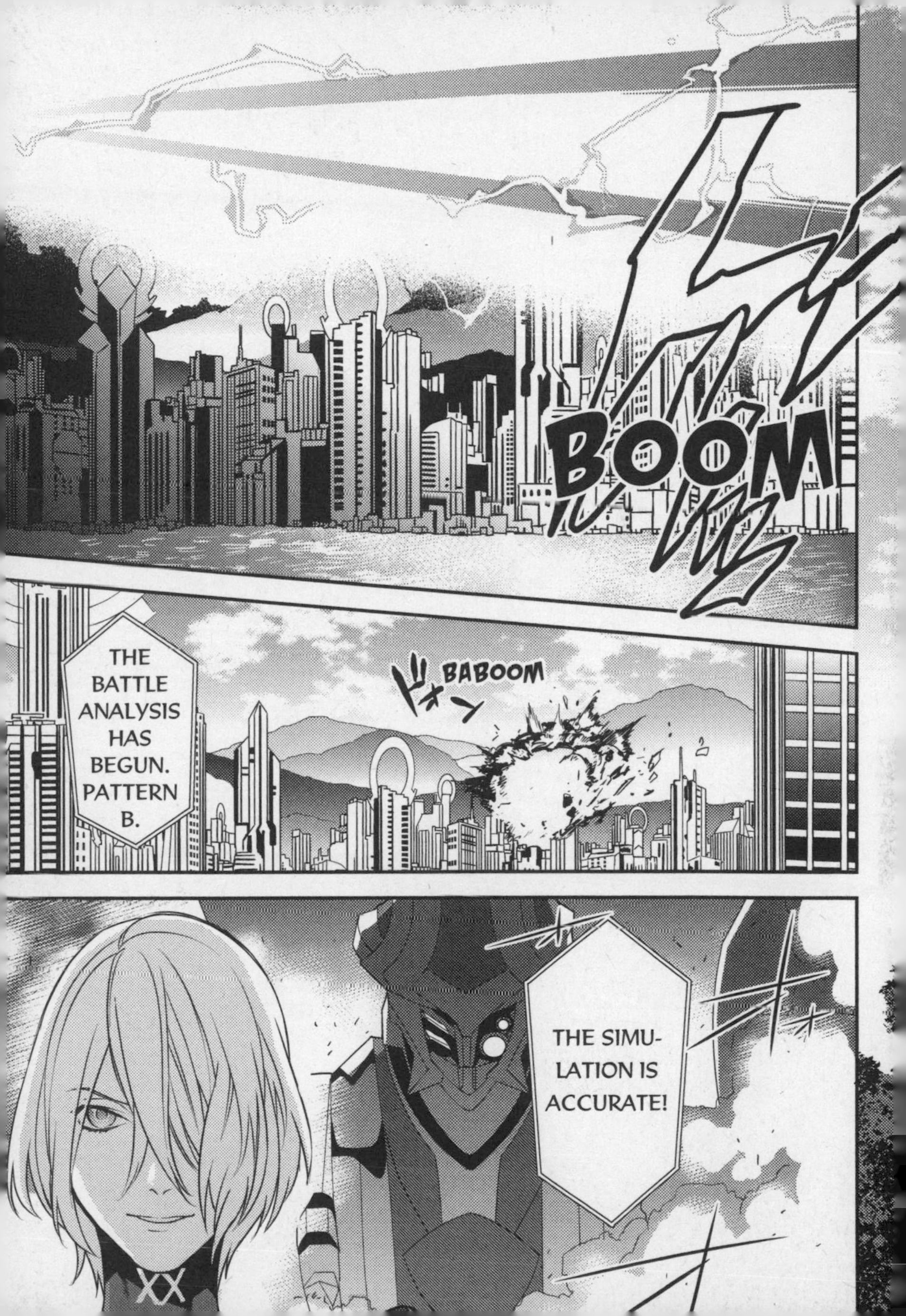
BOOM
BABOOM
ドォン
THE BATTLE ANALYSIS HAS BEGUN. PATTERN B.
THE SIMU-LATION IS ACCURATE!

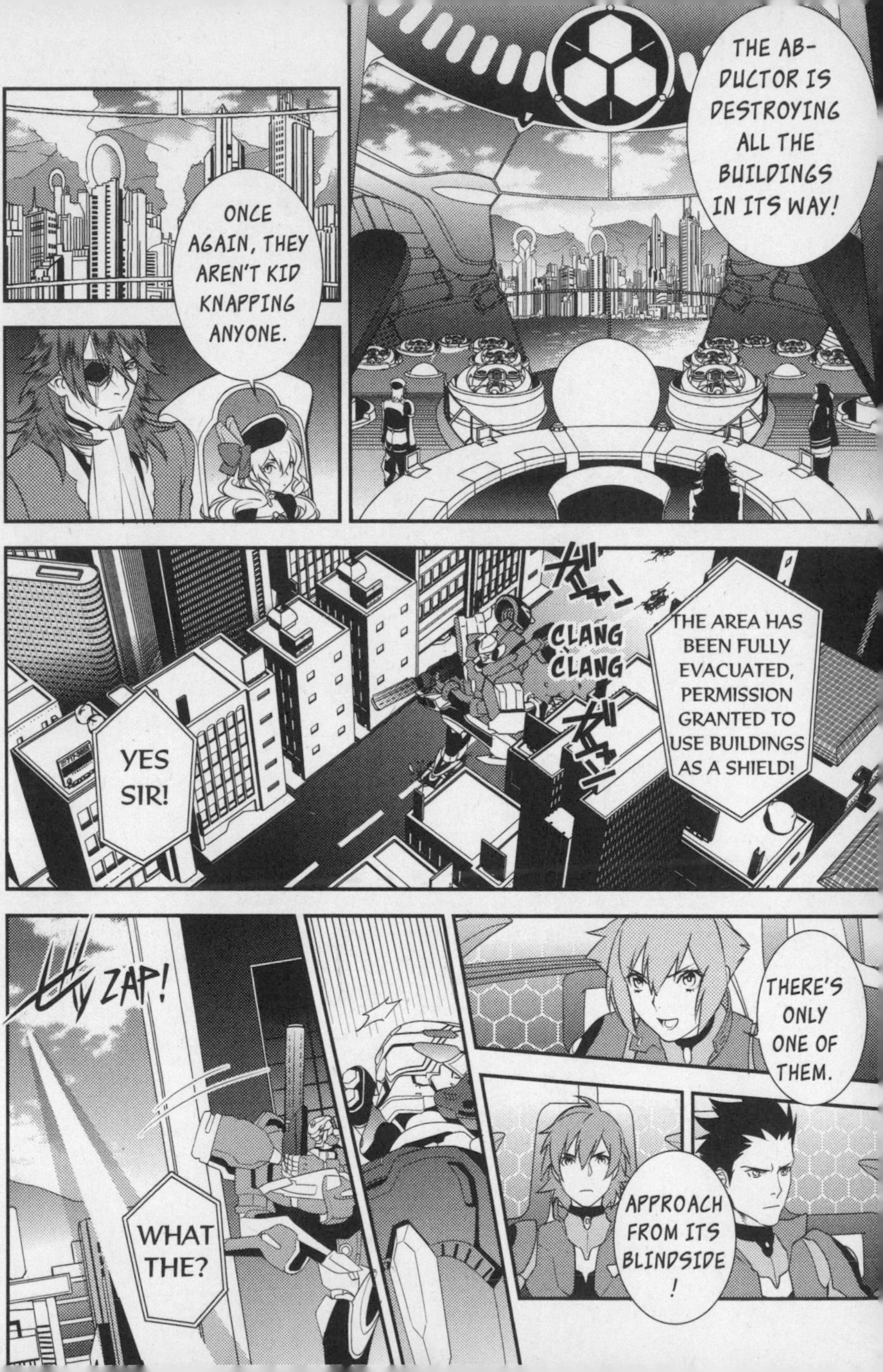
THE AB-DUCTOR IS DESTROYING ALL THE BUILDINGS IN ITS WAY!
ONCE AGAIN, THEY AREN'T KID KNAPPING ANYONE.
THE AREA HAS BEEN FULLY EVACUATED, PERMISSION GRANTED TO USE BUILDINGS AS A SHIELD!
CLANG CLANG
YES SIR!
THERE'S ONLY ONE OF THEM.
APPROACH FROM ITS BLINDSIDE!
ZAP!
WHAT THE?

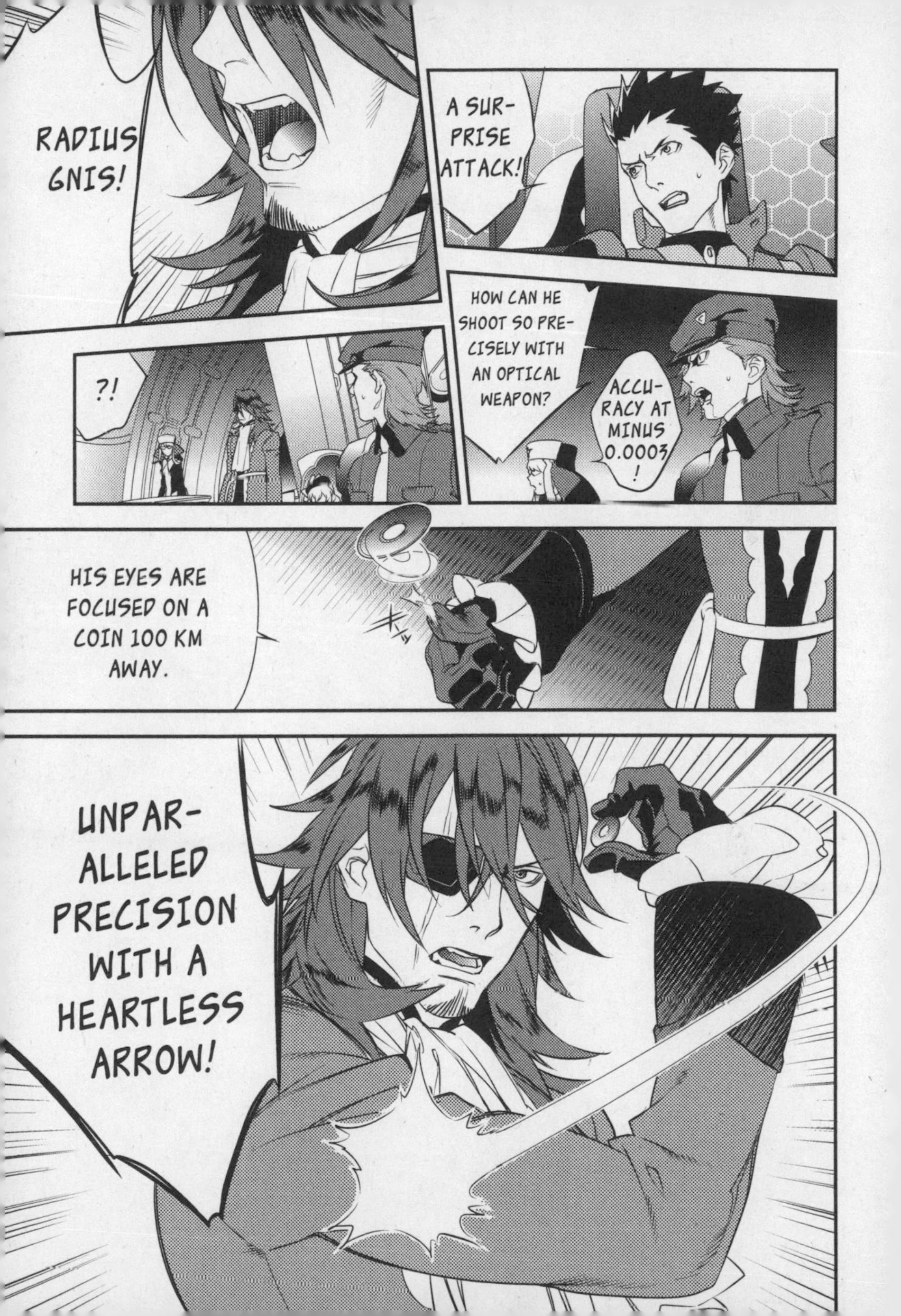
A SURPRISE ATTACK!
RADIUS GNIS!
HOW CAN HE SHOOT SO PRECISELY WITH AN OPTICAL WEAPON?
ACCURACY AT MINUS 0.0003!
?!
HIS EYES ARE FOCUSED ON A COIN 100 KM AWAY.
UNPARALLELED PRECISION WITH A HEARTLESS ARROW!

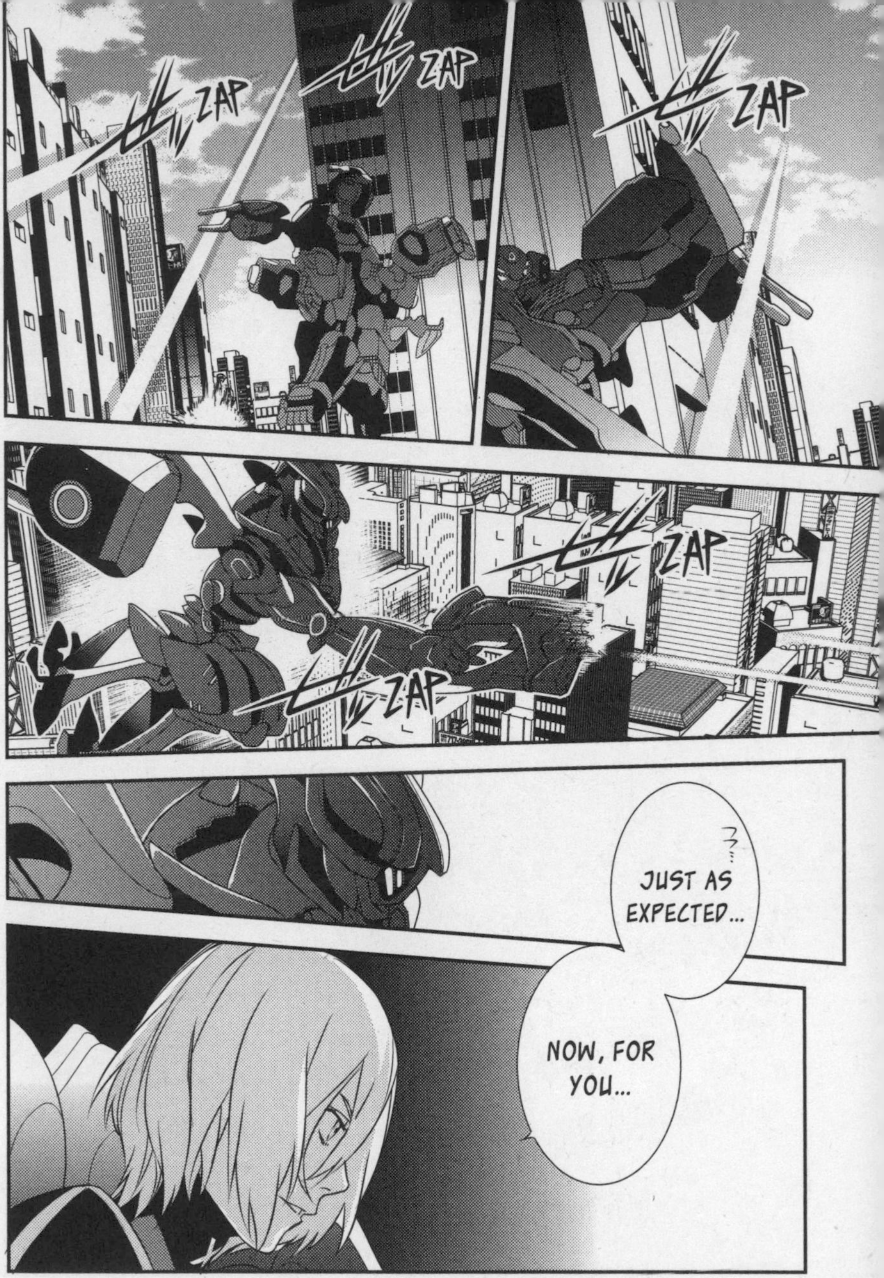
ZAP
ZAP
ZAP
ZAP
ZAP
ZAP
フフ…
JUST AS EXPECTED...
NOW, FOR YOU...

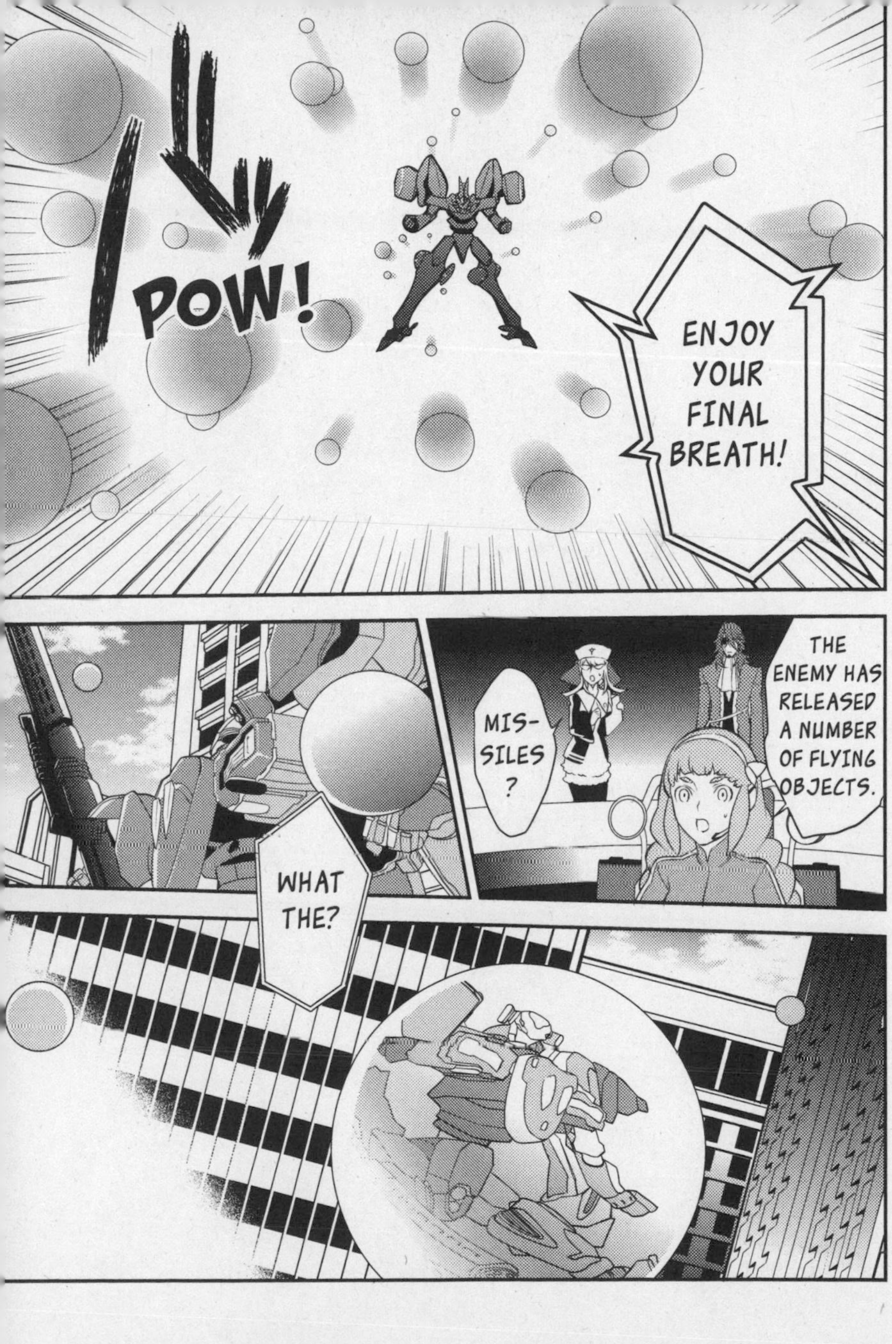
ENJOY YOUR FINAL BREATH!
POW!
THE ENEMY HAS RELEASED A NUMBER OF FLYING OBJECTS.
MIS-SILES?
WHAT THE?

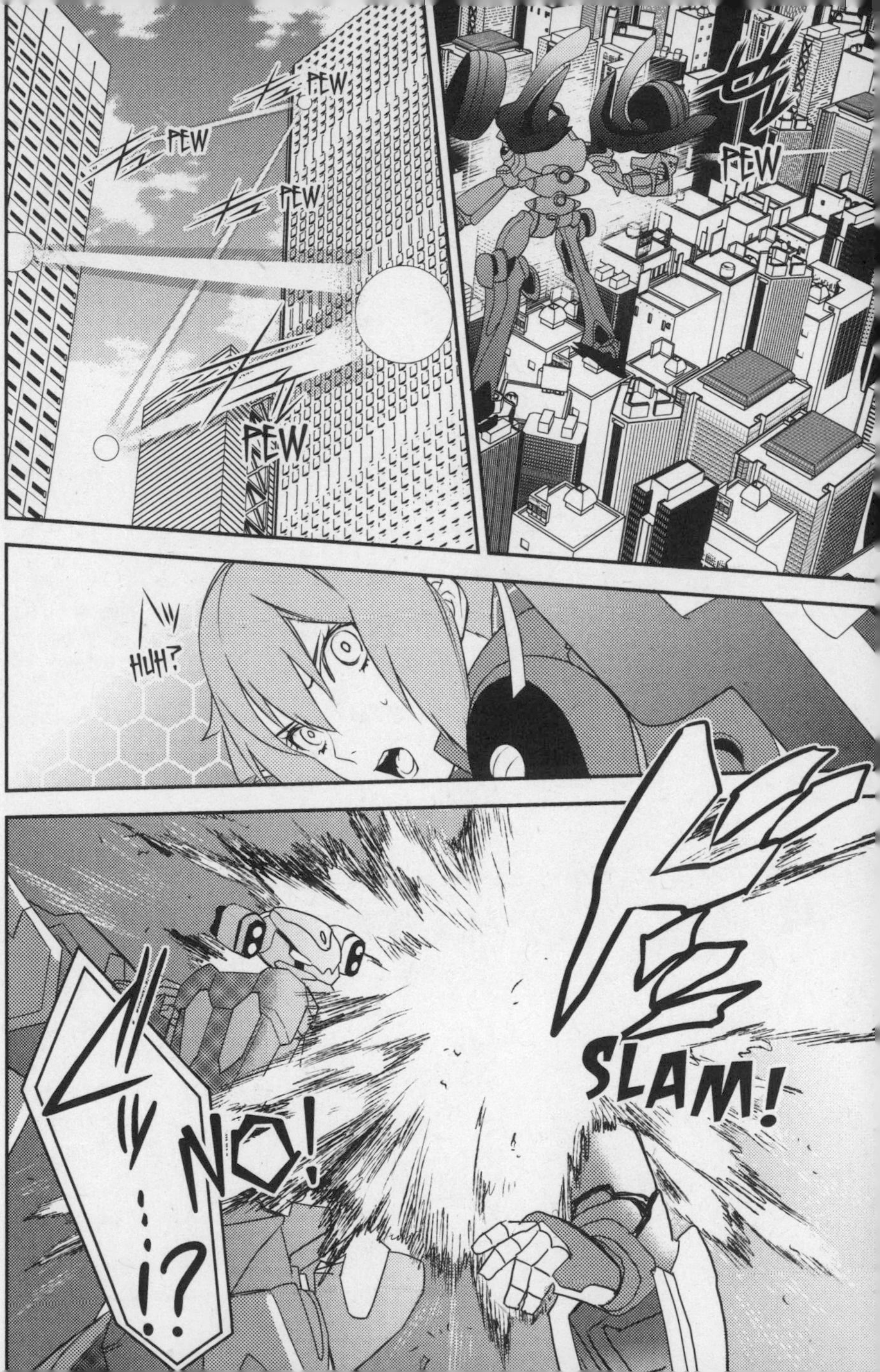
PEW
PEW
PEW
PEW
PEW
HUH?
SLAM!
NO!...!?

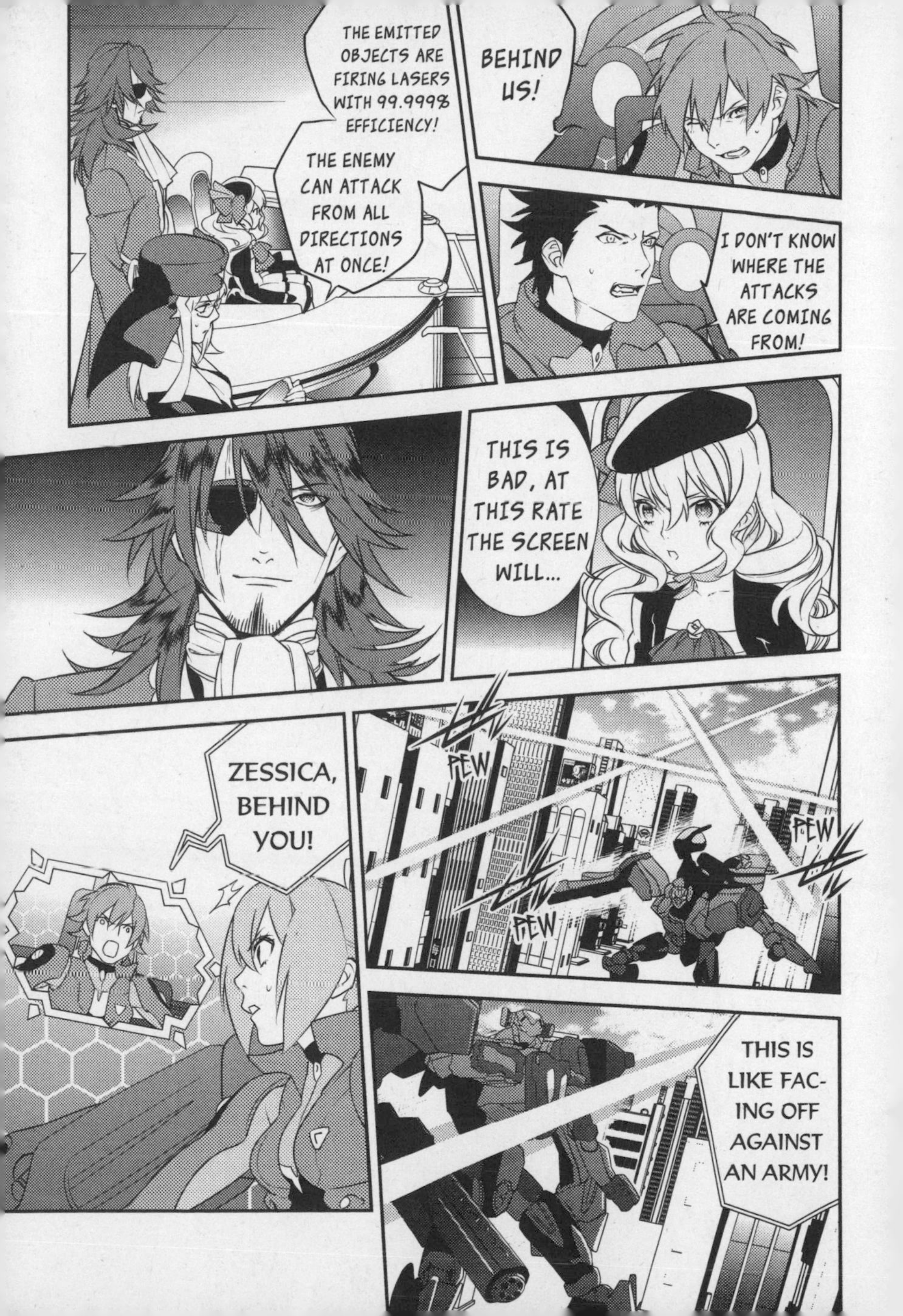
BEHIND US!
I DON'T KNOW WHERE THE ATTACKS ARE COMING FROM!
THE EMITTED OBJECTS ARE FIRING LASERS WITH 99.999% EFFICIENCY!
THE ENEMY CAN ATTACK FROM ALL DIRECTIONS AT ONCE!
THIS IS BAD, AT THIS RATE THE SCREEN WILL...
PEW
PEW
PEW
THIS IS LIKE FAC-ING OFF AGAINST AN ARMY!
ZESSICA, BEHIND YOU!

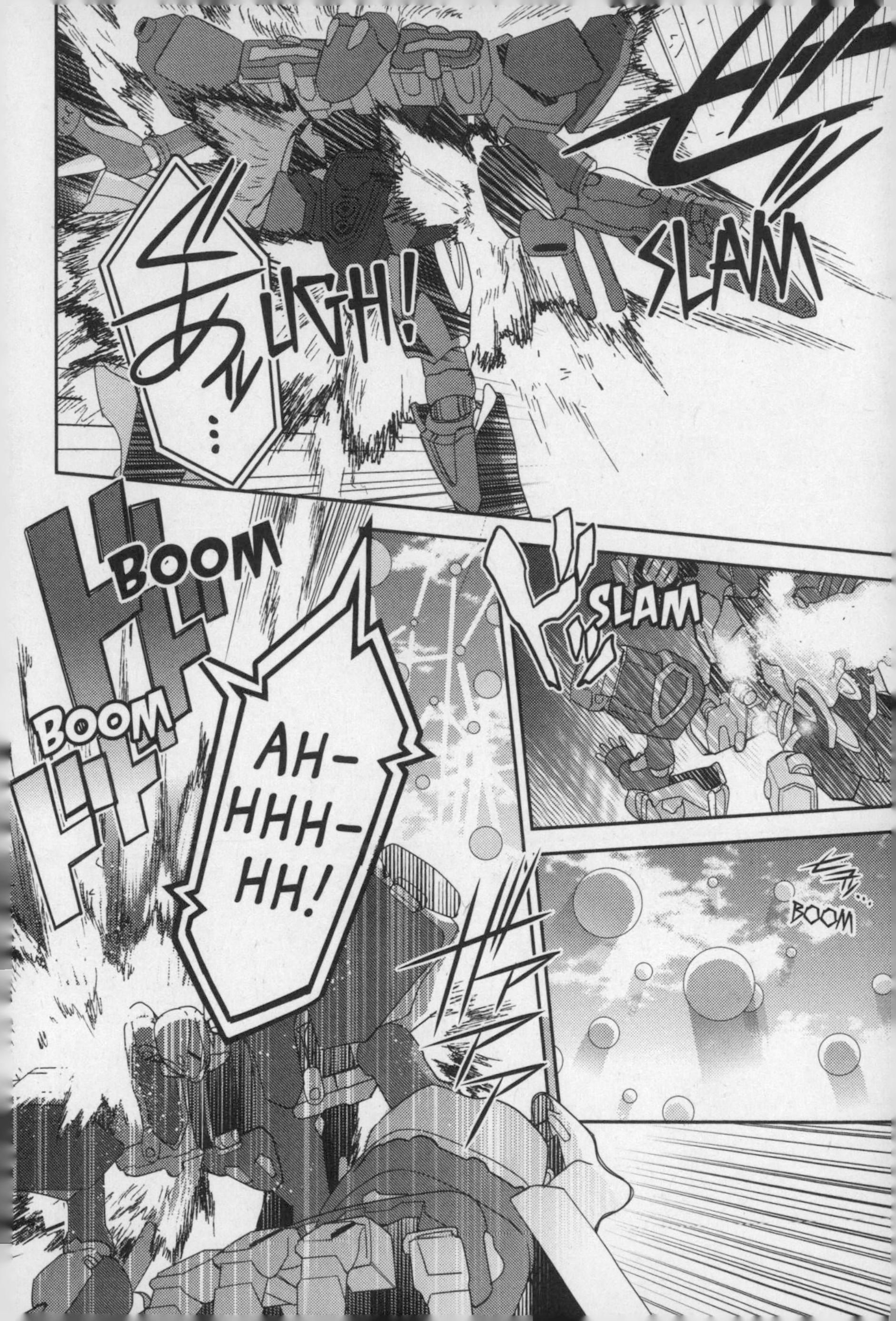
SLAM
UGH! ...
SLAM
AH-HHH-HH!
BOOM
BOOM
BOOM

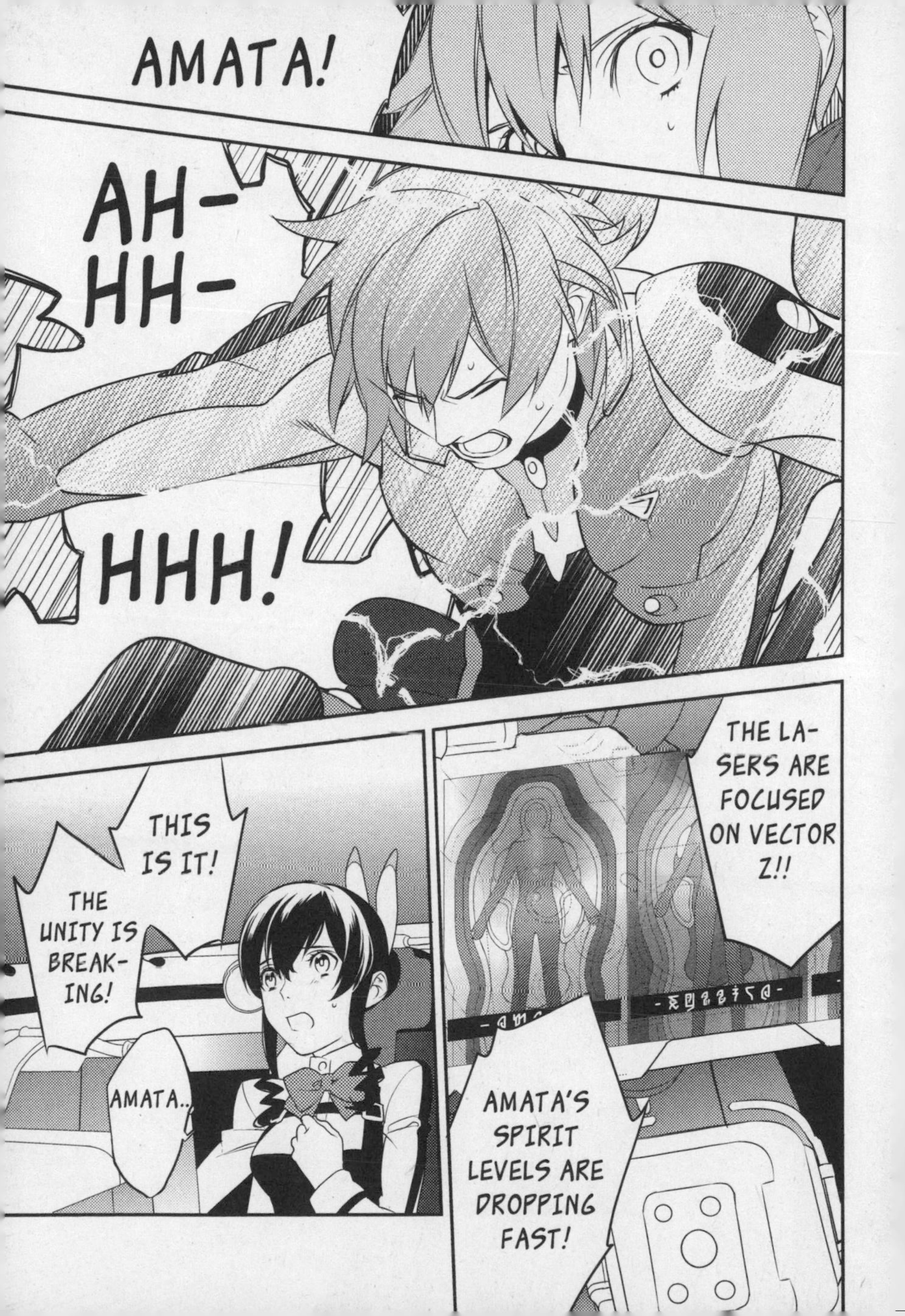
AMATA!
AH-HH-HHH!
THE LA-SERS ARE FOCUSED ON VECTOR Z!!
AMATA'S SPIRIT LEVELS ARE DROPPING FAST!
THIS IS IT!
THE UNITY IS BREAK-ING!
AMATA...

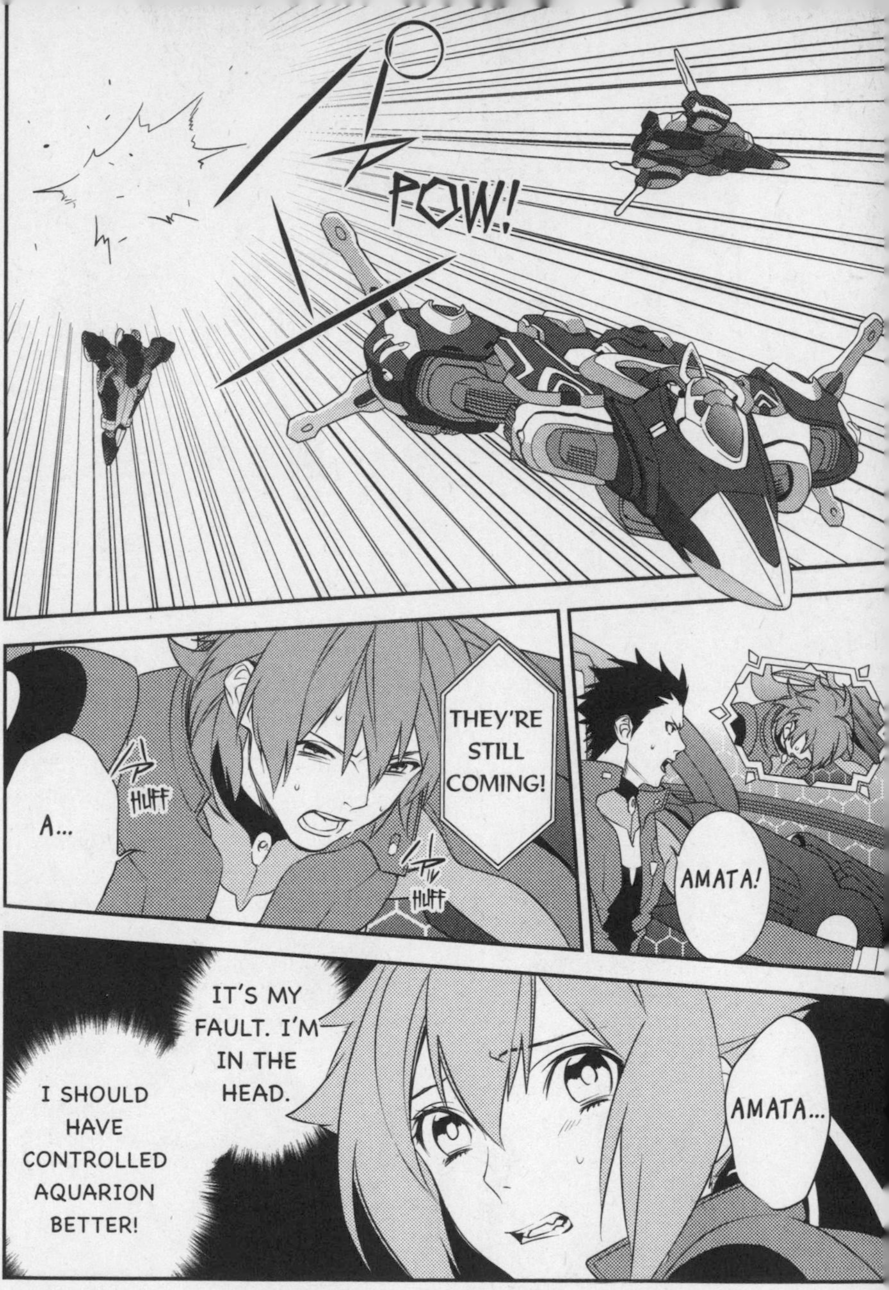
POW!
AMATA!
THEY'RE STILL COMING!
HUFF
A...
HUFF
AMATA...
IT'S MY FAULT. I'M IN THE HEAD.
I SHOULD HAVE CONTROLLED AQUARION BETTER!

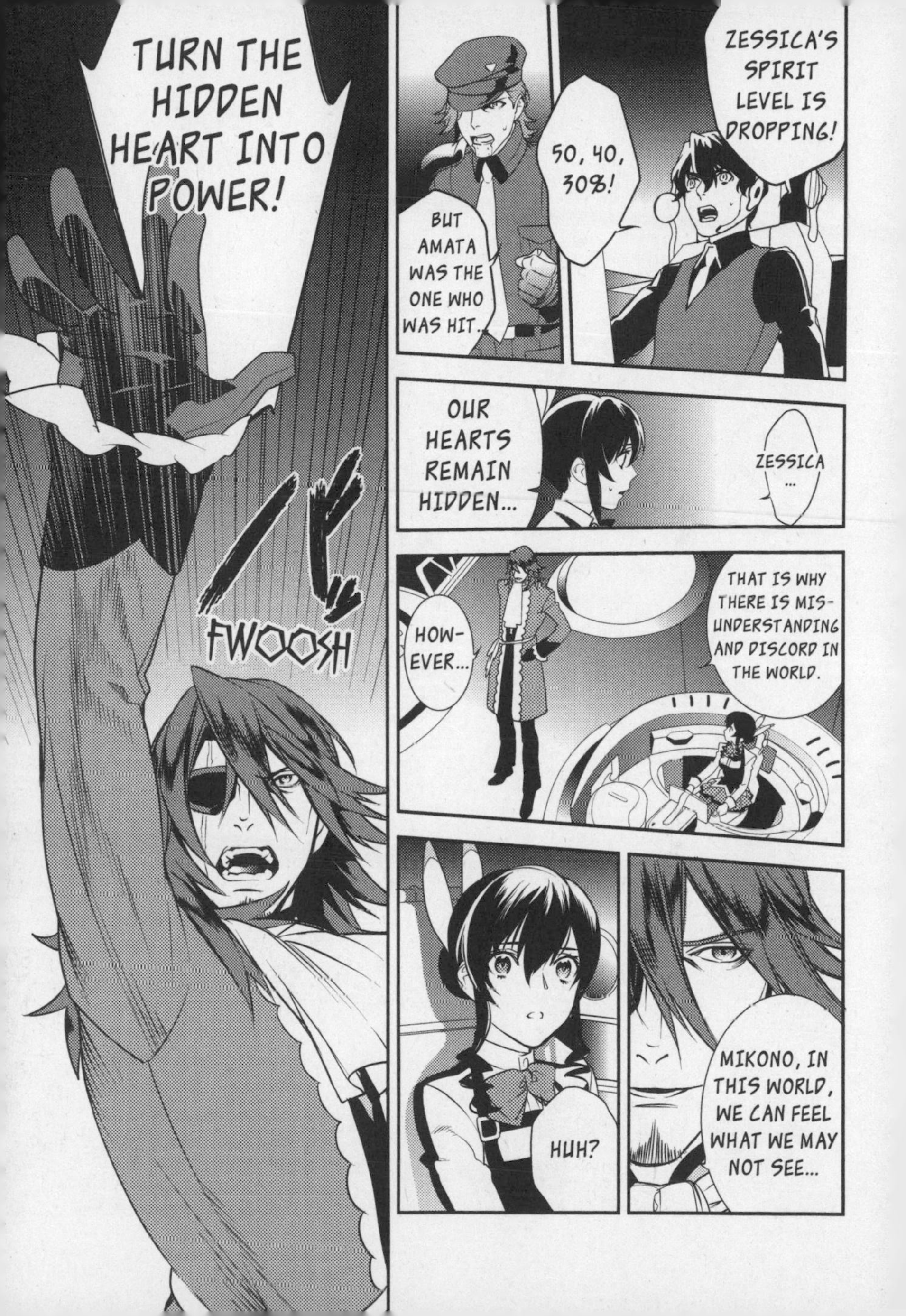
ZESSICA'S SPIRIT LEVEL IS DROPPING!
50, 40, 30%!
BUT AMATA WAS THE ONE WHO WAS HIT..
ZESSICA ...
OUR HEARTS REMAIN HIDDEN...
THAT IS WHY THERE IS MIS-UNDERSTANDING AND DISCORD IN THE WORLD.
HOW-EVER...
MIKONO, IN THIS WORLD, WE CAN FEEL WHAT WE MAY NOT SEE...
HUH?
TURN THE HIDDEN HEART INTO POWER!
FWOOSH

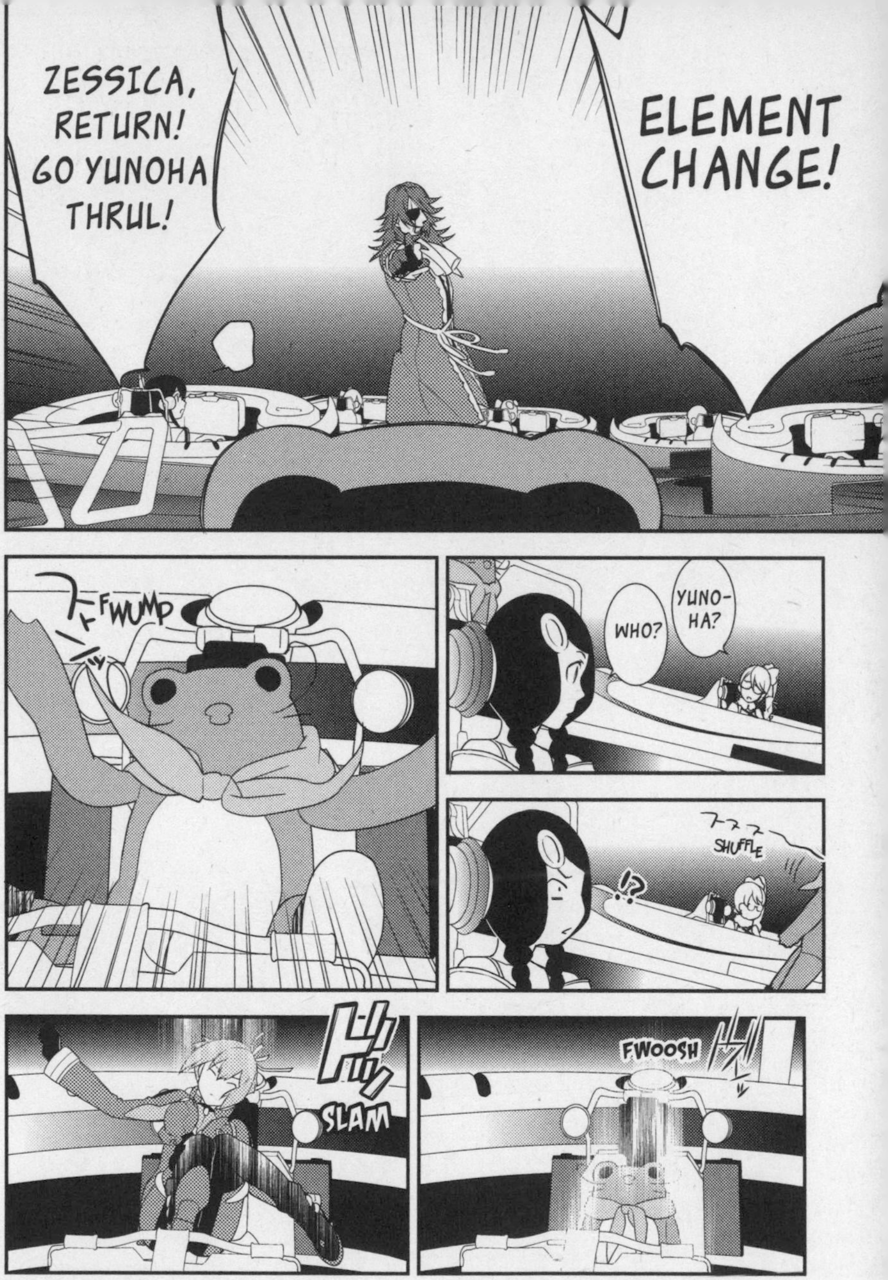
ELEMENT CHANGE!
ZESSICA, RETURN! GO YUNOHA THRUL!
YUNO-HA?
WHO?
SHUFFLE
!?
FWUMP
FWOOSH
SLAM

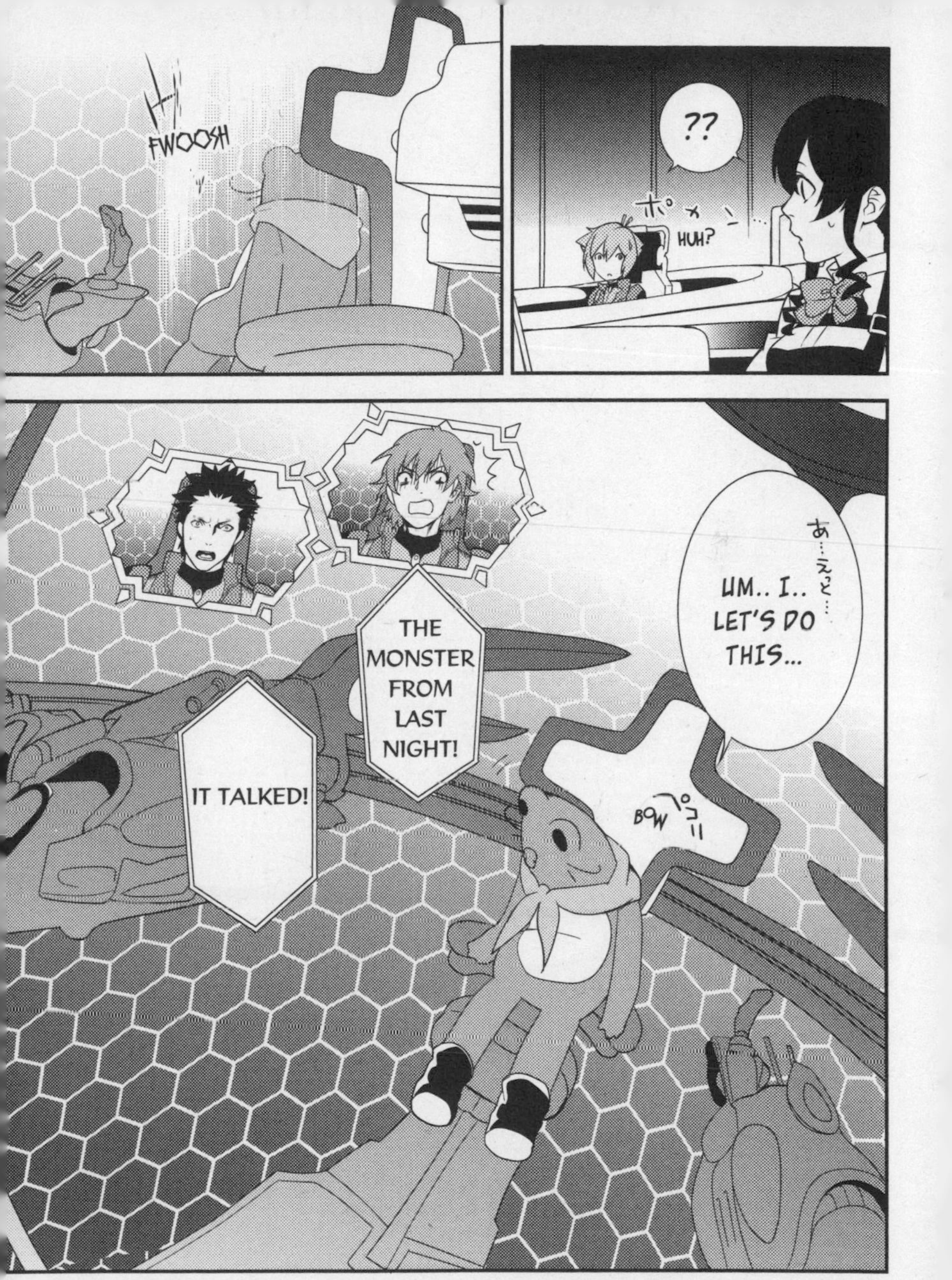
??
ポカン…
HUH?
FWOOSH
あ…えっと…
UM.. I..
LET'S DO
THIS...
ペコ
BOW
THE
MONSTER
FROM
LAST
NIGHT!
IT TALKED!

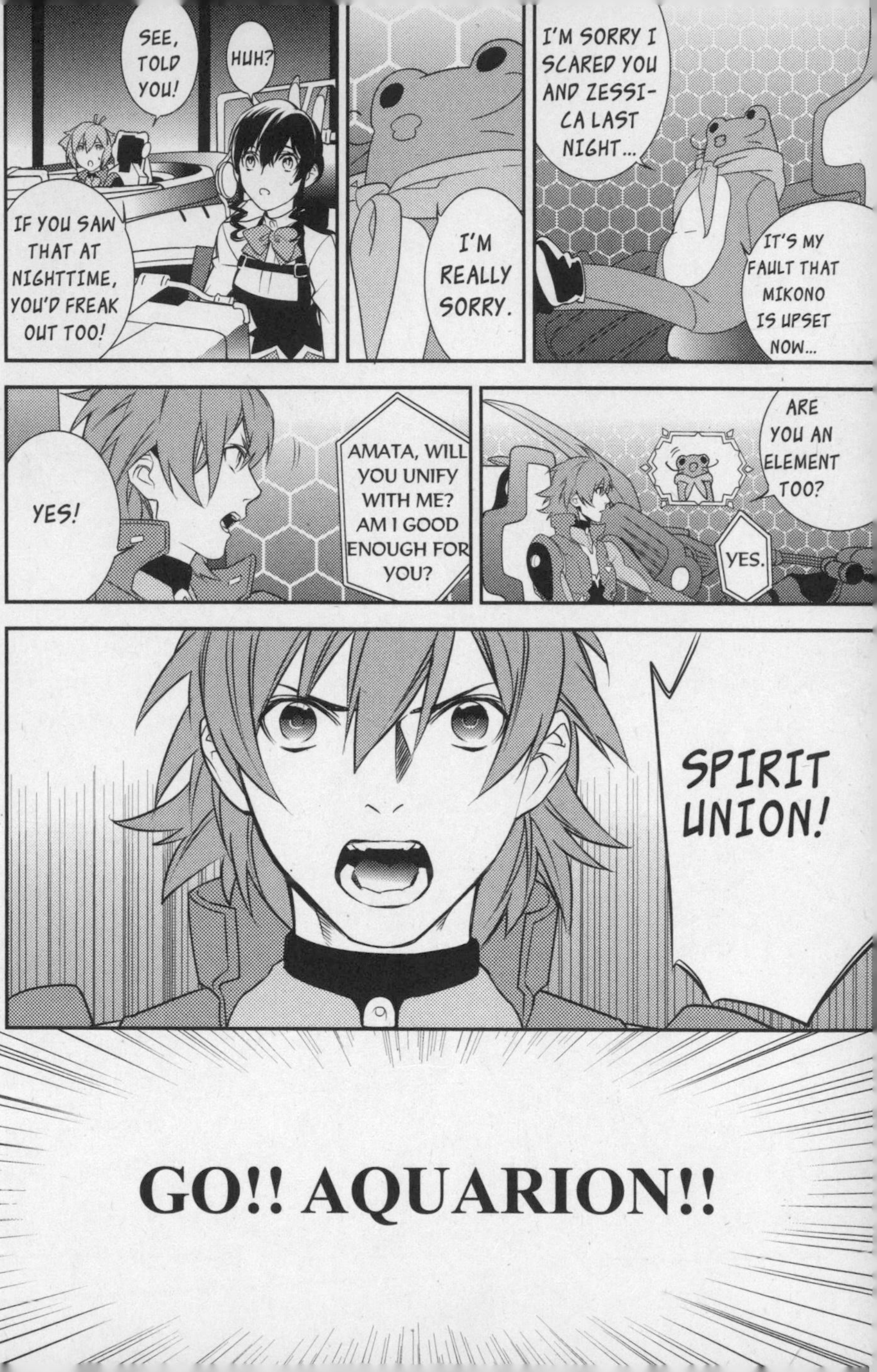
I'M SORRY I SCARED YOU AND ZESSI-CA LAST NIGHT...
IT'S MY FAULT THAT MIKONO IS UPSET NOW...
I'M REALLY SORRY.
SEE, TOLD YOU!
HUH?
IF YOU SAW THAT AT NIGHTTIME, YOU'D FREAK OUT TOO!
ARE YOU AN ELEMENT TOO?
YES.
AMATA, WILL YOU UNIFY WITH ME? AM I GOOD ENOUGH FOR YOU?
YES!
SPIRIT UNION!
GO!! AQUARION!!

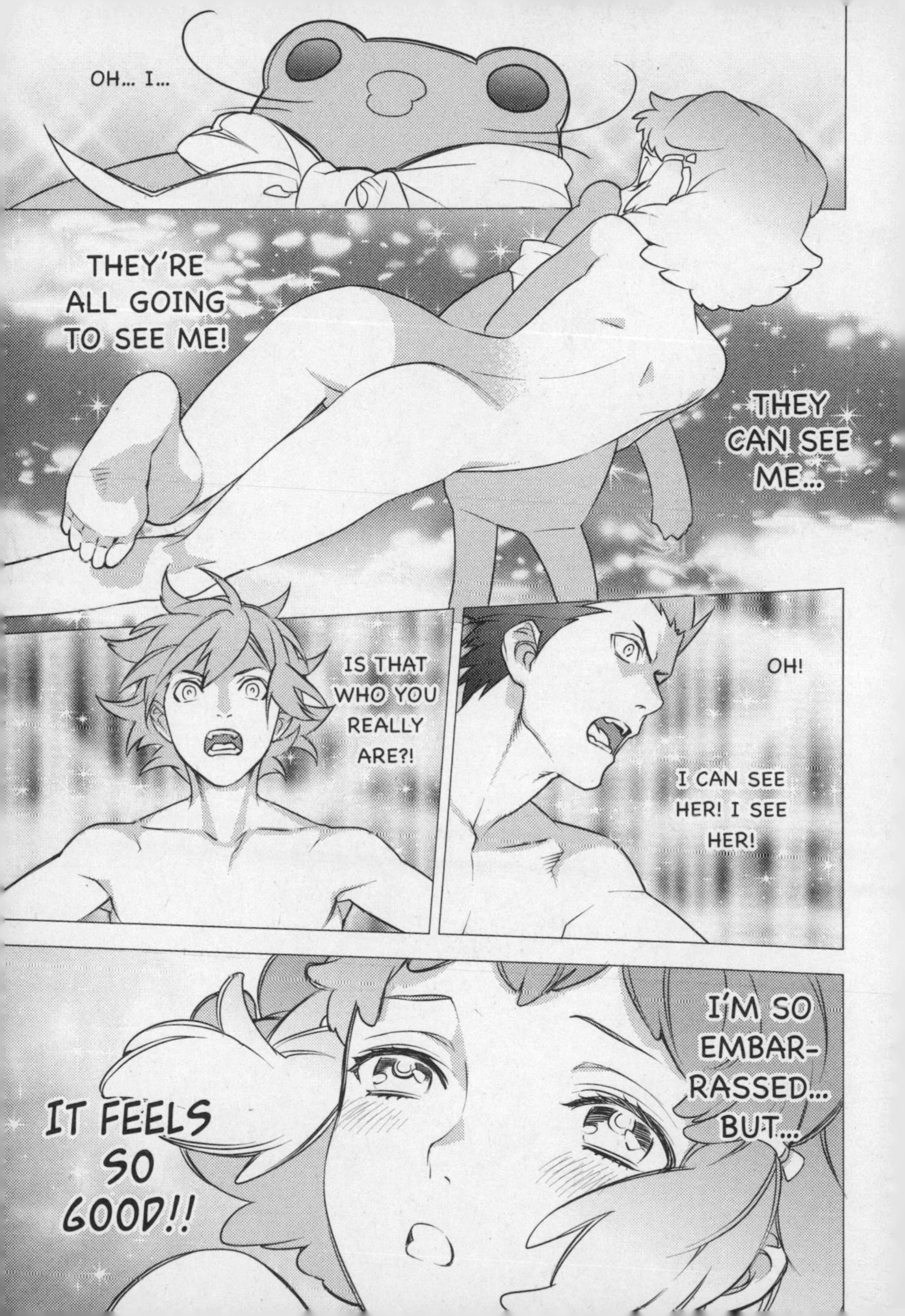
OH... I...
THEY CAN SEE ME...
THEY'RE ALL GOING TO SEE ME!
OH!
I CAN SEE HER! I SEE HER!
IS THAT WHO YOU REALLY ARE?!
I'M SO EMBARRASSED... BUT...
IT FEELS SO GOOD!!

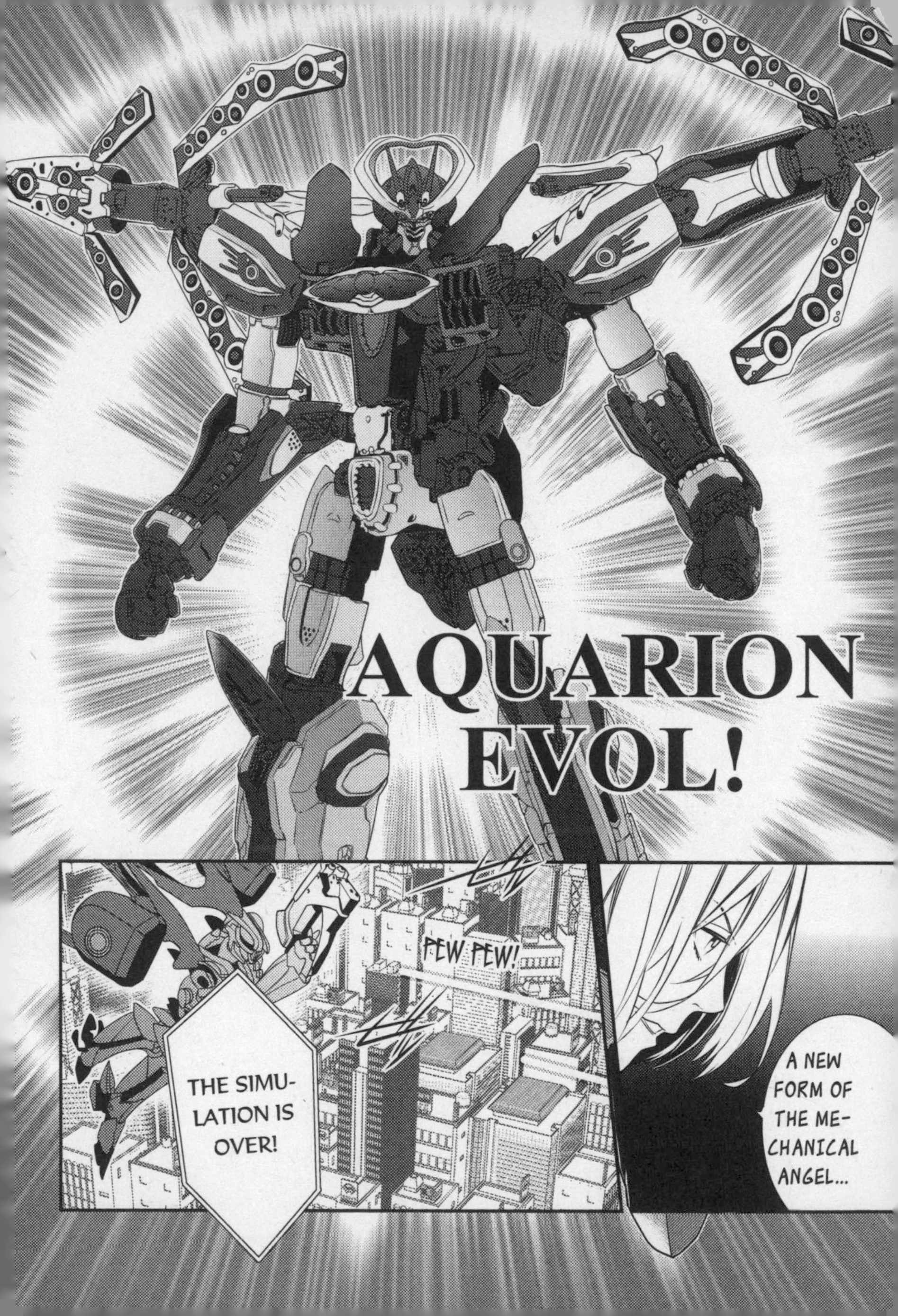
AQUARION EVOL!
A NEW FORM OF THE ME-CHANICAL ANGEL...
PEW PEW!
THE SIMU-LATION IS OVER!

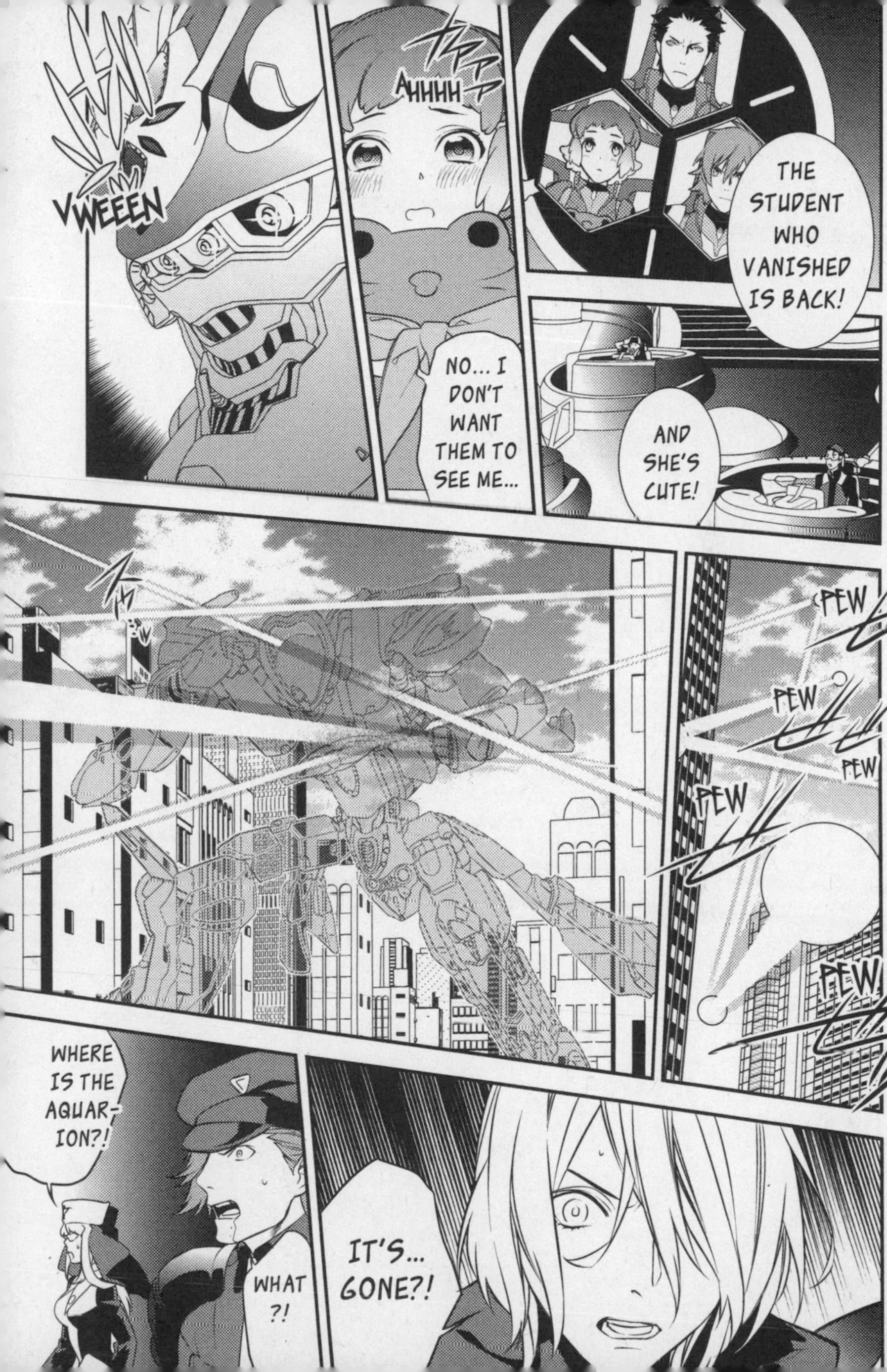
THE STUDENT WHO VANISHED IS BACK!
AND SHE'S CUTE!
AHHHH
NO... I DON'T WANT THEM TO SEE ME...
VWEEEN
PEW
PEW
PEW
PEW
PEW
IT'S... GONE?!
WHERE IS THE AQUAR-ION?!
WHAT?!

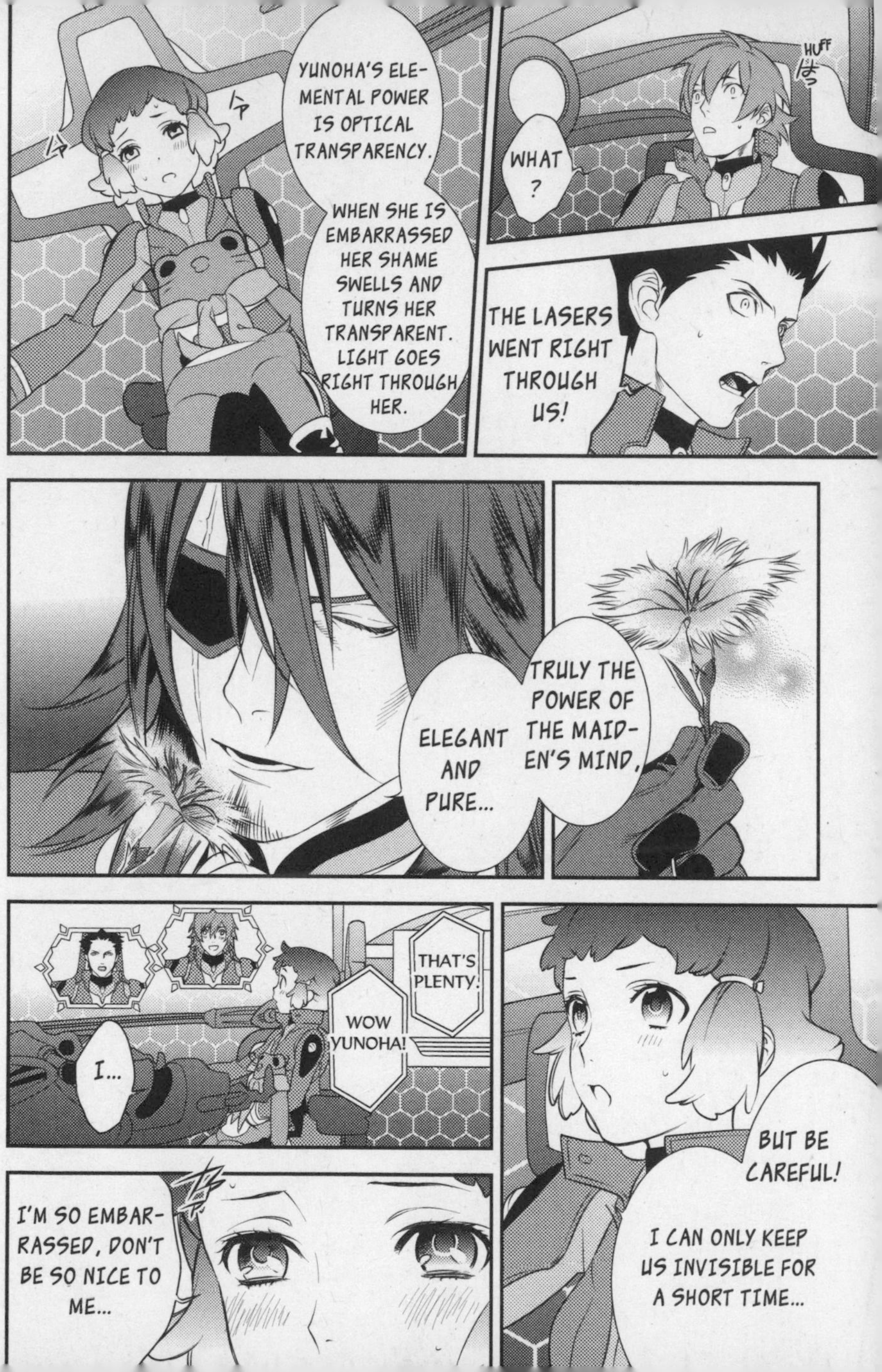
HUFF
はっ
WHAT ?
THE LASERS WENT RIGHT THROUGH US!
ハァ
ハァ
YUNOHA'S ELE-MENTAL POWER IS OPTICAL TRANSPARENCY.
WHEN SHE IS EMBARRASSED HER SHAME SWELLS AND TURNS HER TRANSPARENT. LIGHT GOES RIGHT THROUGH HER.
TRULY THE POWER OF THE MAID-EN'S MIND,
ELEGANT AND PURE...
BUT BE CAREFUL!
I CAN ONLY KEEP US INVISIBLE FOR A SHORT TIME...
THAT'S PLENTY!
WOW YUNOHA!
I...
I'M SO EMBAR-RASSED, DON'T BE SO NICE TO ME...

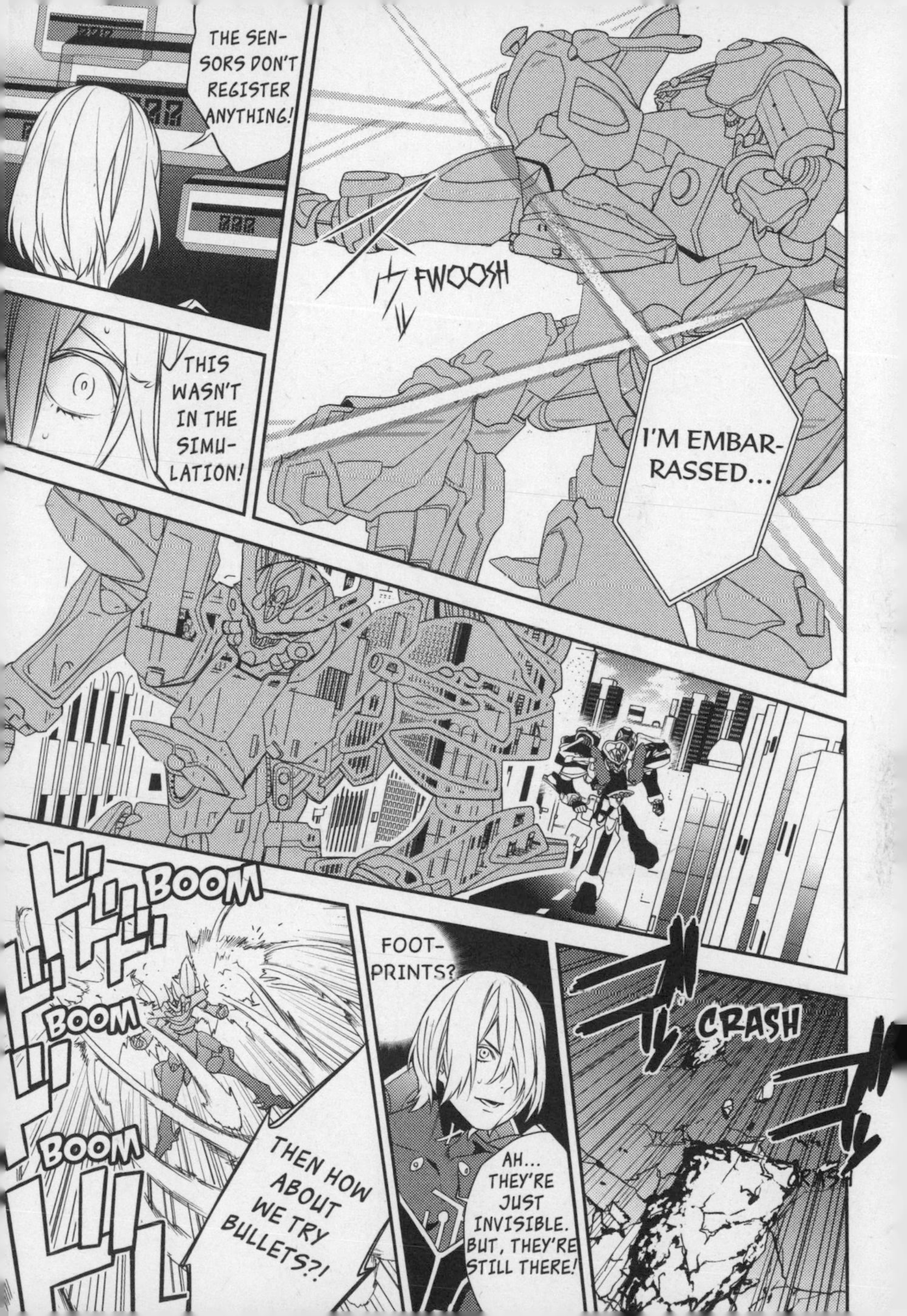
FWOOSH
I'M EMBARRASSED...
THE SENSORS DON'T REGISTER ANYTHING!
THIS WASN'T IN THE SIMULATION!
CRASH
CRASH
FOOT-PRINTS?
AH... THEY'RE JUST INVISIBLE. BUT, THEY'RE STILL THERE!
THEN HOW ABOUT WE TRY BULLETS?!
BOOM
BOOM
BOOM

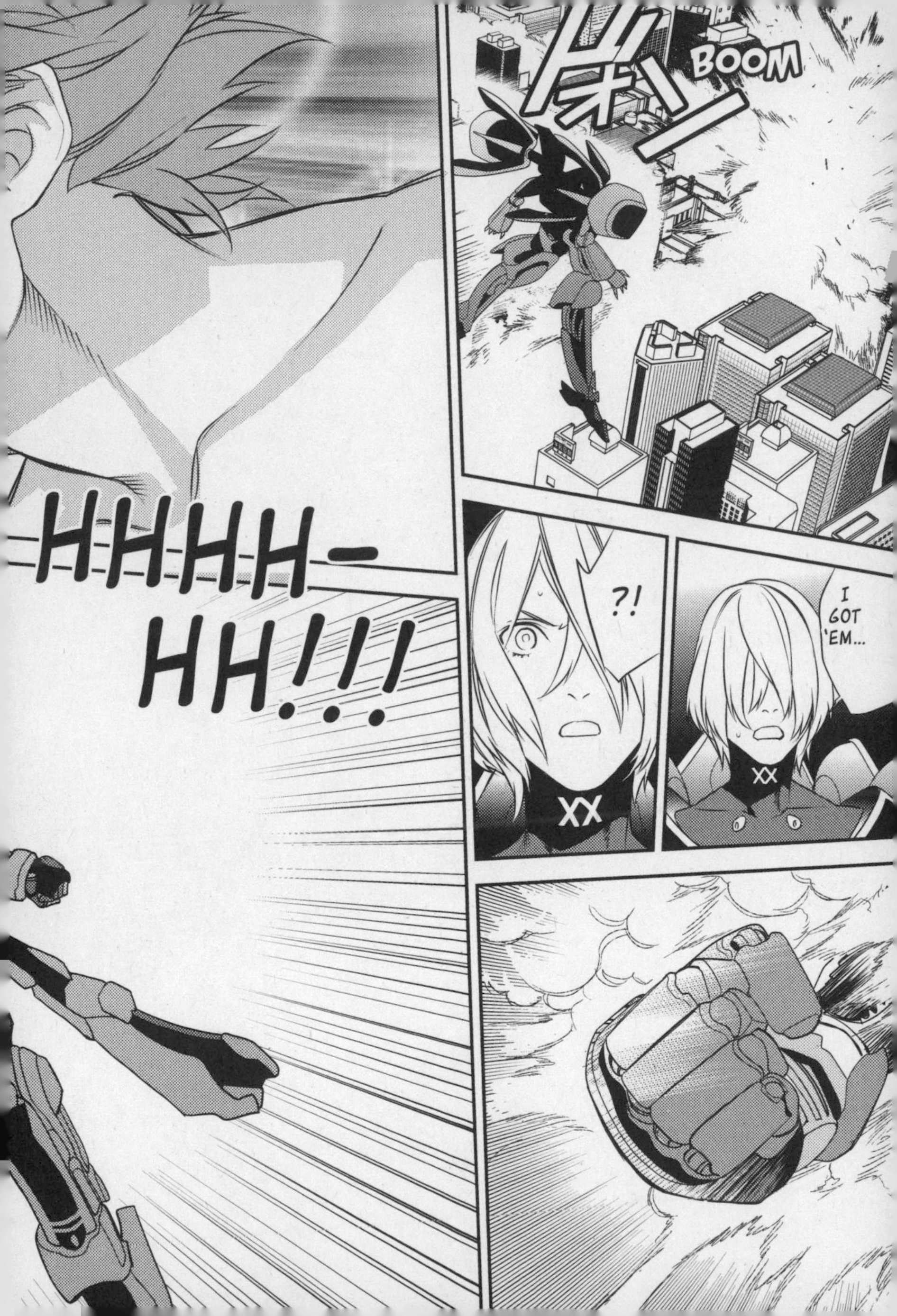
BOOM
I GOT 'EM...
?!
HHHH–
HH!!!

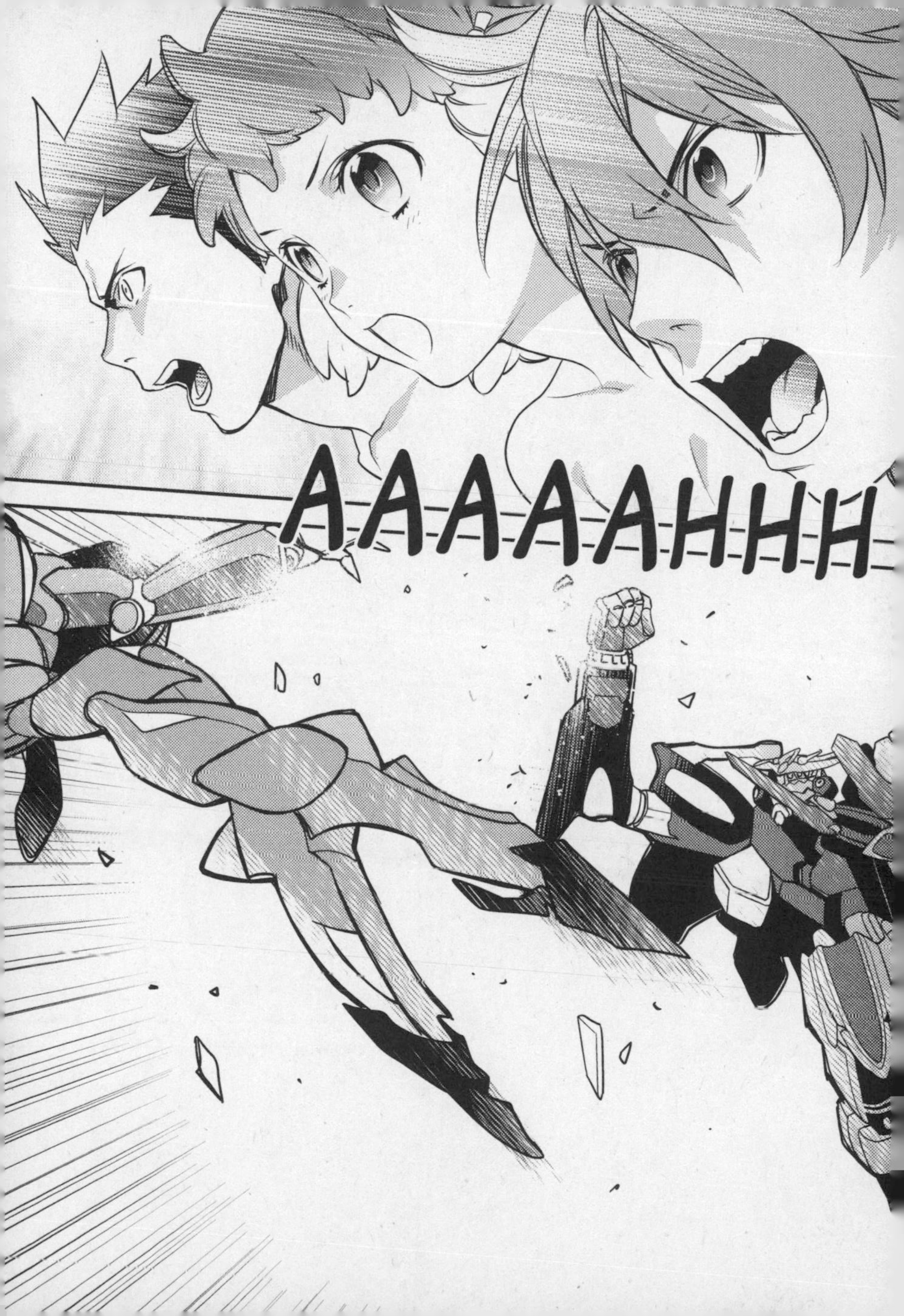
AAAAAAHHH

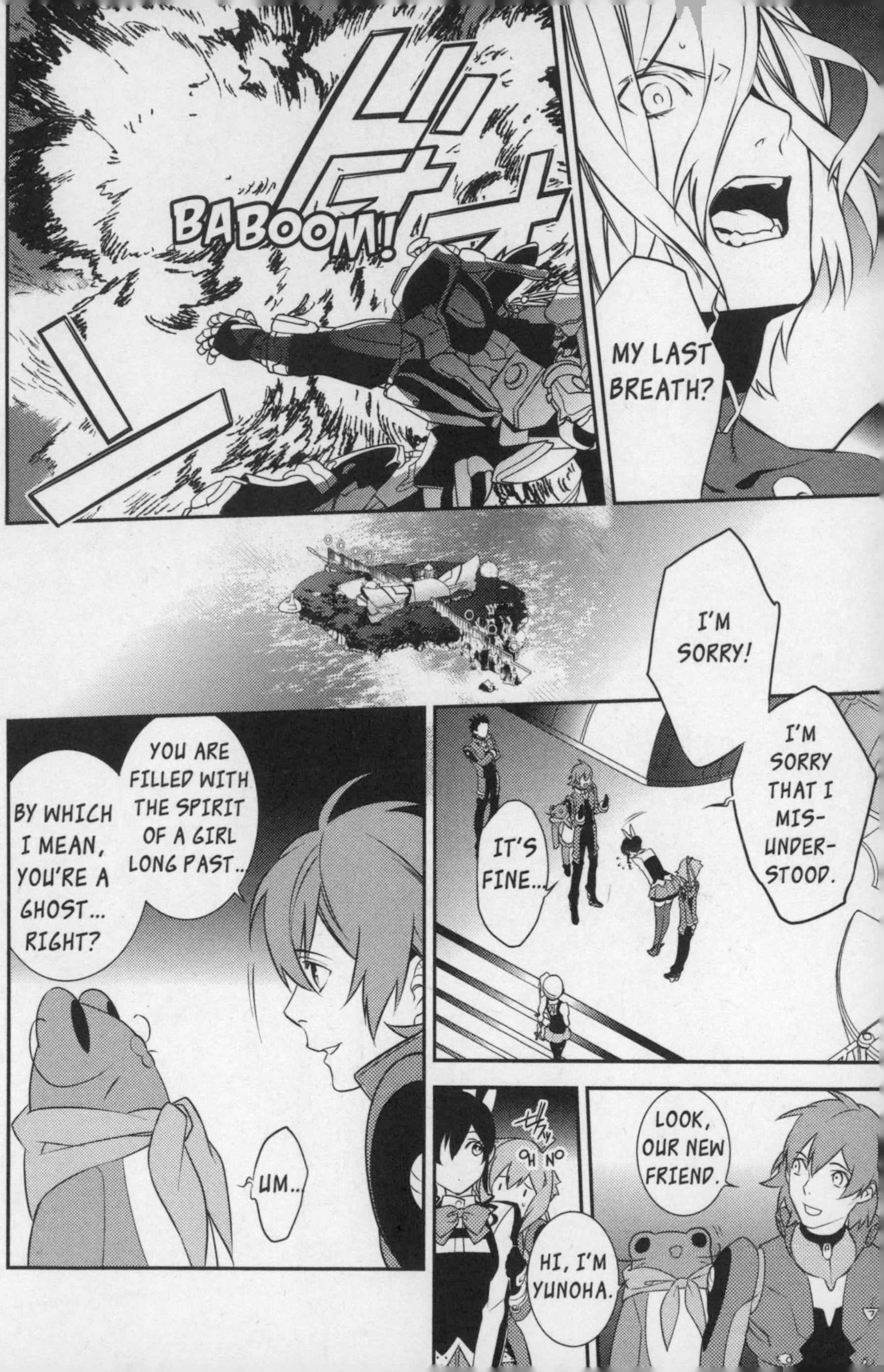
MY LAST BREATH?
BABOOM!
I'M SORRY!
I'M SORRY THAT I MIS-UNDER-STOOD.
IT'S FINE...
LOOK, OUR NEW FRIEND.
OH NO
HI, I'M YUNOHA.
YOU ARE FILLED WITH THE SPIRIT OF A GIRL LONG PAST...
BY WHICH I MEAN, YOU'RE A GHOST... RIGHT?
UM...

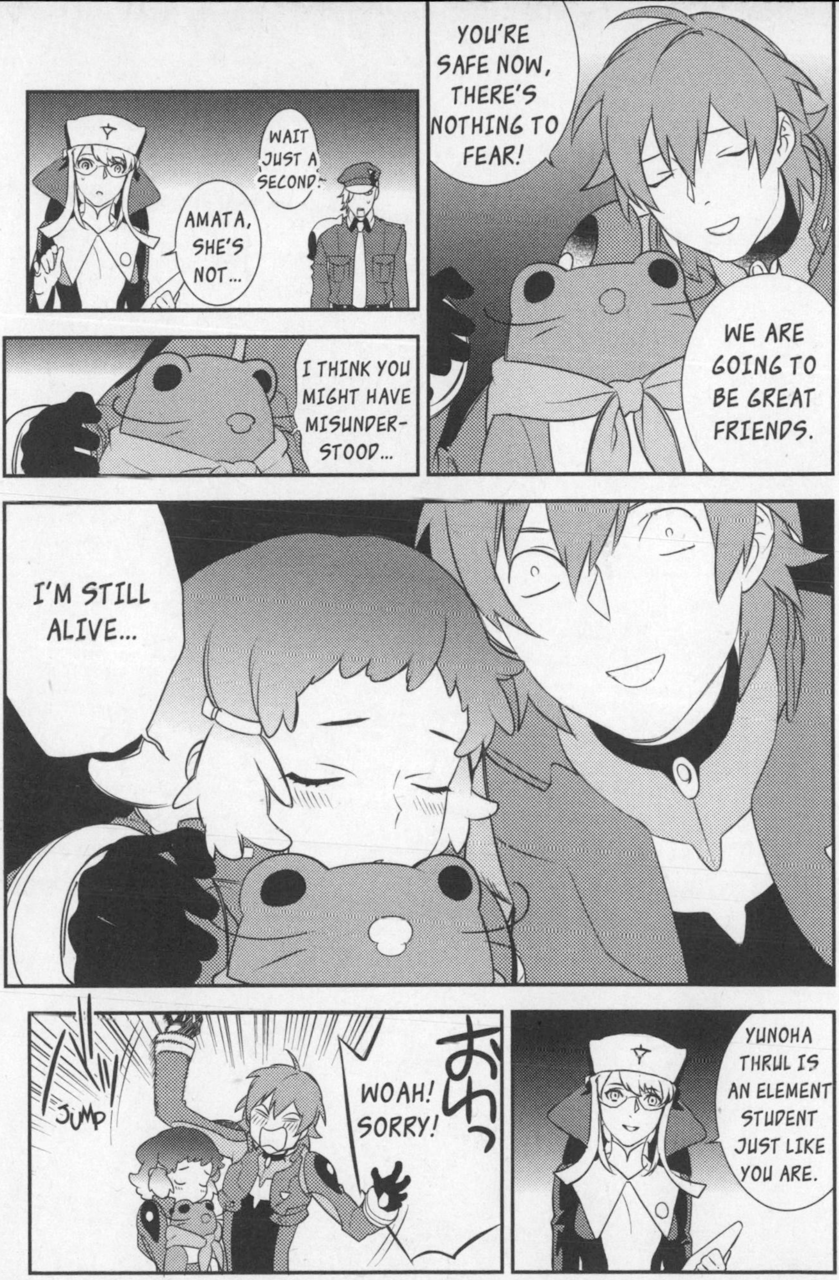
YOU'RE SAFE NOW, THERE'S NOTHING TO FEAR!
WE ARE GOING TO BE GREAT FRIENDS.
WAIT JUST A SECOND.
AMATA, SHE'S NOT...
I THINK YOU MIGHT HAVE MISUNDER-STOOD...
I'M STILL ALIVE...
YUNOHA THRUL IS AN ELEMENT STUDENT JUST LIKE YOU ARE.
おわっ
WOAH! SORRY!
JUMP

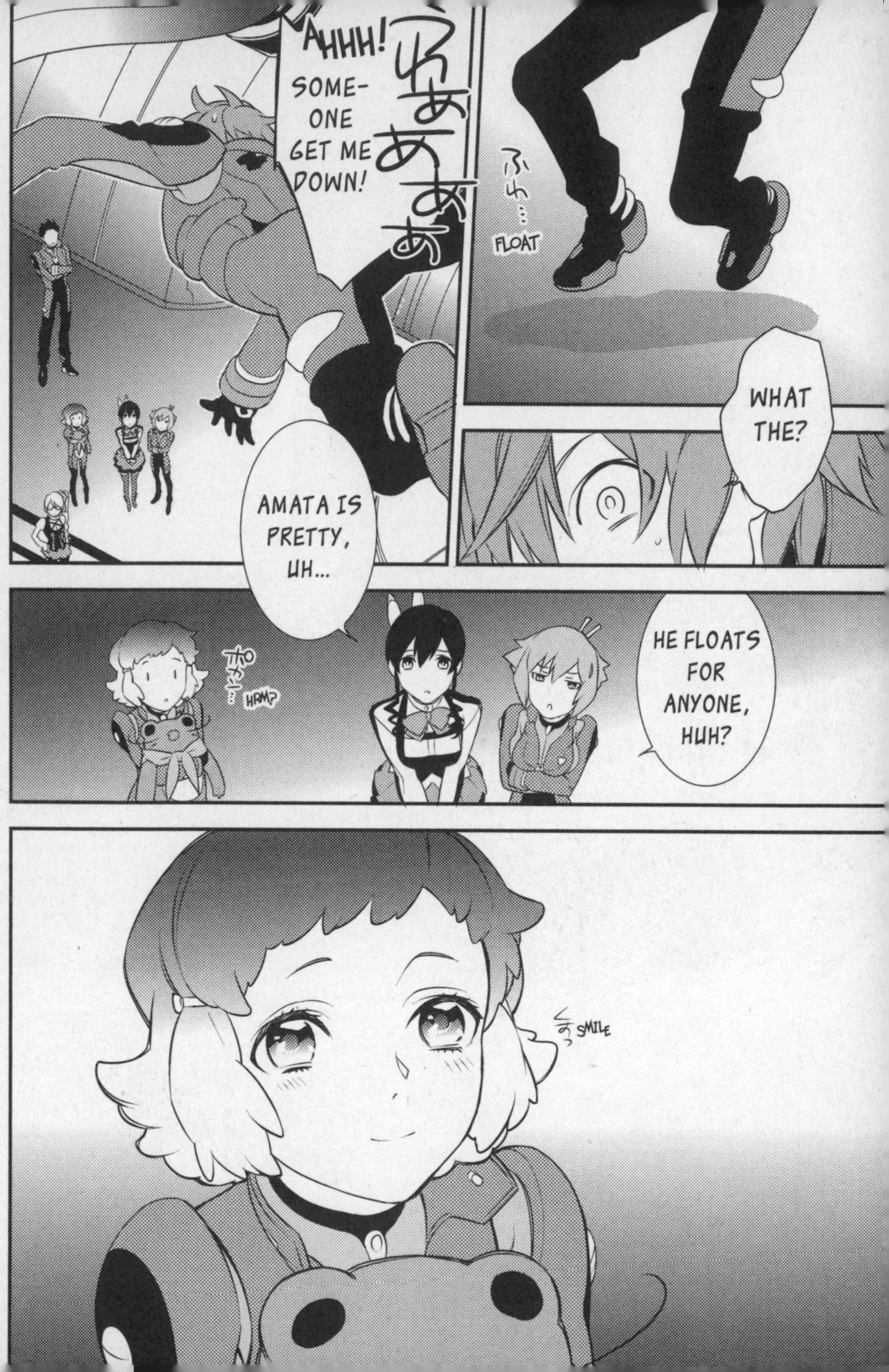
ふわ…
FLOAT
WHAT THE?
AHHH! SOME-ONE GET ME DOWN!
わぁぁぁぁ
AMATA IS PRETTY, UH...
HE FLOATS FOR ANYONE, HUH?
HRM?
SMILE

AQUARION EVOL

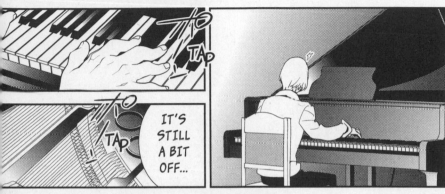

IT'S STILL A BIT OFF...

IT SHOULD BE PERFECTLY IN TIME THOUGH...

THIS IS OUR NEW TRANSFER STUDENT.

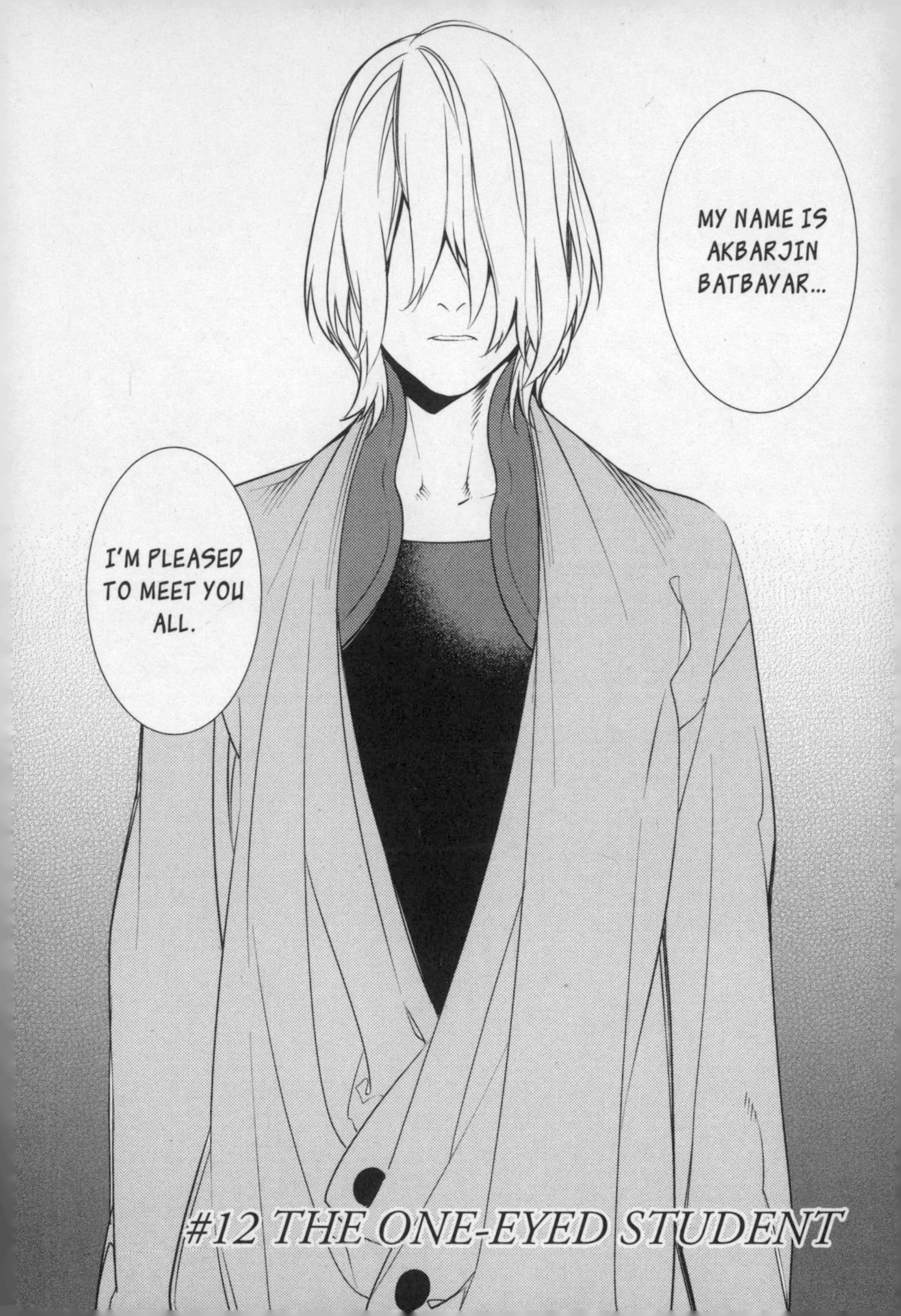
MY NAME IS AKBARJIN BATBAYAR...
I'M PLEASED TO MEET YOU ALL.

#12 THE ONE-EYED STUDENT

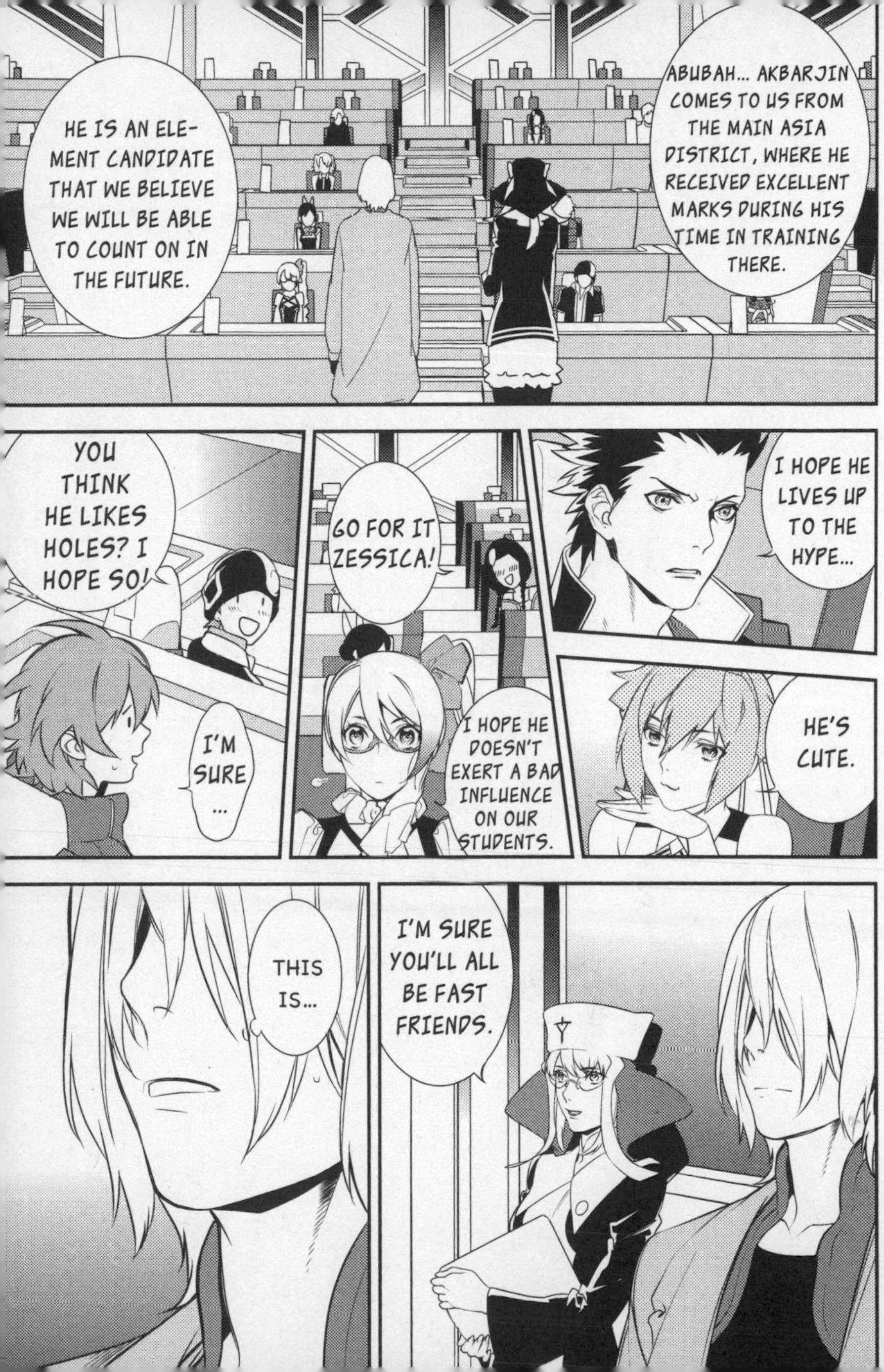
ABUBAH... AKBARJIN COMES TO US FROM THE MAIN ASIA DISTRICT, WHERE HE RECEIVED EXCELLENT MARKS DURING HIS TIME IN TRAINING THERE.
HE IS AN ELE-MENT CANDIDATE THAT WE BELIEVE WE WILL BE ABLE TO COUNT ON IN THE FUTURE.
I HOPE HE LIVES UP TO THE HYPE...
HE'S CUTE.
GO FOR IT ZESSICA!
I HOPE HE DOESN'T EXERT A BAD INFLUENCE ON OUR STUDENTS.
YOU THINK HE LIKES HOLES? I HOPE SO!
I'M SURE ...
I'M SURE YOU'LL ALL BE FAST FRIENDS.
THIS IS...

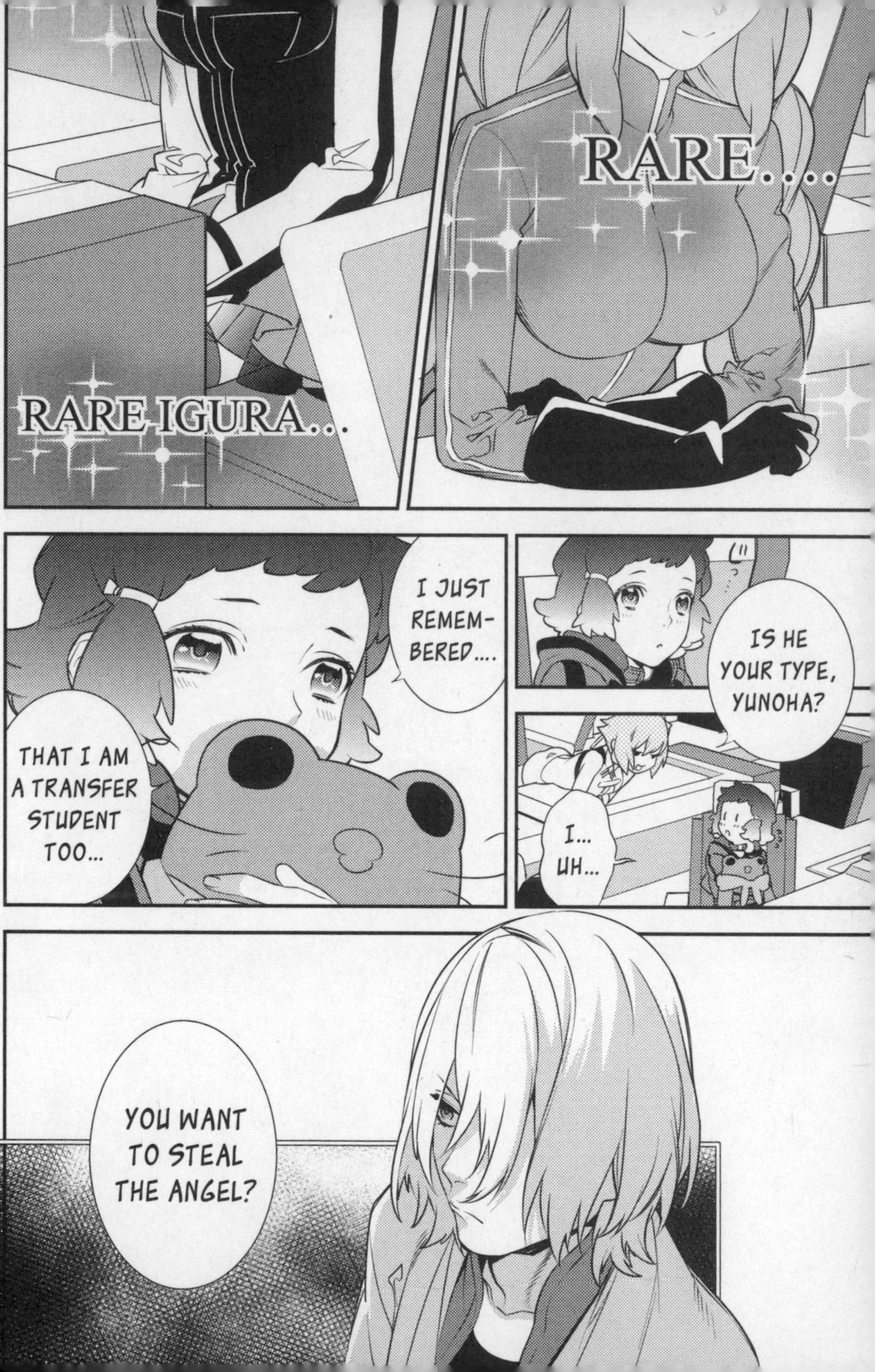
RARE....
RARE IGURA...
IS HE YOUR TYPE, YUNOHA?
I... UH...
I JUST REMEM-BERED....
THAT I AM A TRANSFER STUDENT TOO...
YOU WANT TO STEAL THE ANGEL?

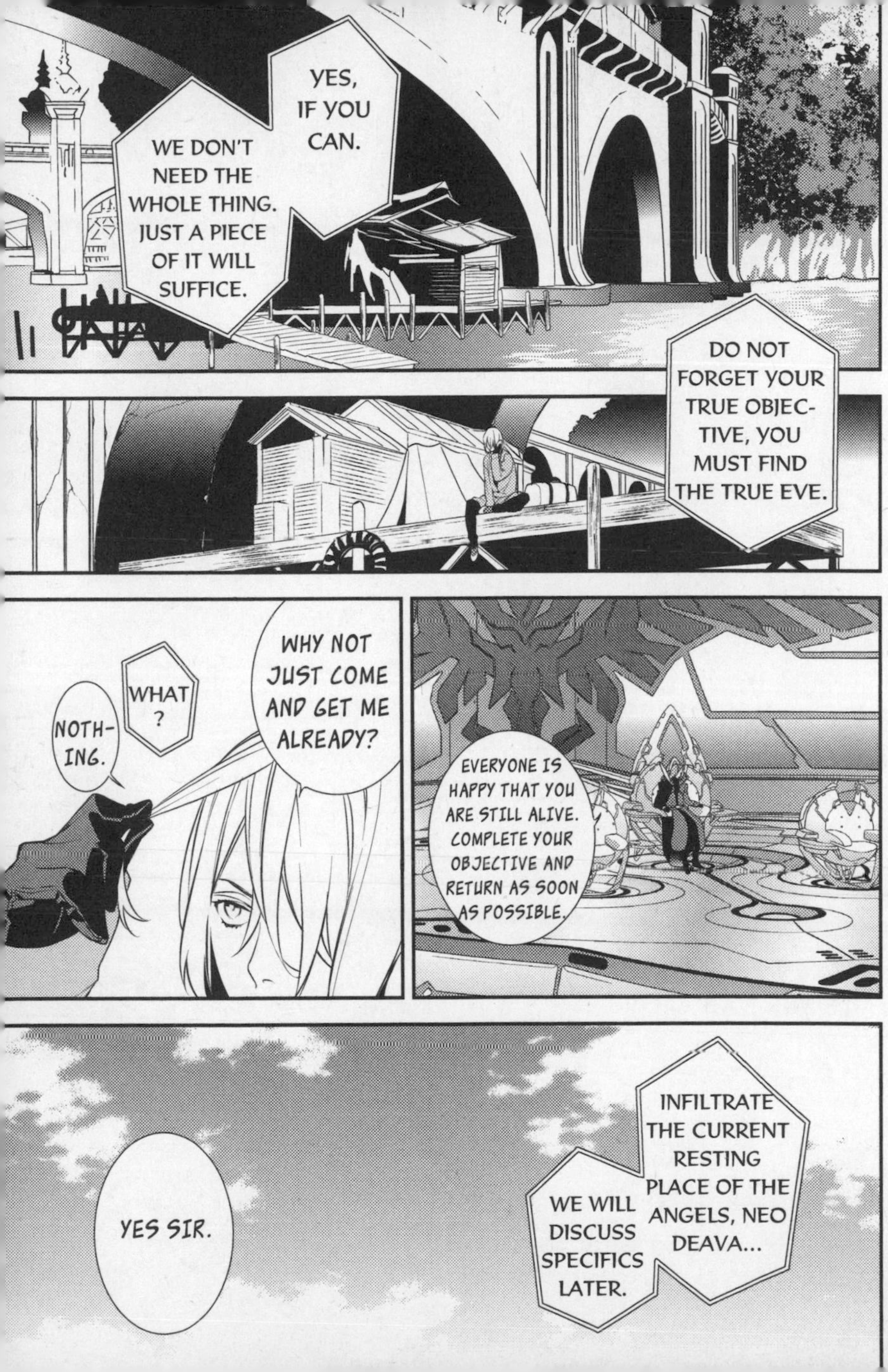
YES, IF YOU CAN.
WE DON'T NEED THE WHOLE THING. JUST A PIECE OF IT WILL SUFFICE.
DO NOT FORGET YOUR TRUE OBJEC-TIVE, YOU MUST FIND THE TRUE EVE.
EVERYONE IS HAPPY THAT YOU ARE STILL ALIVE. COMPLETE YOUR OBJECTIVE AND RETURN AS SOON AS POSSIBLE.
WHY NOT JUST COME AND GET ME ALREADY?
WHAT?
NOTH-ING.
INFILTRATE THE CURRENT RESTING PLACE OF THE ANGELS, NEO DEAVA...
WE WILL DISCUSS SPECIFICS LATER.
YES SIR.

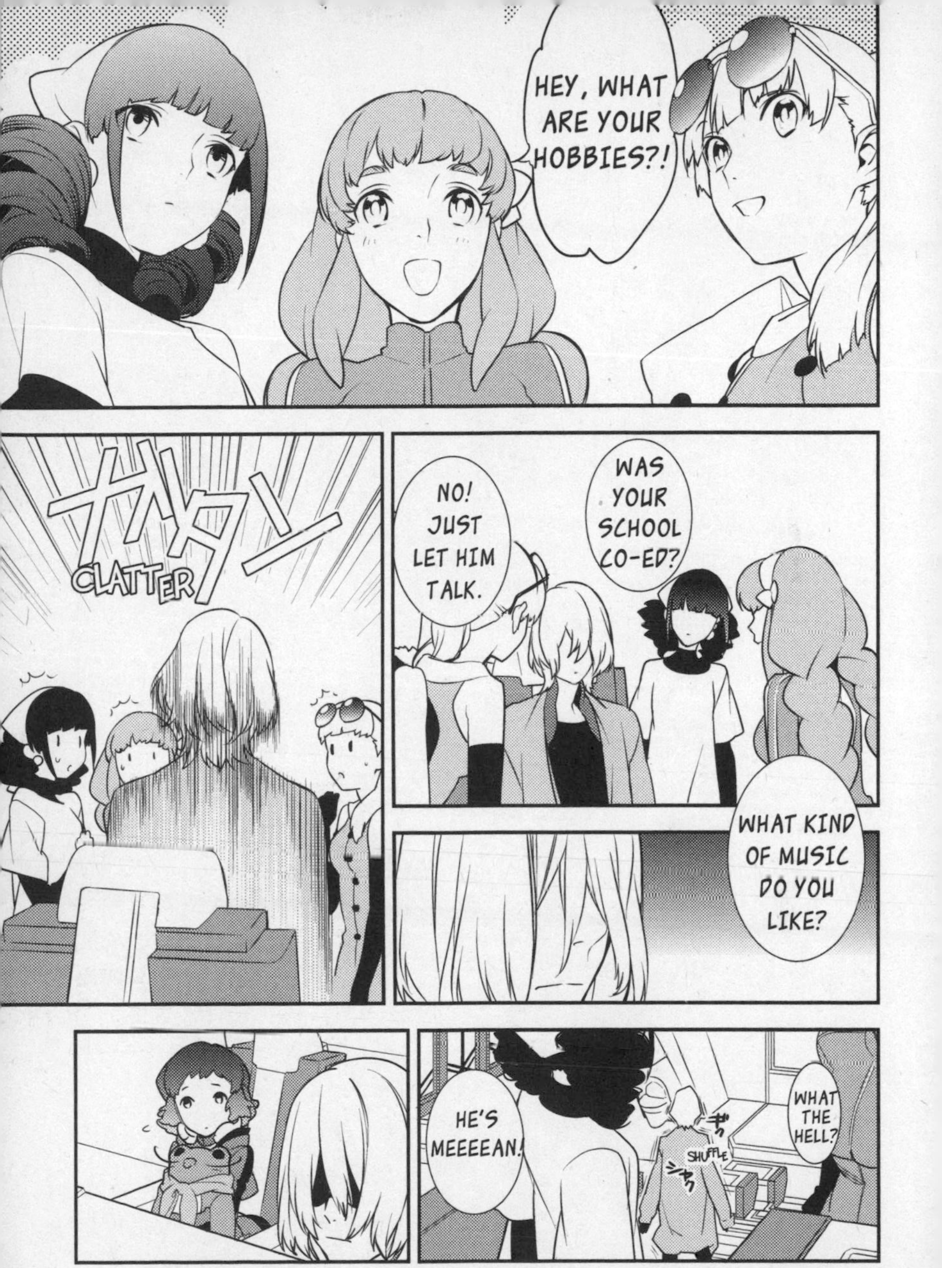
HEY, WHAT ARE YOUR HOBBIES?!
WAS YOUR SCHOOL CO-ED?
NO! JUST LET HIM TALK.
WHAT KIND OF MUSIC DO YOU LIKE?
CLATTER
WHAT THE HELL?
SHUFFLE
HE'S MEEEEAN!

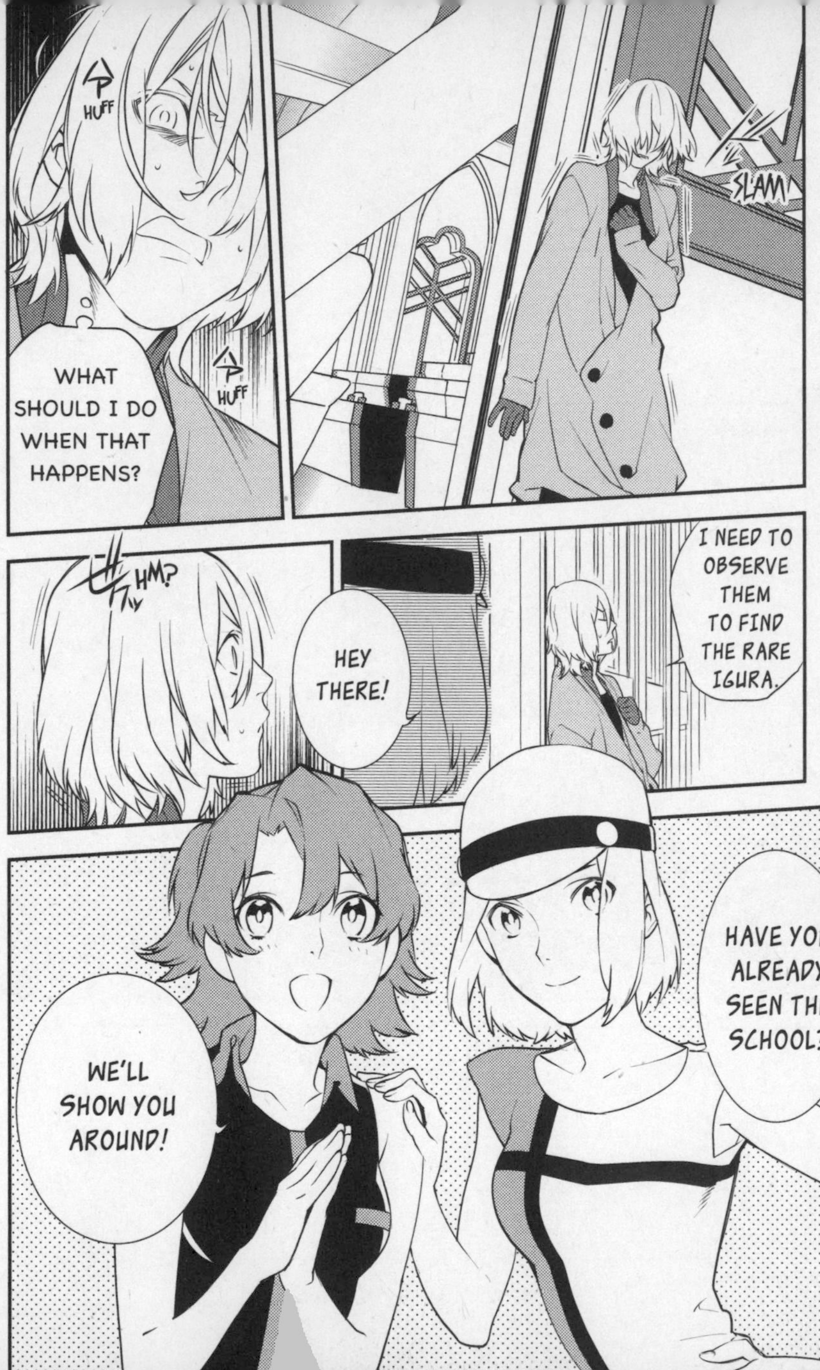
SLAM
HUFF
WHAT SHOULD I DO WHEN THAT HAPPENS?
HUFF
I NEED TO OBSERVE THEM TO FIND THE RARE IGURA.
HM?
HEY THERE!
HAVE YOU ALREADY SEEN THE SCHOOL?
WE'LL SHOW YOU AROUND!

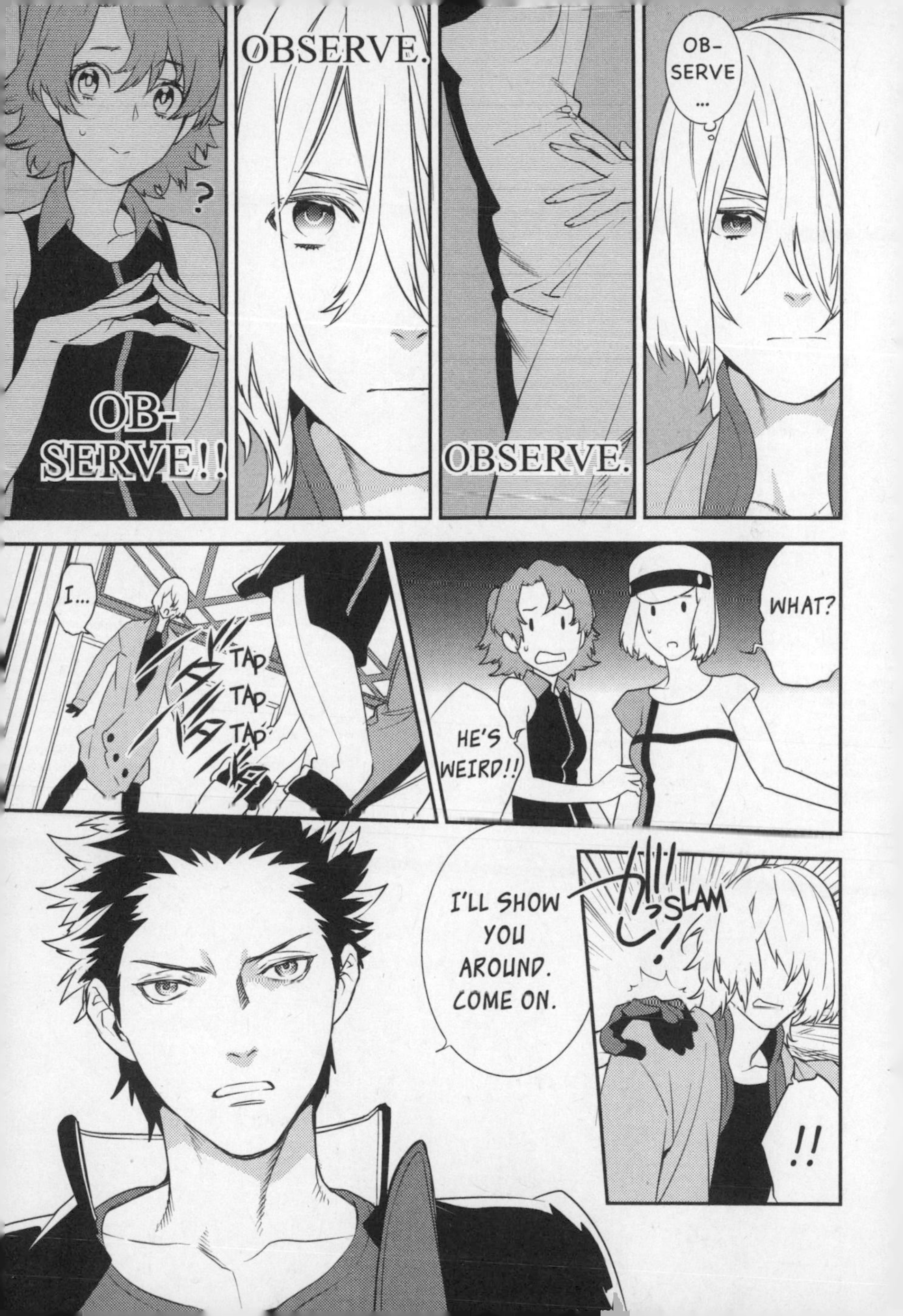
OB-SERVE ...
OBSERVE.
OBSERVE.
?
OB-SERVE!!
WHAT?
HE'S WEIRD!!
TAP TAP TAP
I...
SLAM
!!
I'LL SHOW YOU AROUND. COME ON.

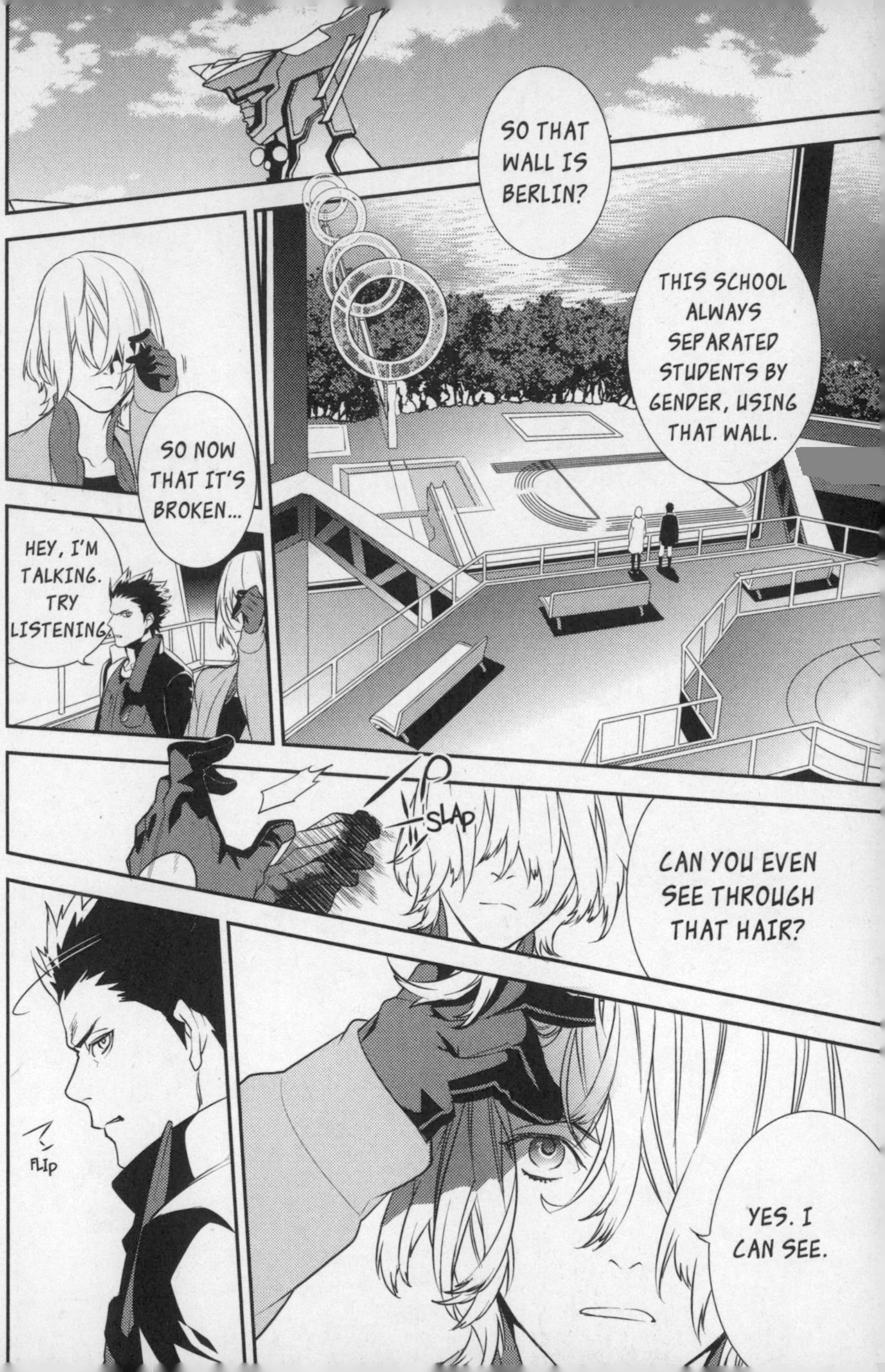
SO THAT WALL IS BERLIN?
THIS SCHOOL ALWAYS SEPARATED STUDENTS BY GENDER, USING THAT WALL.
SO NOW THAT IT'S BROKEN...
HEY, I'M TALKING. TRY LISTENING.
SLAP
CAN YOU EVEN SEE THROUGH THAT HAIR?
FLIP
YES. I CAN SEE.

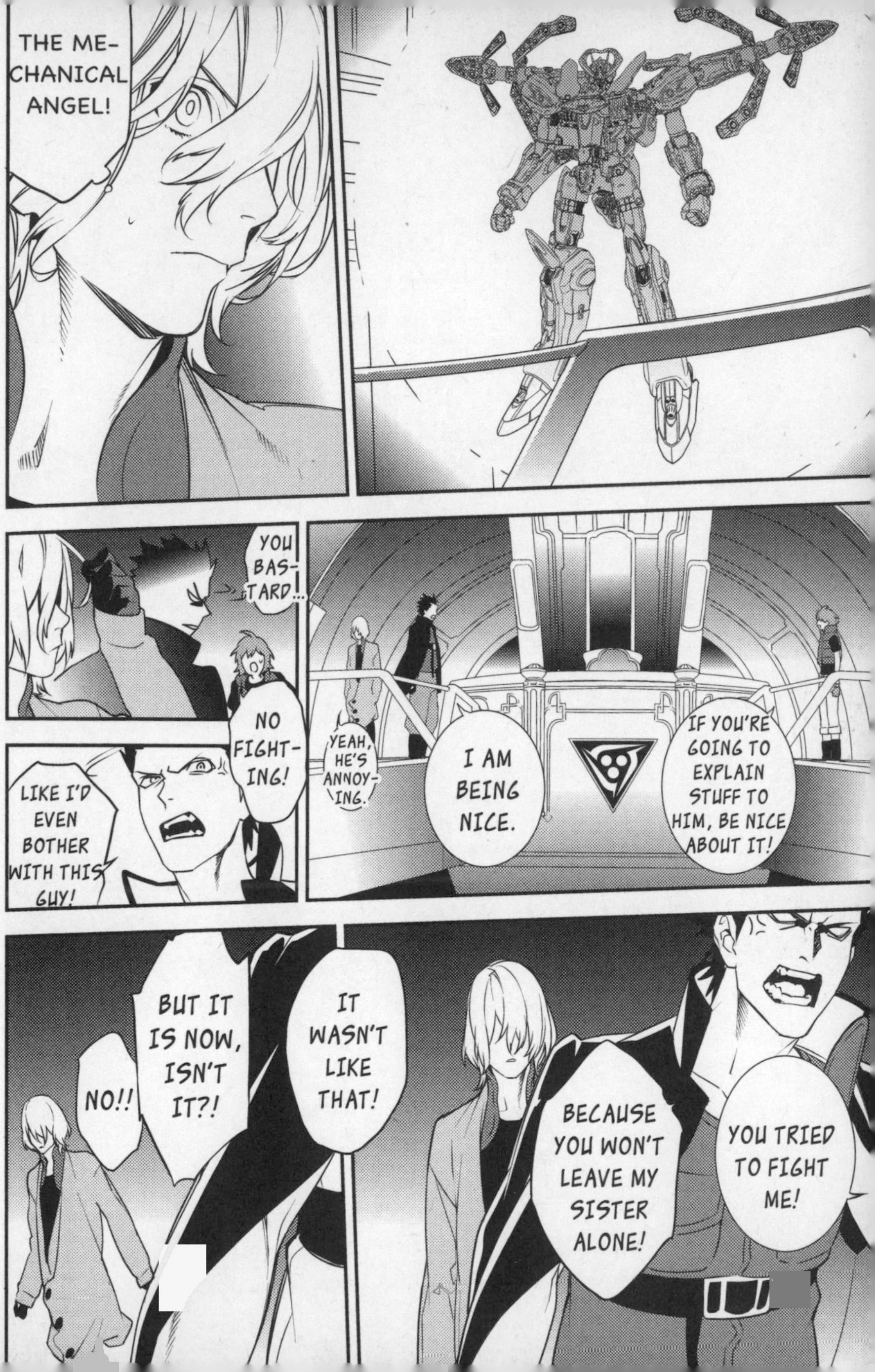
THE ME-CHANICAL ANGEL!
IF YOU'RE GOING TO EXPLAIN STUFF TO HIM, BE NICE ABOUT IT!
I AM BEING NICE.
YEAH, HE'S ANNOY-ING.
YOU BAS-TARD...
NO FIGHT-ING!
LIKE I'D EVEN BOTHER WITH THIS GUY!
YOU TRIED TO FIGHT ME!
BECAUSE YOU WON'T LEAVE MY SISTER ALONE!
IT WASN'T LIKE THAT!
BUT IT IS NOW, ISN'T IT?!
NO!!

I COULD USE ONE OF THEM...

SO THESE ARE THE PARTS THAT MAKE UP THE MECHANICAL ANGEL...

GO TAKE A LOOK.

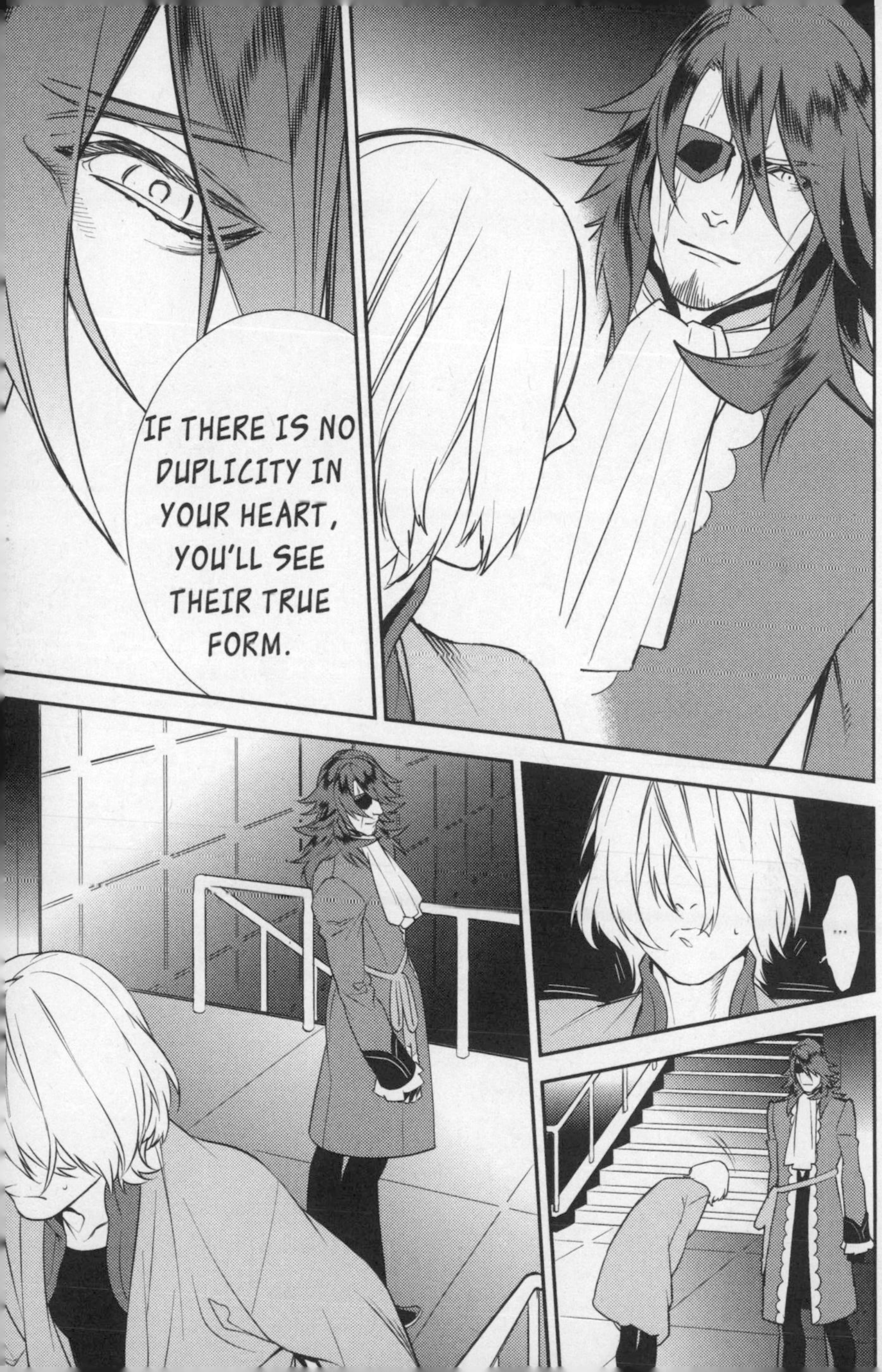
IF THERE IS NO DUPLICITY IN YOUR HEART, YOU'LL SEE THEIR TRUE FORM.
...

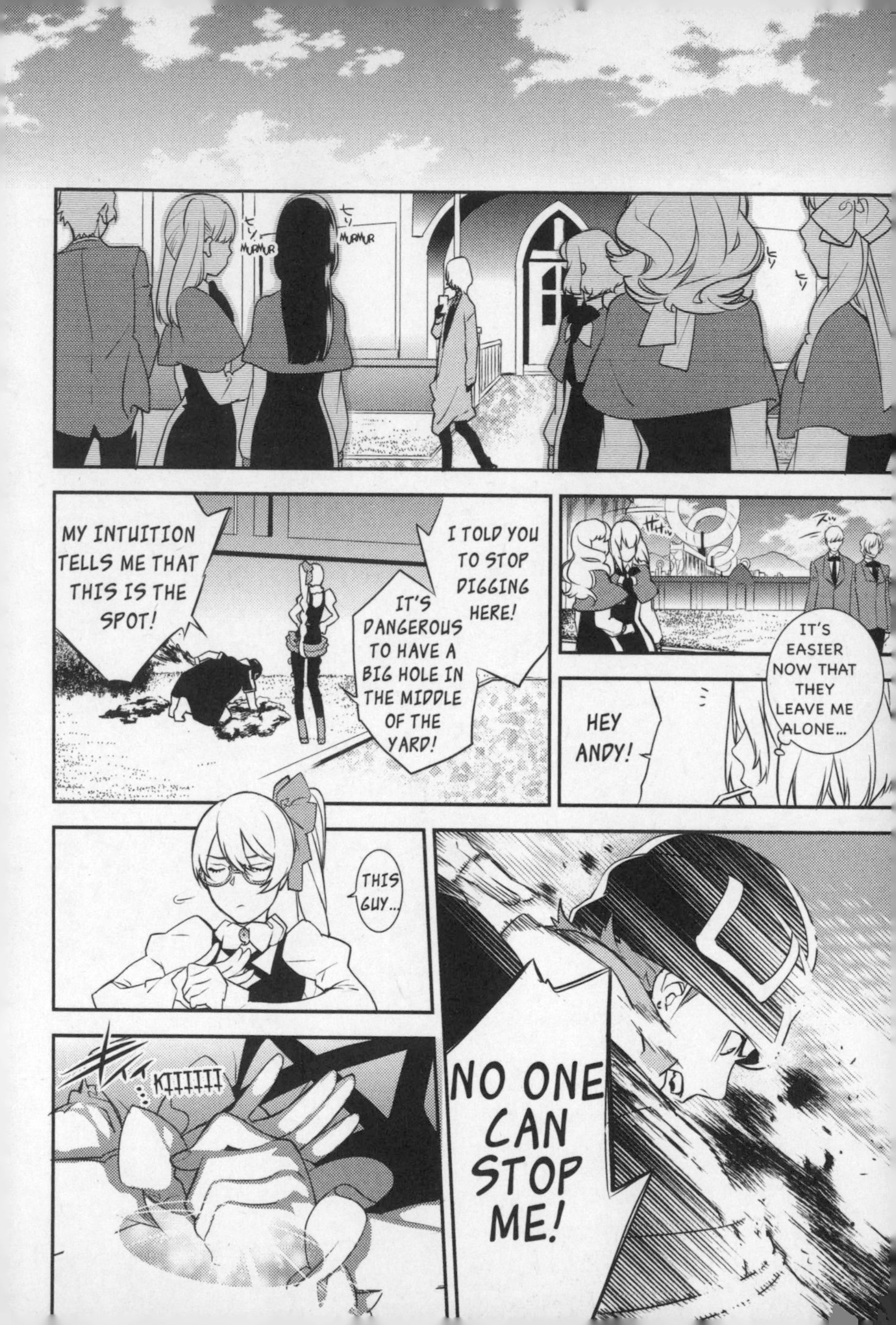
MURMUR
MURMUR
IT'S EASIER NOW THAT THEY LEAVE ME ALONE...
HEY ANDY!
I TOLD YOU TO STOP DIGGING HERE!
IT'S DANGEROUS TO HAVE A BIG HOLE IN THE MIDDLE OF THE YARD!
MY INTUITION TELLS ME THAT THIS IS THE SPOT!
NO ONE CAN STOP ME!
THIS GUY...
KIIIIII

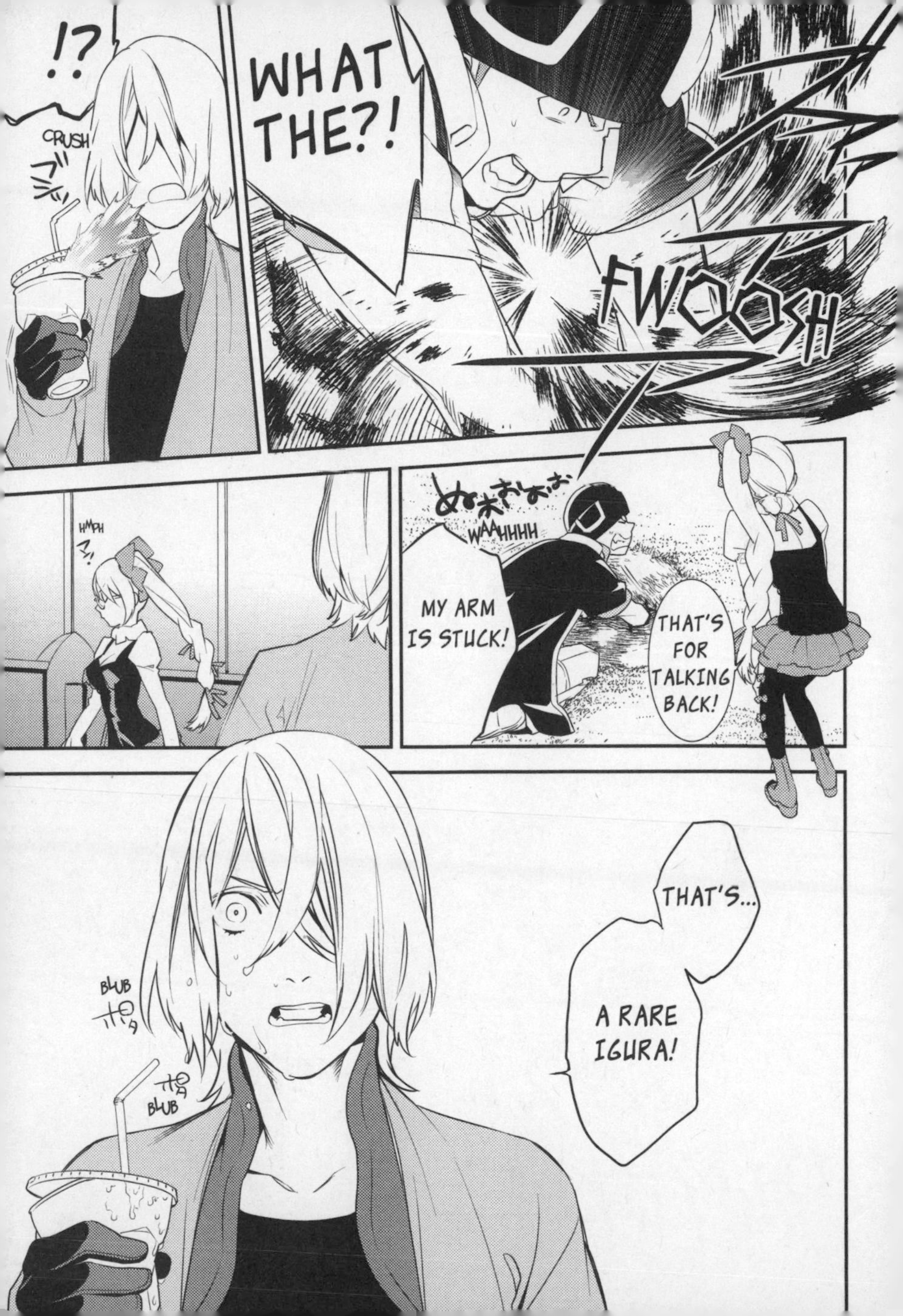
WHAT THE?!
FWOOSH
!?
CRUSH
WAAHHHH
THAT'S FOR TALKING BACK!
MY ARM IS STUCK!
HMPH
THAT'S...
A RARE IGURA!
BLUB
BLUB

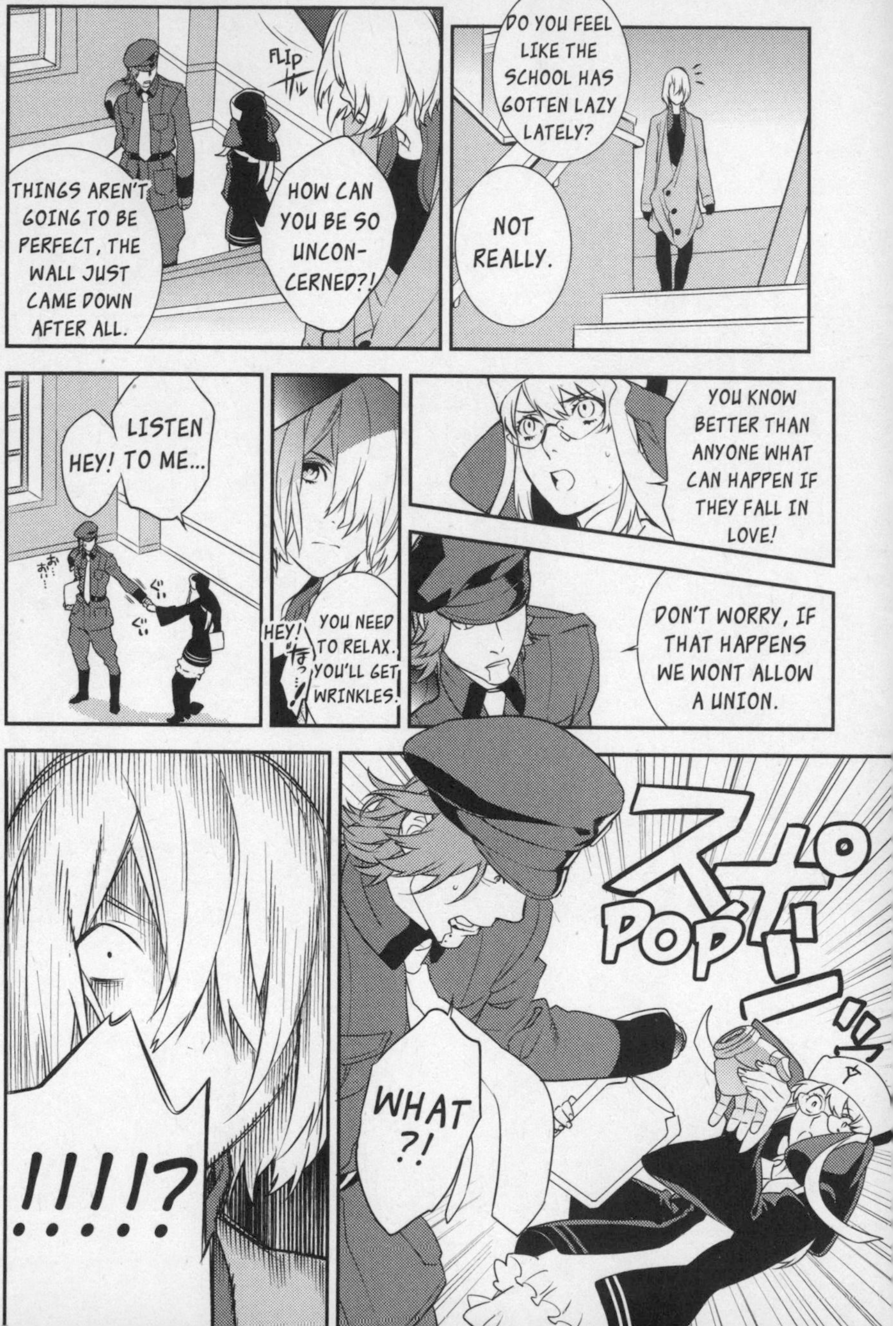
DO YOU FEEL LIKE THE SCHOOL HAS GOTTEN LAZY LATELY?
NOT REALLY.
FLIP
HOW CAN YOU BE SO UNCON-CERNED?!
THINGS AREN'T GOING TO BE PERFECT, THE WALL JUST CAME DOWN AFTER ALL.
YOU KNOW BETTER THAN ANYONE WHAT CAN HAPPEN IF THEY FALL IN LOVE!
DON'T WORRY, IF THAT HAPPENS WE WONT ALLOW A UNION.
YOU NEED TO RELAX. YOU'LL GET WRINKLES!
HEY!
LISTEN TO ME...
HEY!
POP
WHAT?!
!!!!?

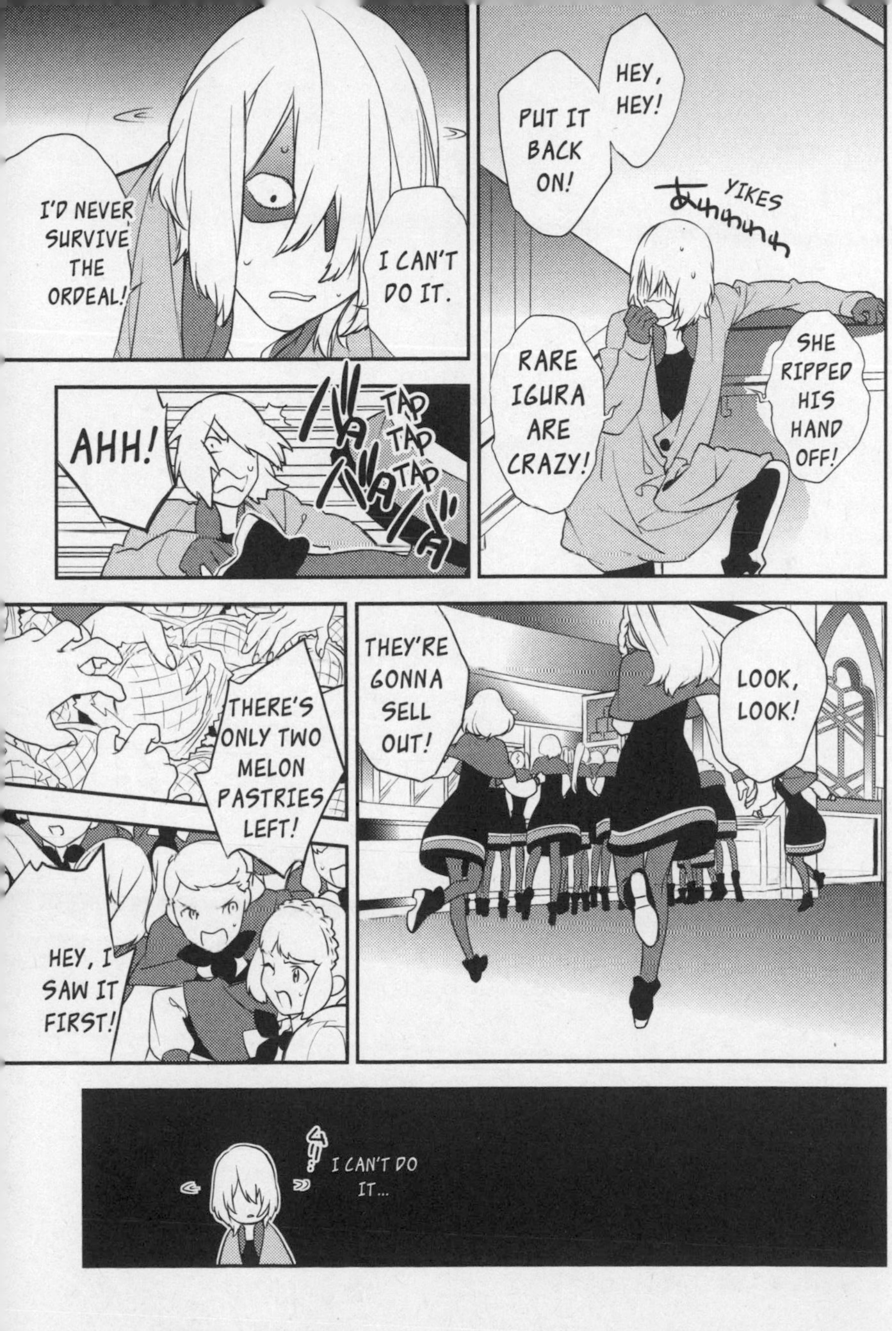
HEY, HEY!
PUT IT BACK ON!
YIKES
SHE RIPPED HIS HAND OFF!
RARE IGURA ARE CRAZY!
I CAN'T DO IT.
I'D NEVER SURVIVE THE ORDEAL!
AHH!
TAP TAP TAP TAP
LOOK, LOOK!
THEY'RE GONNA SELL OUT!
THERE'S ONLY TWO MELON PASTRIES LEFT!
HEY, I SAW IT FIRST!
I CAN'T DO IT...

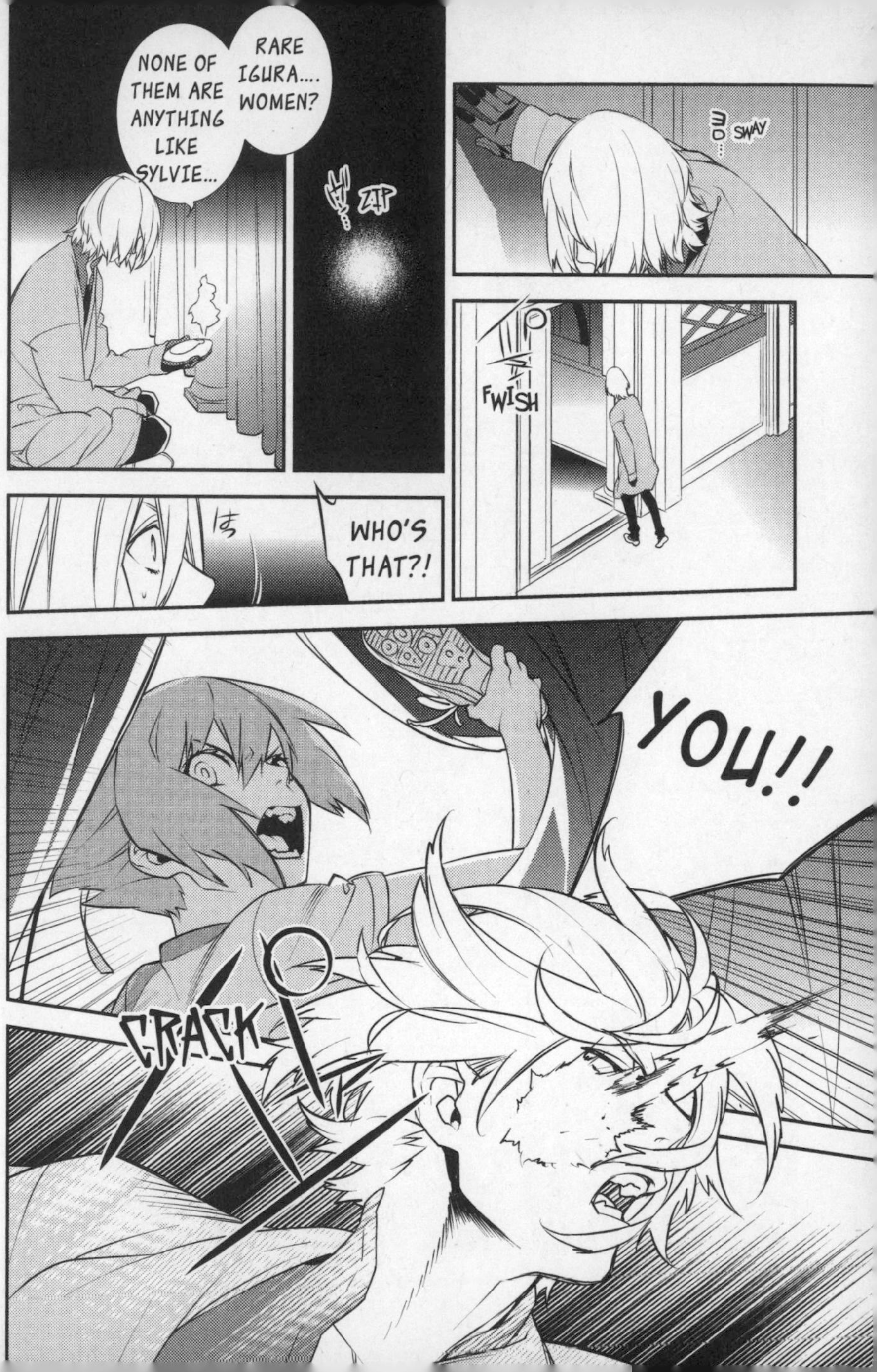
SWAY
FWISH
ZAP
RARE IGURA.... WOMEN?
NONE OF THEM ARE ANYTHING LIKE SYLVIE...
WHO'S THAT?!
YOU!!
CRACK

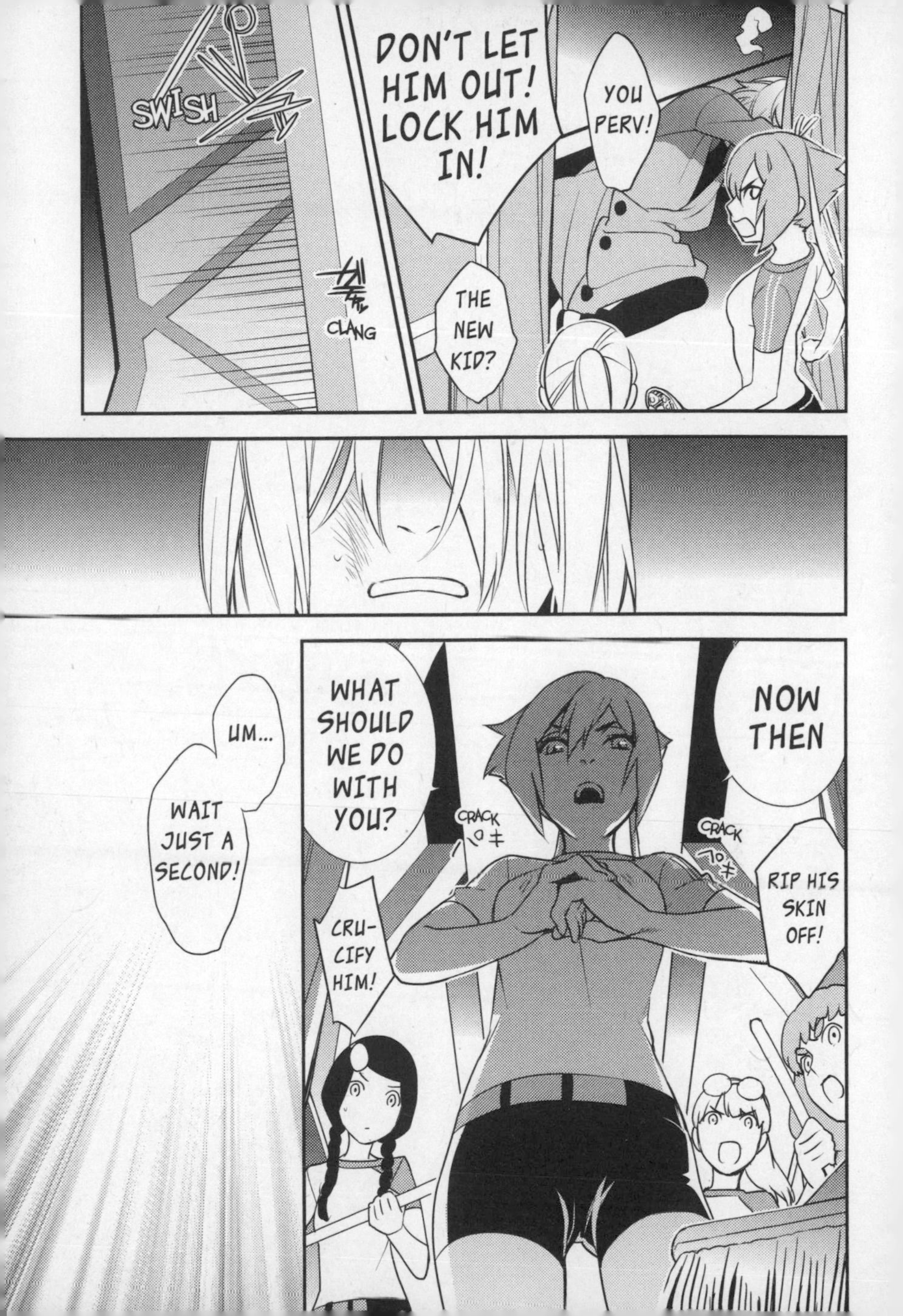
YOU PERV!
DON'T LET HIM OUT! LOCK HIM IN!
THE NEW KID?
SWISH
CLANG
NOW THEN
WHAT SHOULD WE DO WITH YOU?
CRACK
CRACK
RIP HIS SKIN OFF!
CRU-CIFY HIM!
UM...
WAIT JUST A SECOND!

WHO?

DID YOU?

SO EMBAR-RAS-SING...

WHEN I FIRST CAME HERE I ACCIDENTLY WENT TO THE BOY'S BATH-ROOM ALL THE TIME,

I DON'T THINK HE DID IT ON PURPOSE...

DID YOU COME IN HERE ON ACCIDENT?

HUH?

YES! IT WAS JUST AN ACCIDENT!

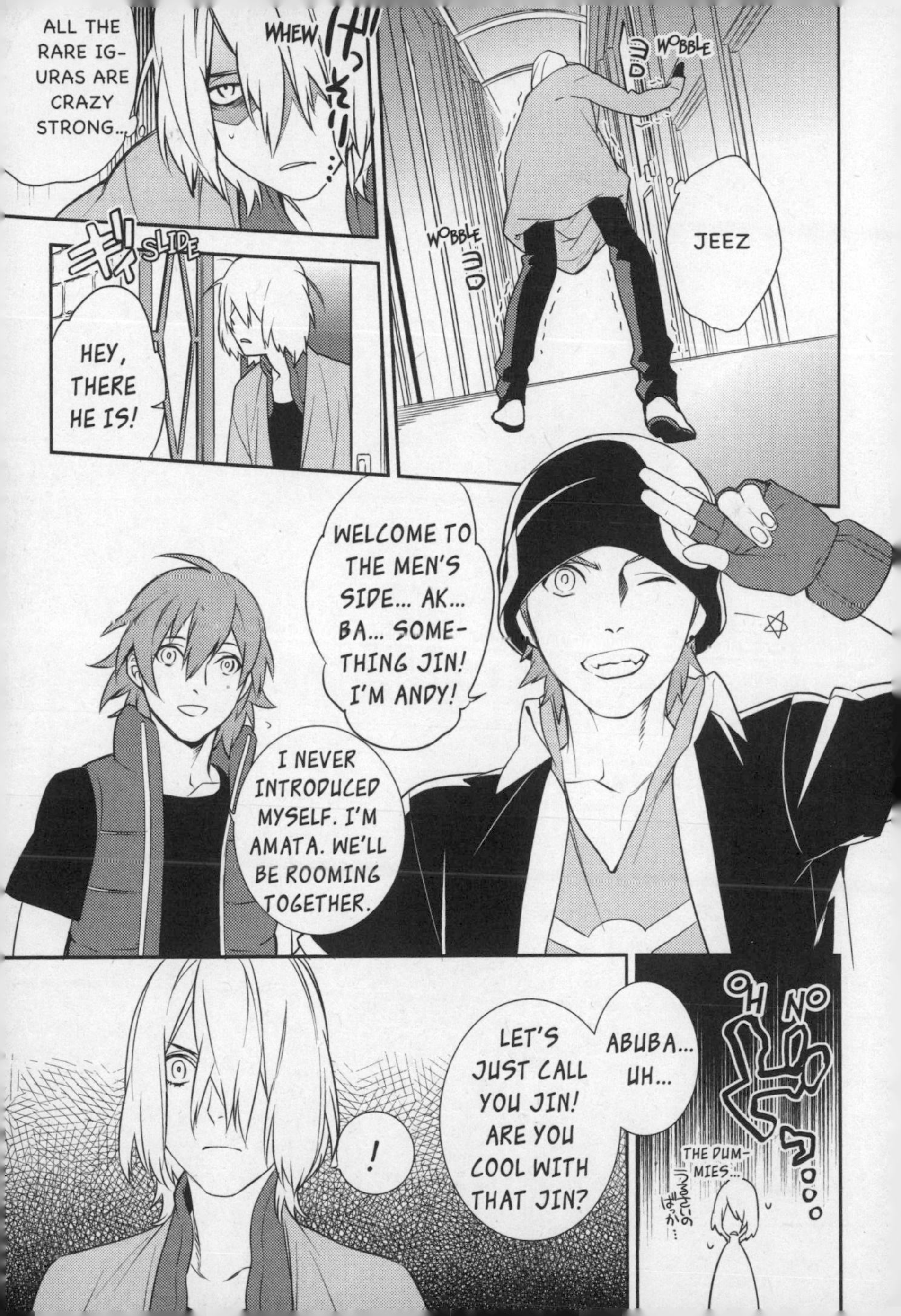

WOBBLE
ヨロ
JEEZ
WOBBLE
ヨロ
WHEW
ALL THE RARE IG-URAS ARE CRAZY STRONG...
SLIDE
HEY, THERE HE IS!
WELCOME TO THE MEN'S SIDE... AK... BA... SOME-THING JIN! I'M ANDY!
I NEVER INTRODUCED MYSELF. I'M AMATA. WE'LL BE ROOMING TOGETHER.
OH NO
THE DUM-MIES...
ABUBA... UH...
LET'S JUST CALL YOU JIN! ARE YOU COOL WITH THAT JIN?
!

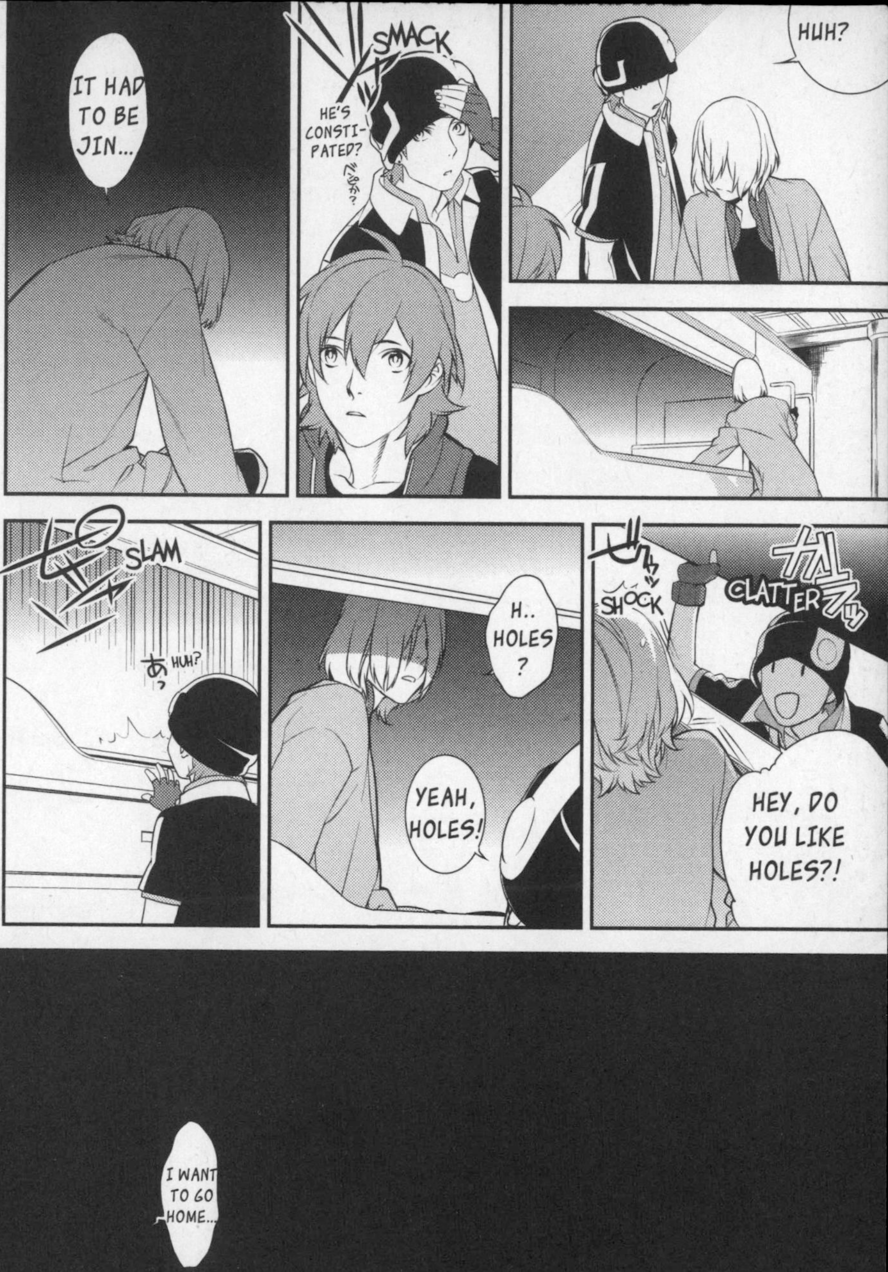
HUH?
SMACK
HE'S CONSTI-PATED?
IT HAD TO BE JIN...
SHOCK
CLATTER
HEY, DO YOU LIKE HOLES?!
H.. HOLES?
YEAH, HOLES!
SLAM
HUH?
I WANT TO GO HOME...

aquarion evol

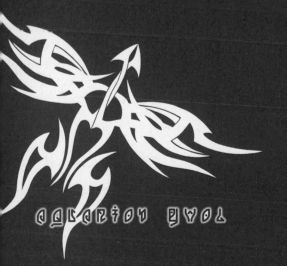

#13 WAVERING SOUNDS

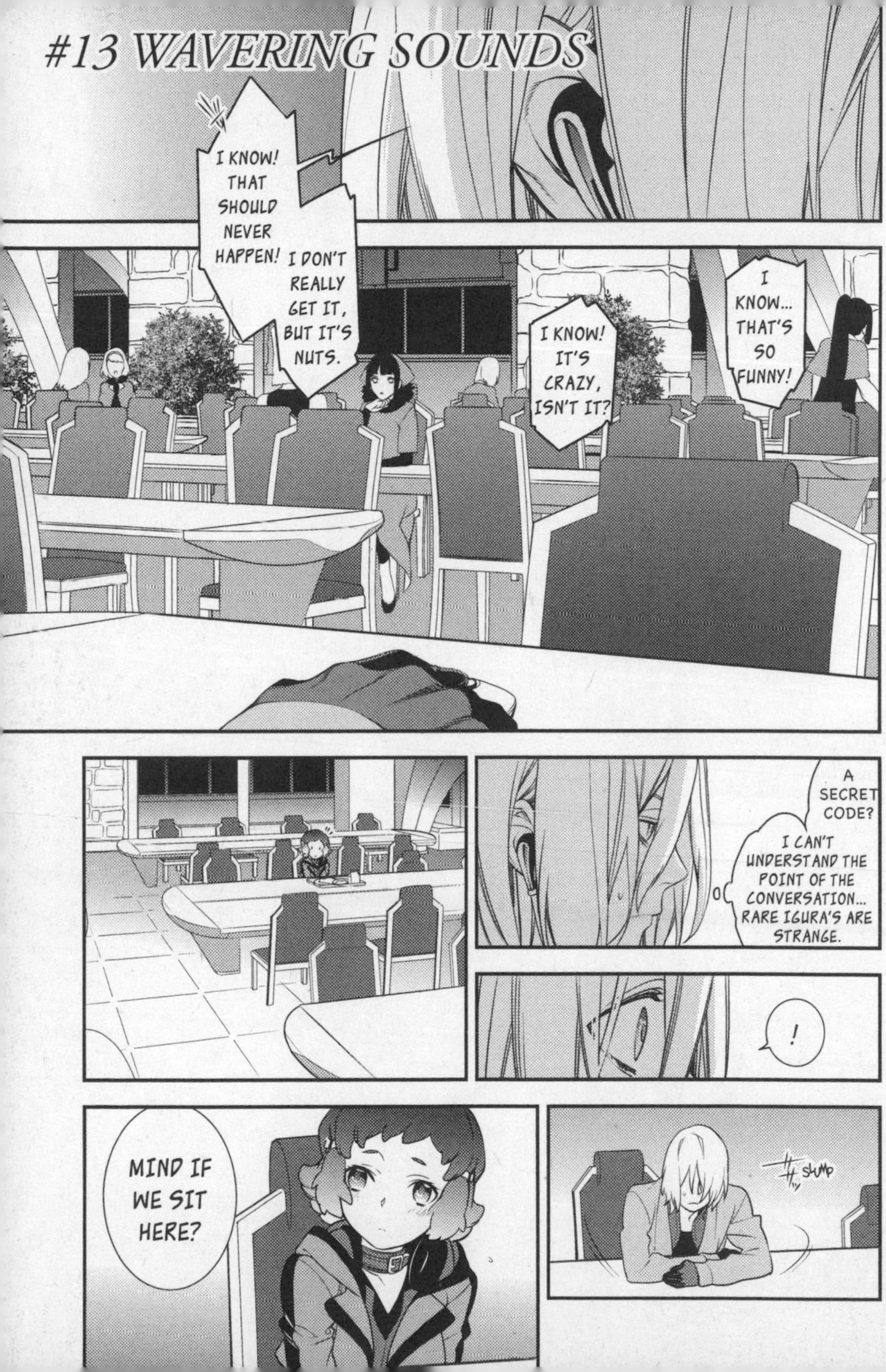
I KNOW! THAT SHOULD NEVER HAPPEN!
I KNOW... THAT'S SO FUNNY!
I KNOW! IT'S CRAZY, ISN'T IT?
I DON'T REALLY GET IT, BUT IT'S NUTS.
A SECRET CODE?
I CAN'T UNDERSTAND THE POINT OF THE CONVERSATION... RARE IGURA'S ARE STRANGE.
!
SLUMP
MIND IF WE SIT HERE?

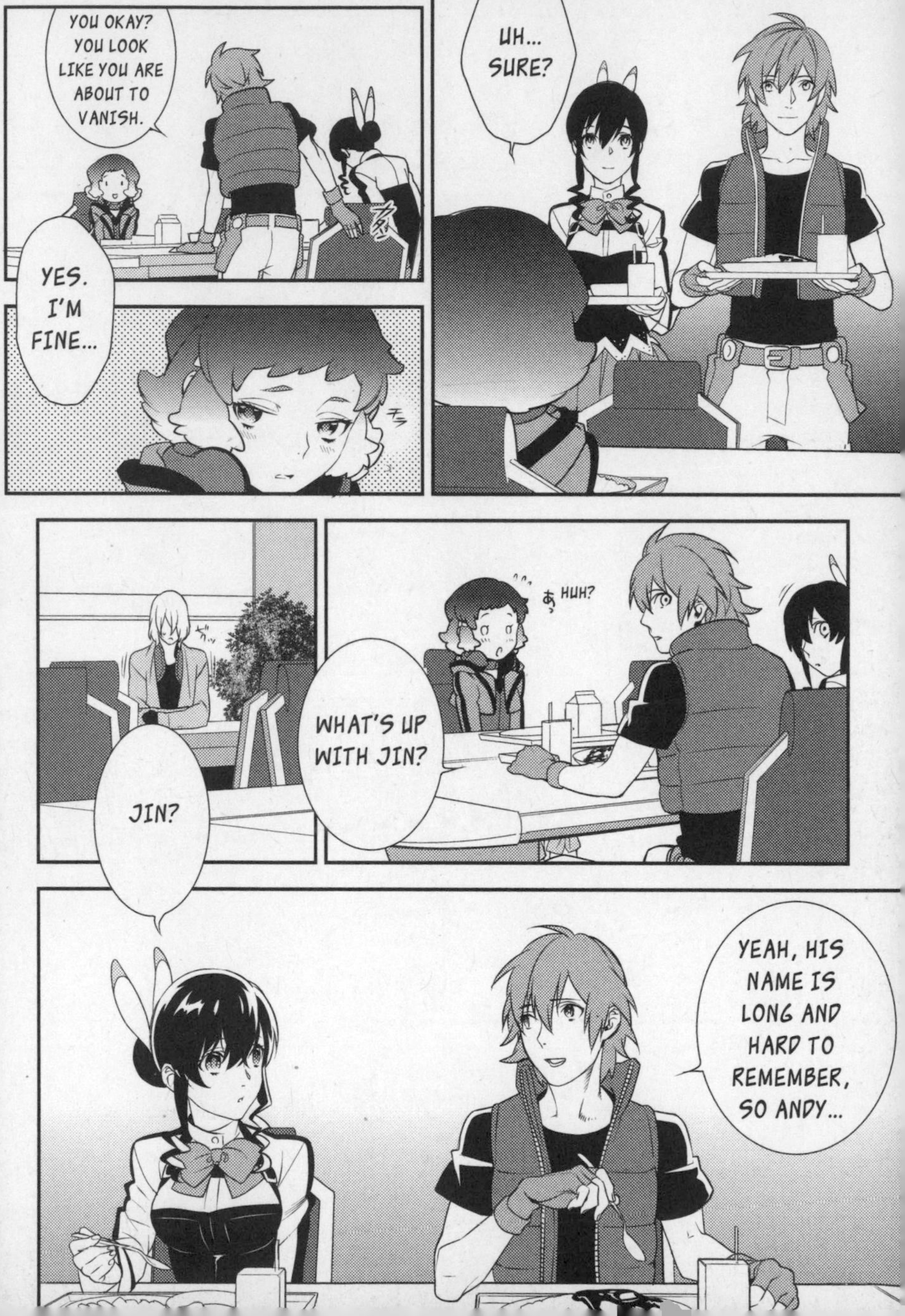
UH... SURE?
YOU OKAY? YOU LOOK LIKE YOU ARE ABOUT TO VANISH.
YES. I'M FINE...
あ HUH?
WHAT'S UP WITH JIN?
JIN?
YEAH, HIS NAME IS LONG AND HARD TO REMEMBER, SO ANDY...

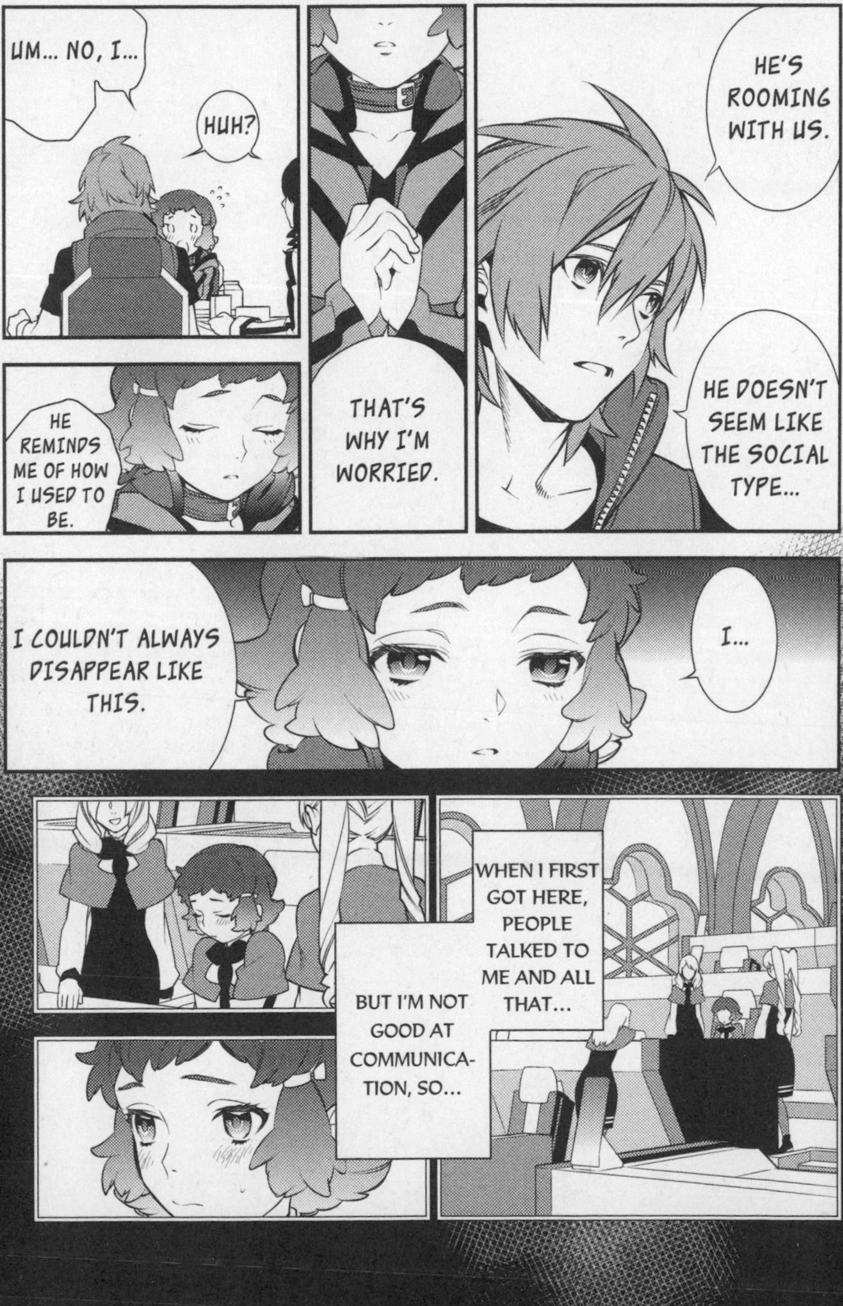
HE'S ROOMING WITH US.
HE DOESN'T SEEM LIKE THE SOCIAL TYPE...
THAT'S WHY I'M WORRIED.
UM... NO, I...
HUH?
HE REMINDS ME OF HOW I USED TO BE.
I...
I COULDN'T ALWAYS DISAPPEAR LIKE THIS.
WHEN I FIRST GOT HERE, PEOPLE TALKED TO ME AND ALL THAT...
BUT I'M NOT GOOD AT COMMUNICA-TION, SO...

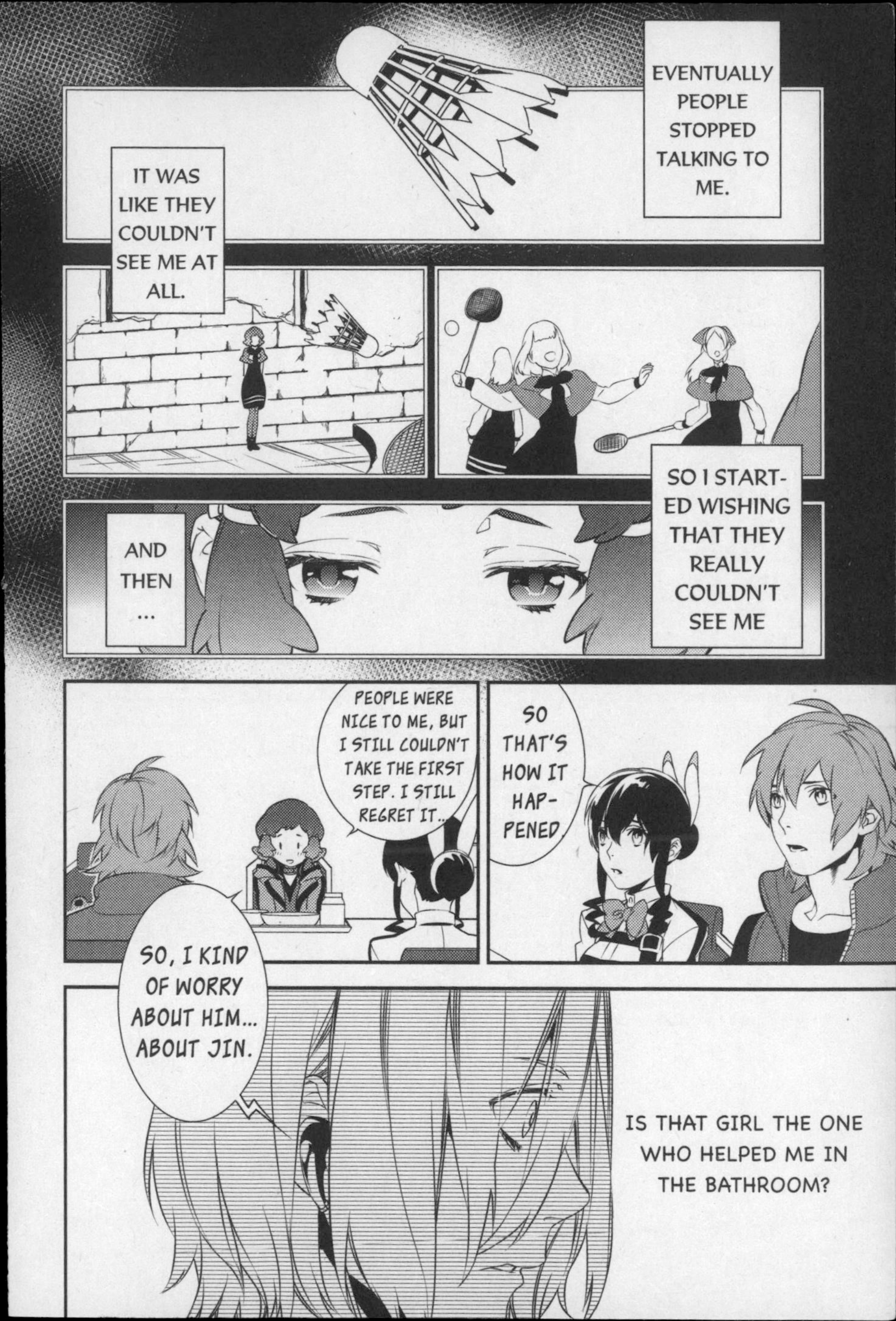
EVENTUALLY PEOPLE STOPPED TALKING TO ME.
IT WAS LIKE THEY COULDN'T SEE ME AT ALL.
SO I START-ED WISHING THAT THEY REALLY COULDN'T SEE ME
AND THEN ...
SO THAT'S HOW IT HAP-PENED.
PEOPLE WERE NICE TO ME, BUT I STILL COULDN'T TAKE THE FIRST STEP. I STILL REGRET IT..
SO, I KIND OF WORRY ABOUT HIM... ABOUT JIN.
IS THAT GIRL THE ONE WHO HELPED ME IN THE BATHROOM?

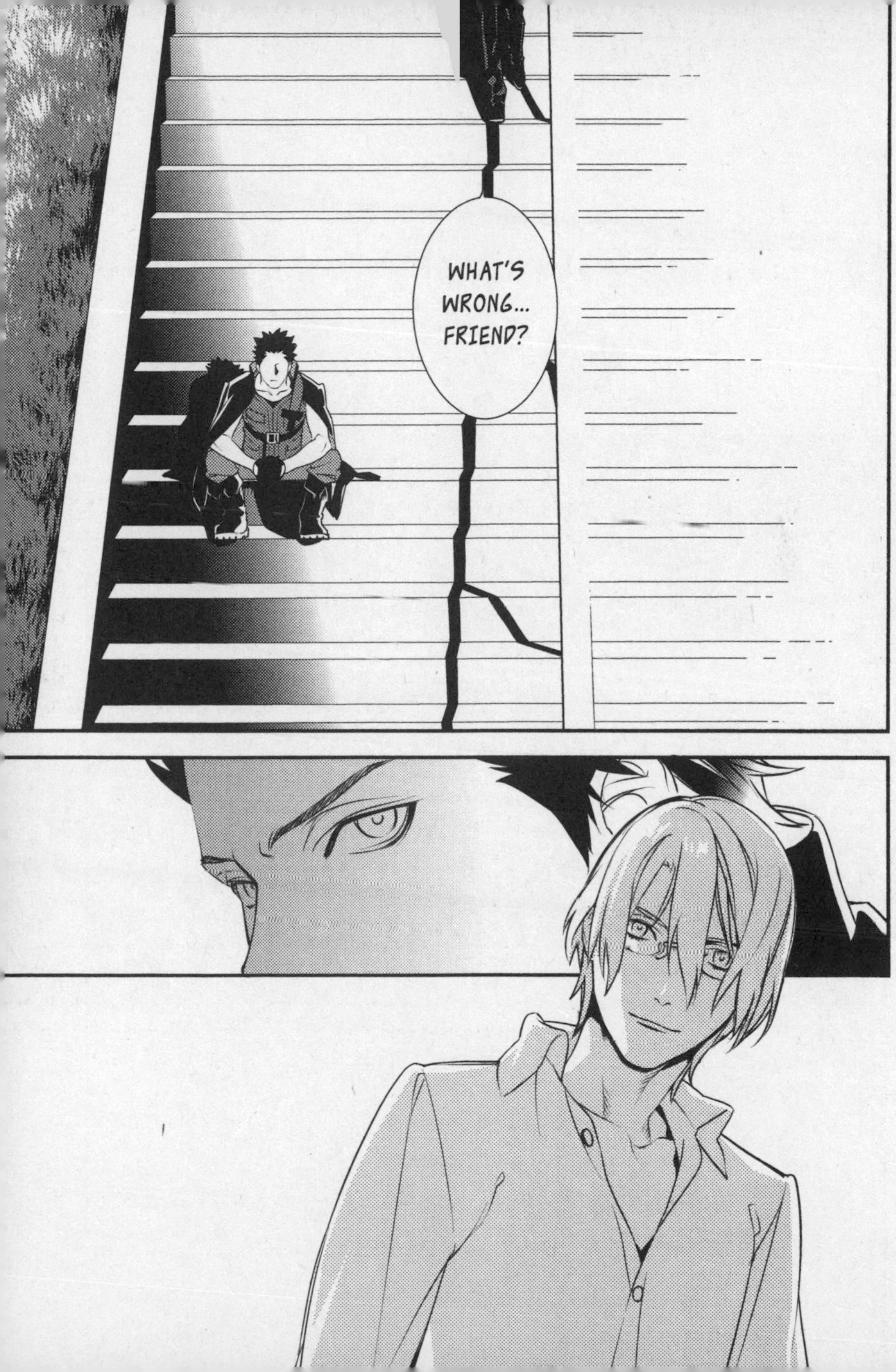
WHAT'S WRONG... FRIEND?

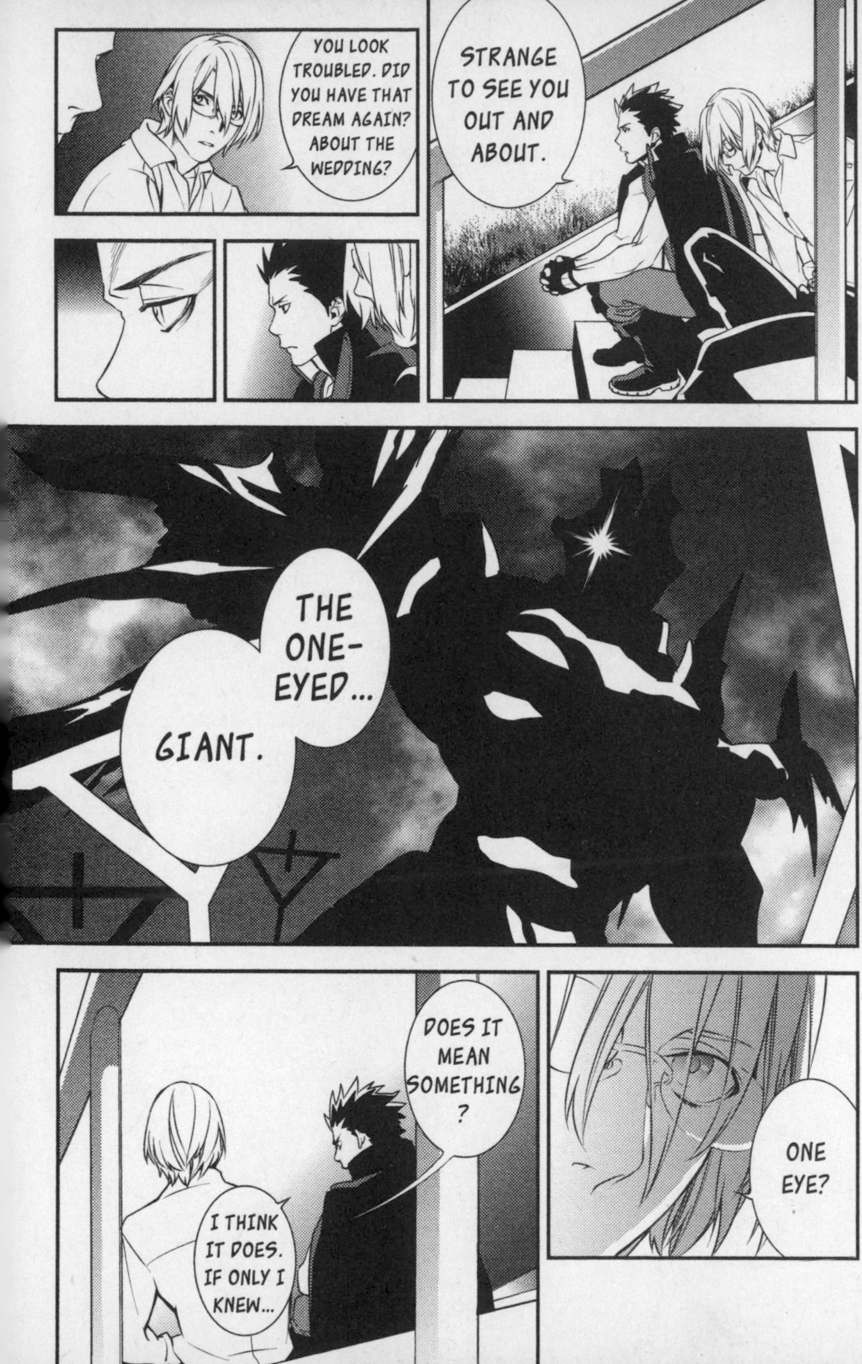
STRANGE TO SEE YOU OUT AND ABOUT.
YOU LOOK TROUBLED. DID YOU HAVE THAT DREAM AGAIN? ABOUT THE WEDDING?
THE ONE-EYED...
GIANT.
ONE EYE?
DOES IT MEAN SOMETHING?
I THINK IT DOES. IF ONLY I KNEW...

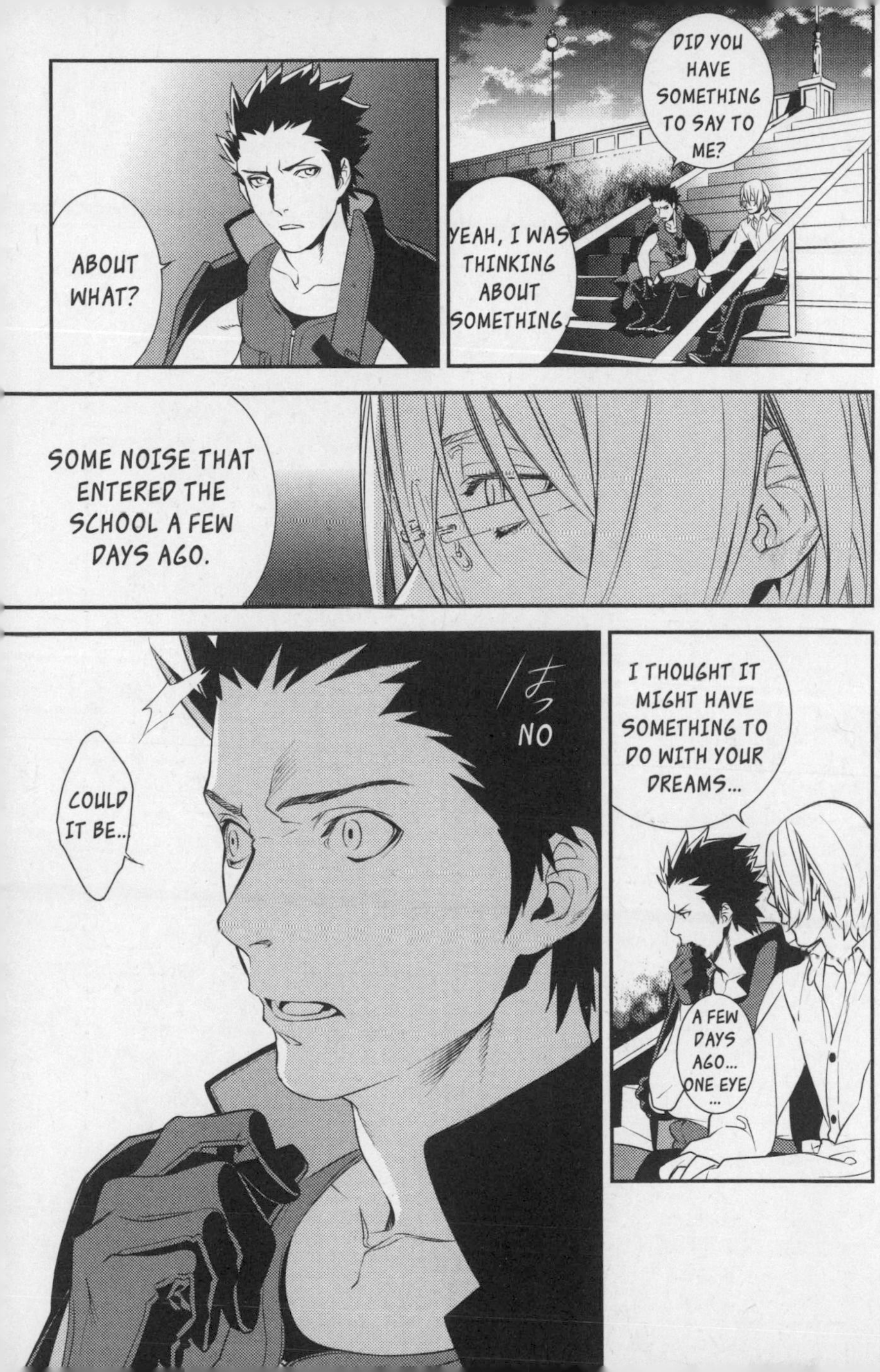
DID YOU HAVE SOMETHING TO SAY TO ME?
YEAH, I WAS THINKING ABOUT SOMETHING.
ABOUT WHAT?
SOME NOISE THAT ENTERED THE SCHOOL A FEW DAYS AGO.
I THOUGHT IT MIGHT HAVE SOMETHING TO DO WITH YOUR DREAMS...
A FEW DAYS AGO... ONE EYE ...
はっ
NO
COULD IT BE...

HE'S
WEIRD
...

I DON'T
UNDER-
STAND.

WHAT'S
WITH
HIM...

SLAM

NO NEED
TO LOOK
AT THIS
ANY
MORE.

RARE
IGURA'S
ARE A
COMPLETE
MYSTERY

UM
...

HRM?
?

CLATTER

SHUU

ボスン
SLAM

I'M SORRY!

WHAT THE?!

SHHHHHH

...

THAT'S MY DOLL...

OH, JIN!

SHE'S... GONE?!

THANK YOU.

IS YOUR LITTLE GADGET OKAY?

HERE.

YOU CAN BE ALONE WHENEVER YOU FEEL LIKE IT! PEOPLE CAN'T BOTHER YOU!

THAT'S TRUE...

I CAN'T BELIEVE YOU CAN DISAPPEAR. THAT'S AMAZING!

AMAZING?

WHAT DO YOU MEAN?

I'M SORRY... BUT I THINK YOU HAVE GOOD TASTE.

BUT IT'S EASY.

BUT...

WHY?

WHY? BECAUSE IT'S LONELY

HUG

BUT I DON'T WANT TO BE ALONE.

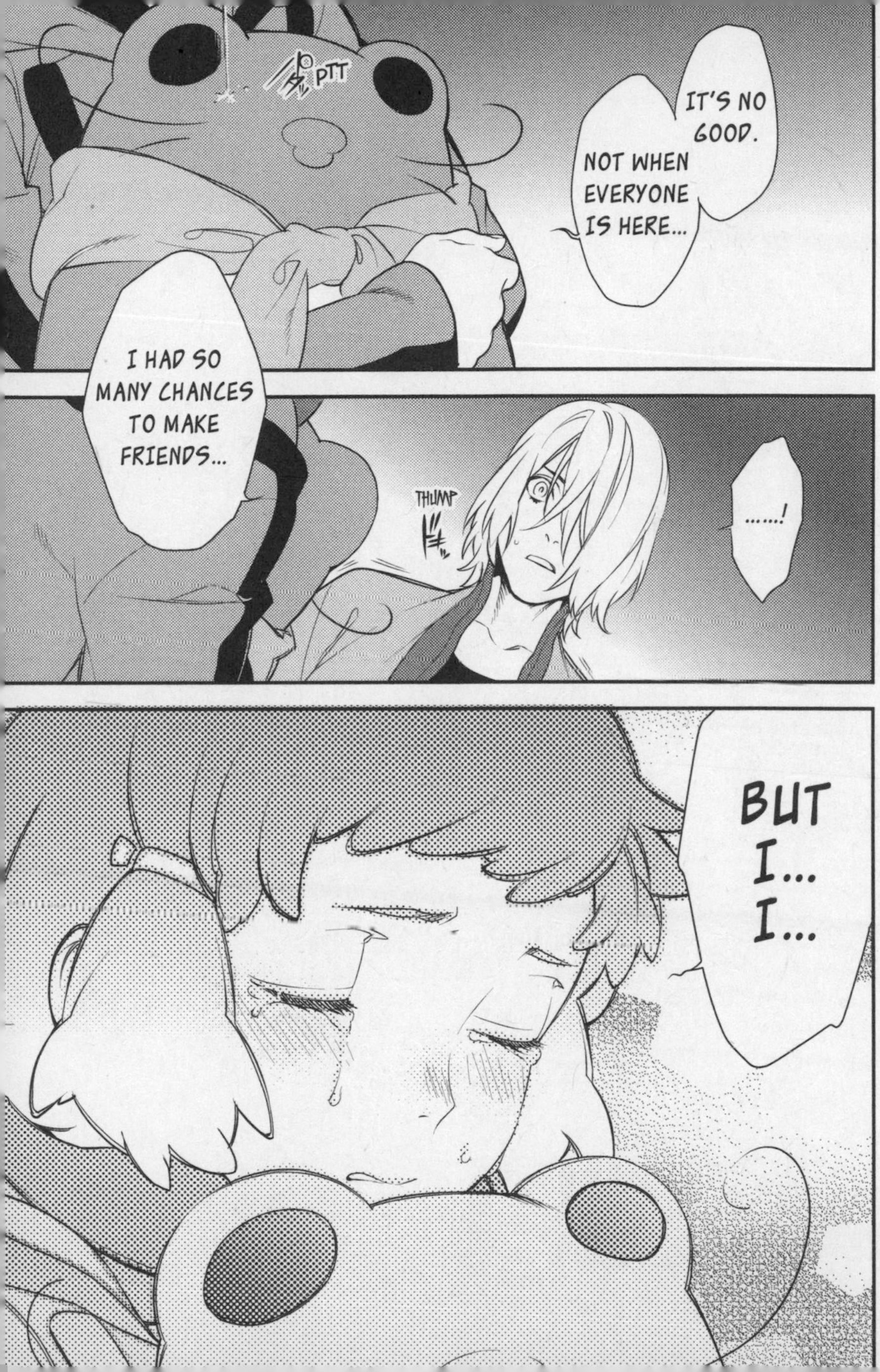
IT'S NO GOOD.
NOT WHEN EVERYONE IS HERE...
PTT
I HAD SO MANY CHANCES TO MAKE FRIENDS...
......!
THUMP
BUT I... I...

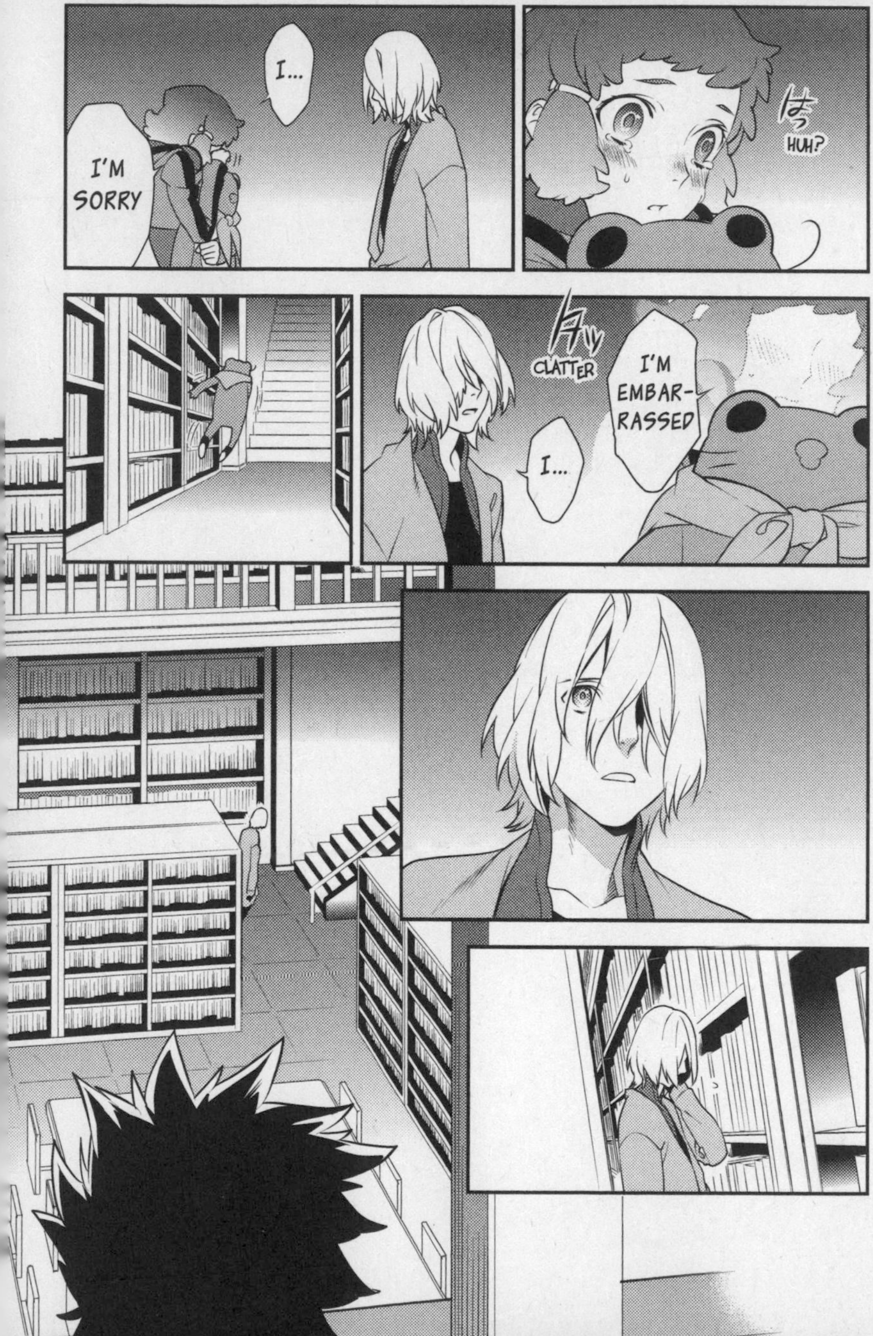
HUH?
I...
I'M SORRY
I'M EMBAR-RASSED
CLATTER
I...

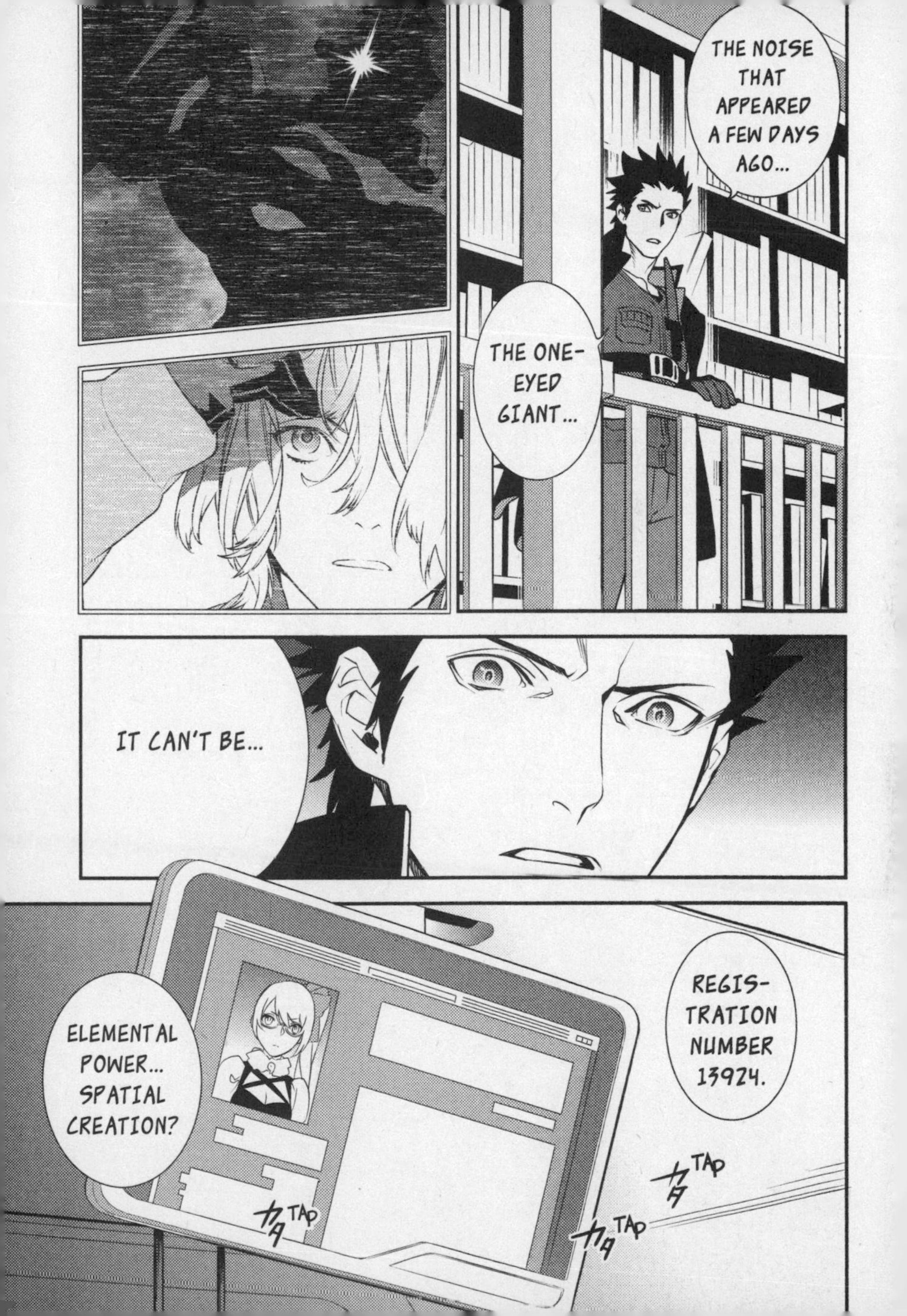
THE NOISE THAT APPEARED A FEW DAYS AGO...
THE ONE-EYED GIANT...
IT CAN'T BE...
REGIS-TRATION NUMBER 13924.
ELEMENTAL POWER... SPATIAL CREATION?
カタ TAP
カタ TAP
カタ TAP

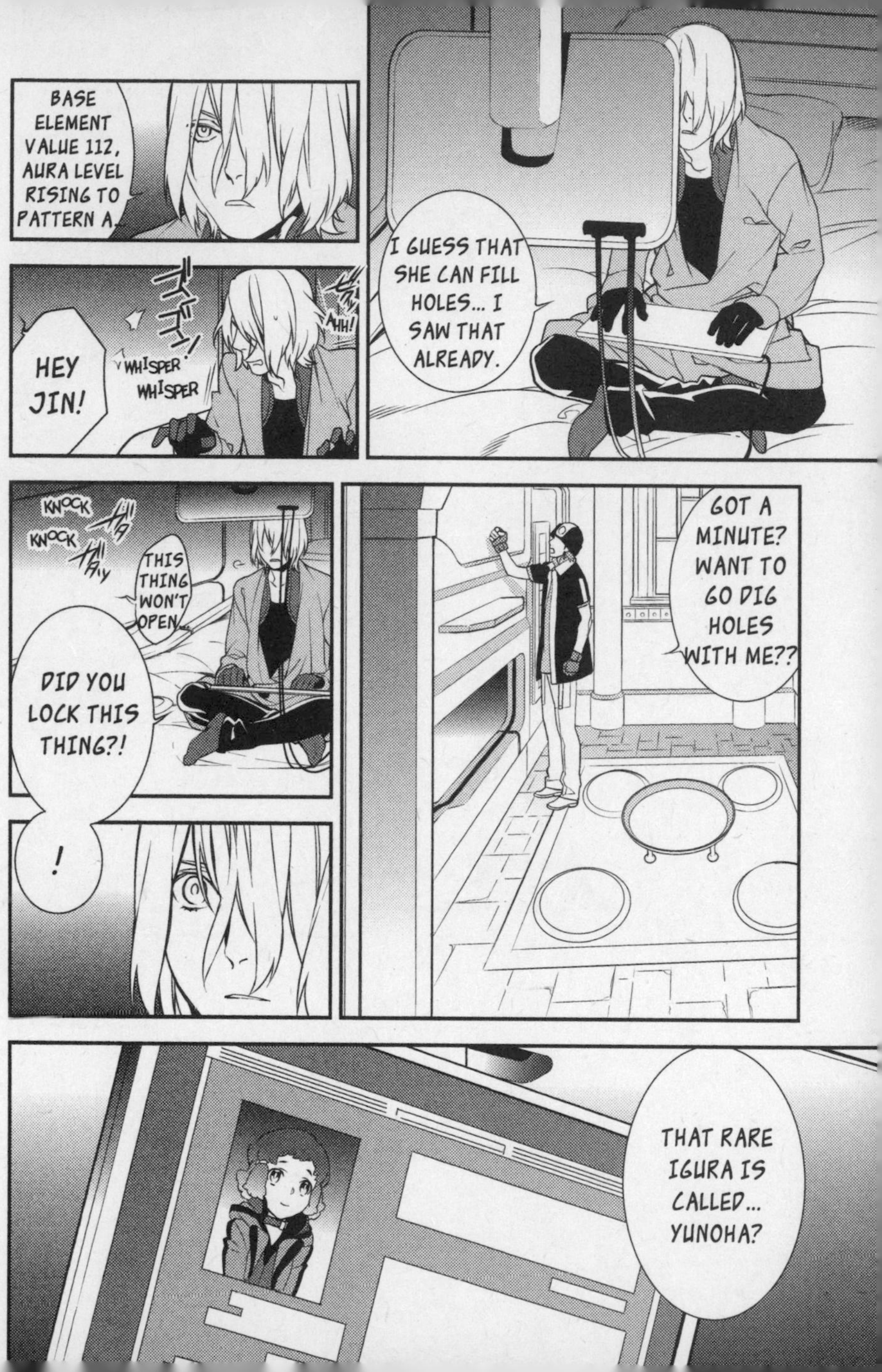
I GUESS THAT SHE CAN FILL HOLES... I SAW THAT ALREADY.
BASE ELEMENT VALUE 112, AURA LEVEL RISING TO PATTERN A...
AHH!
WHISPER WHISPER
HEY JIN!
GOT A MINUTE? WANT TO GO DIG HOLES WITH ME??
KNOCK KNOCK
THIS THING WON'T OPEN...
DID YOU LOCK THIS THING?!
!
THAT RARE IGURA IS CALLED... YUNOHA?

OPTICAL... TRANS- PARENCY?

ELEMENTAL POWER... OPTICAL TRANSPAR- ENCY...

YUNOHA THRUL.

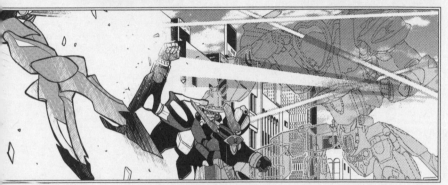

THEN... THE ONE WHO BEAT ME IN THAT BATTLE...?

BEEP

BEEP

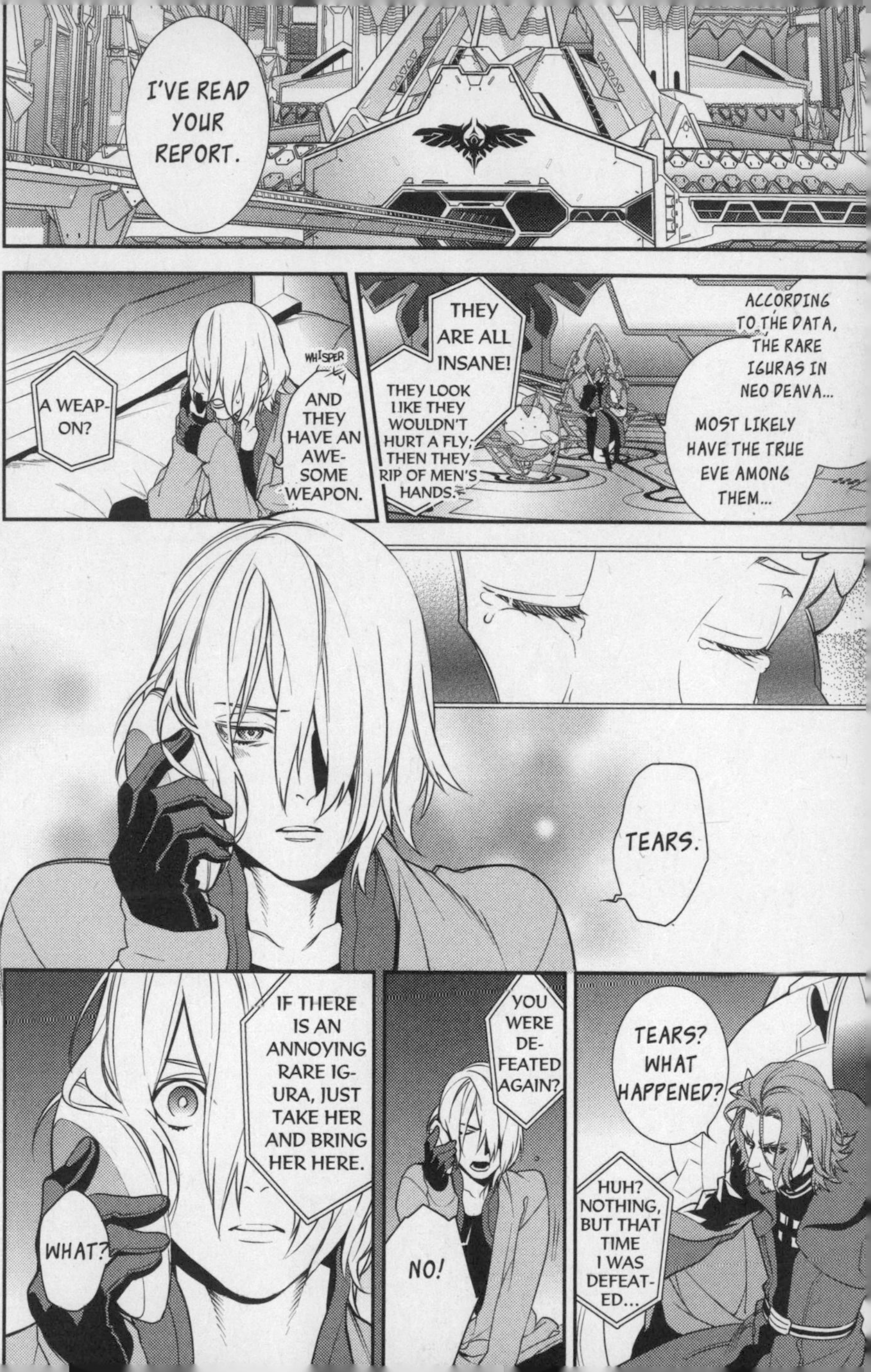
I'VE READ YOUR REPORT.
ACCORDING TO THE DATA, THE RARE IGURAS IN NEO DEAVA...
MOST LIKELY HAVE THE TRUE EVE AMONG THEM...
THEY ARE ALL INSANE!
THEY LOOK LIKE THEY WOULDN'T HURT A FLY; THEN THEY RIP OF MEN'S HANDS.
WHISPER
AND THEY HAVE AN AWESOME WEAPON.
A WEAPON?
TEARS.
TEARS? WHAT HAPPENED?
HUH? NOTHING, BUT THAT TIME I WAS DEFEATED...
YOU WERE DEFEATED AGAIN?
NO!
IF THERE IS AN ANNOYING RARE IGURA, JUST TAKE HER AND BRING HER HERE.
WHAT?

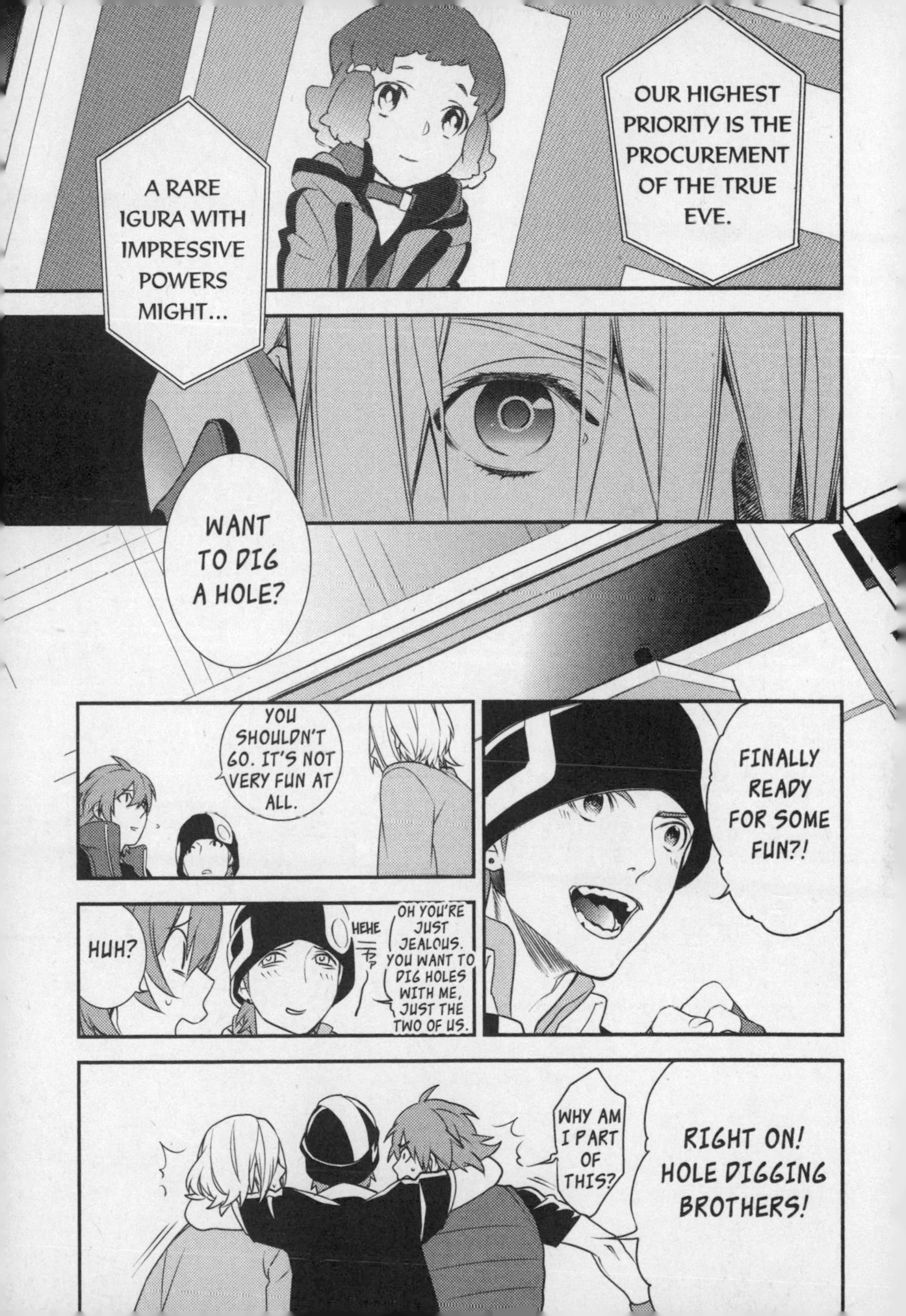
OUR HIGHEST PRIORITY IS THE PROCUREMENT OF THE TRUE EVE.
A RARE IGURA WITH IMPRESSIVE POWERS MIGHT...
WANT TO DIG A HOLE?
FINALLY READY FOR SOME FUN?!
YOU SHOULDN'T GO. IT'S NOT VERY FUN AT ALL.
OH YOU'RE JUST JEALOUS. YOU WANT TO DIG HOLES WITH ME, JUST THE TWO OF US.
HEHE
HUH?
RIGHT ON! HOLE DIGGING BROTHERS!
WHY AM I PART OF THIS?

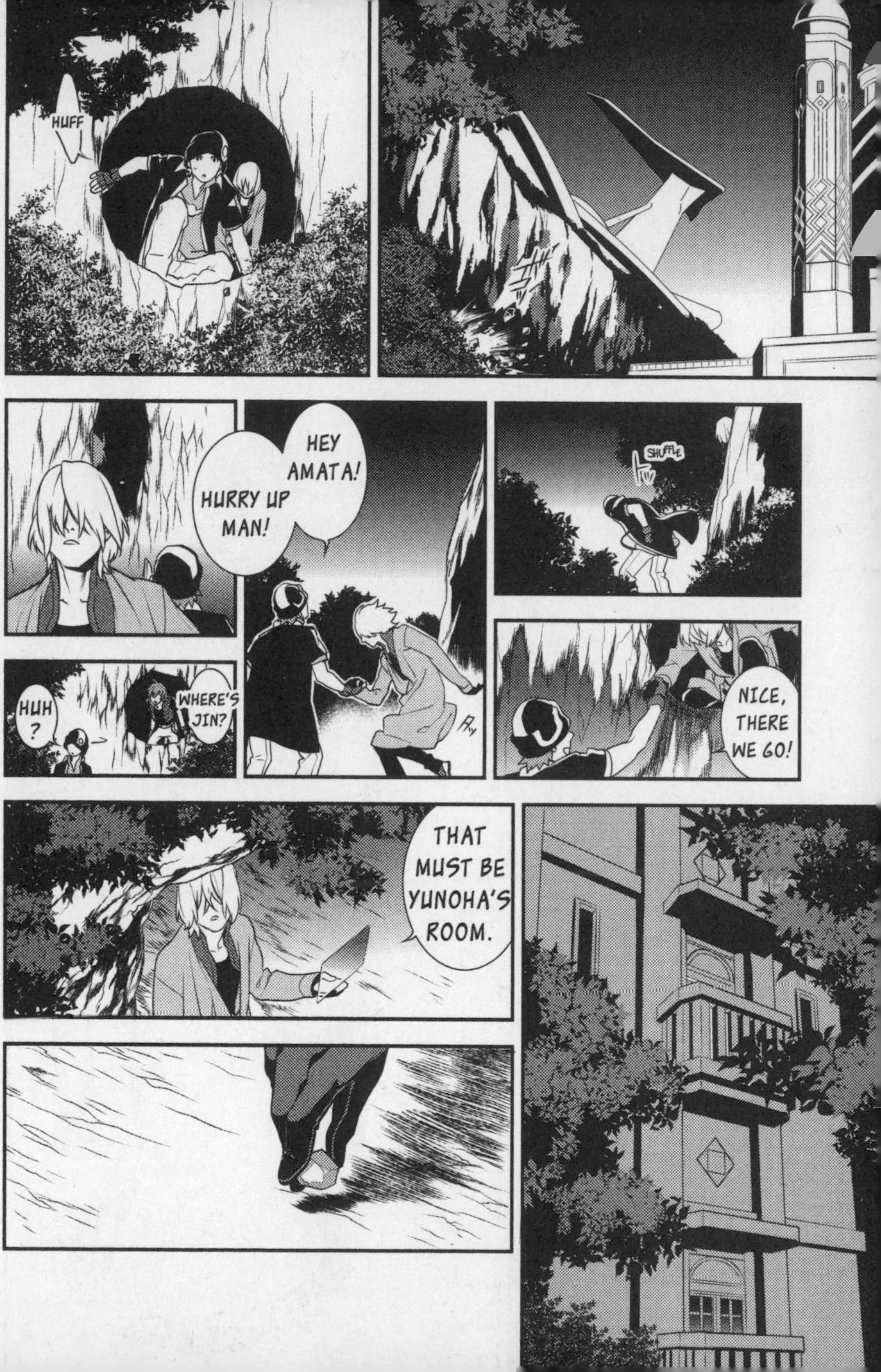
HUFF
SHUFFLE
NICE, THERE WE GO!
HEY AMATA!
HURRY UP MAN!
WHERE'S JIN?
HUH?
THAT MUST BE YUNOHA'S ROOM.

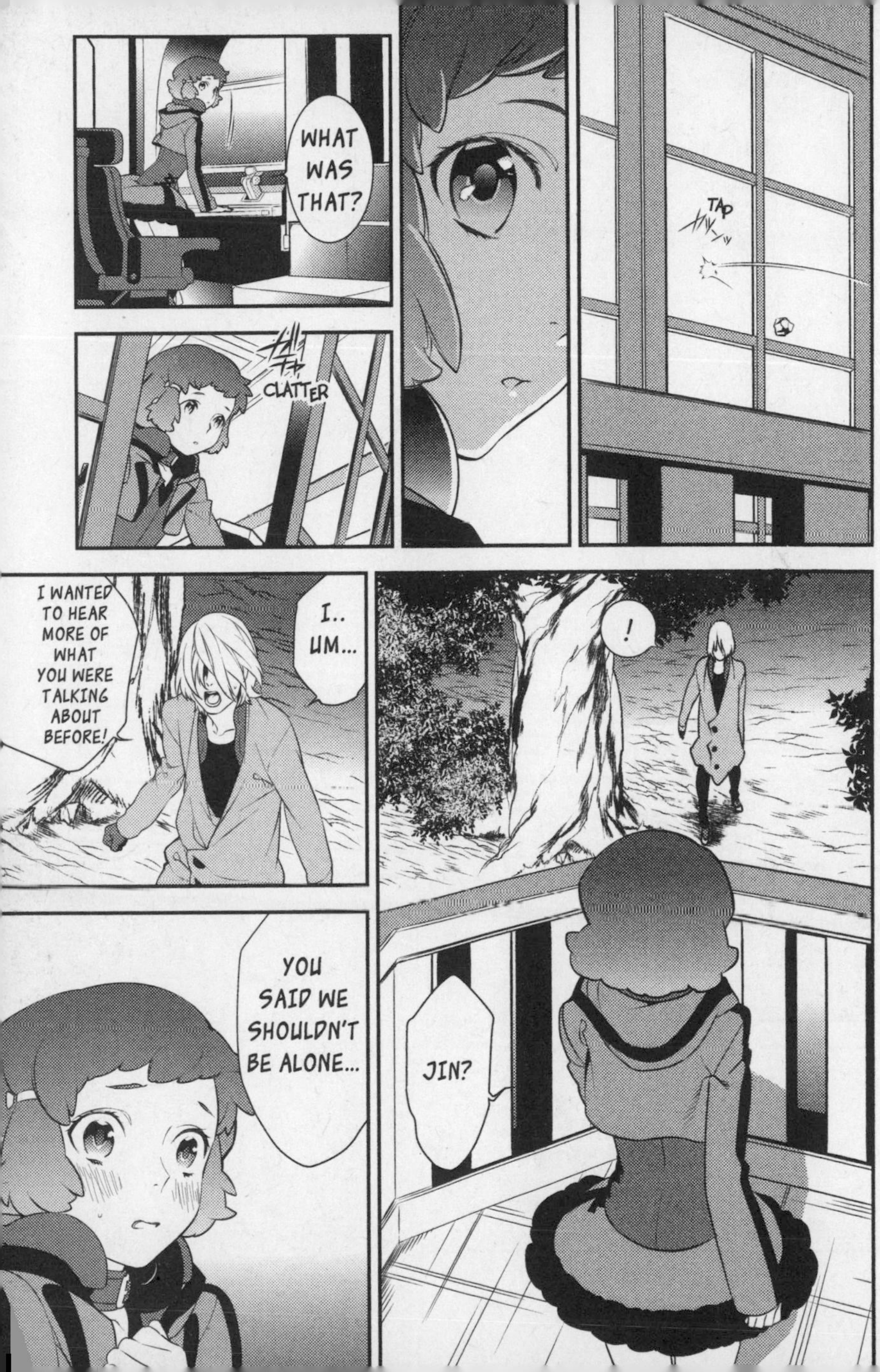
TAP
WHAT WAS THAT?
CLATTER
!
I.. UM...
I WANTED TO HEAR MORE OF WHAT YOU WERE TALKING ABOUT BEFORE!
JIN?
YOU SAID WE SHOULDN'T BE ALONE...

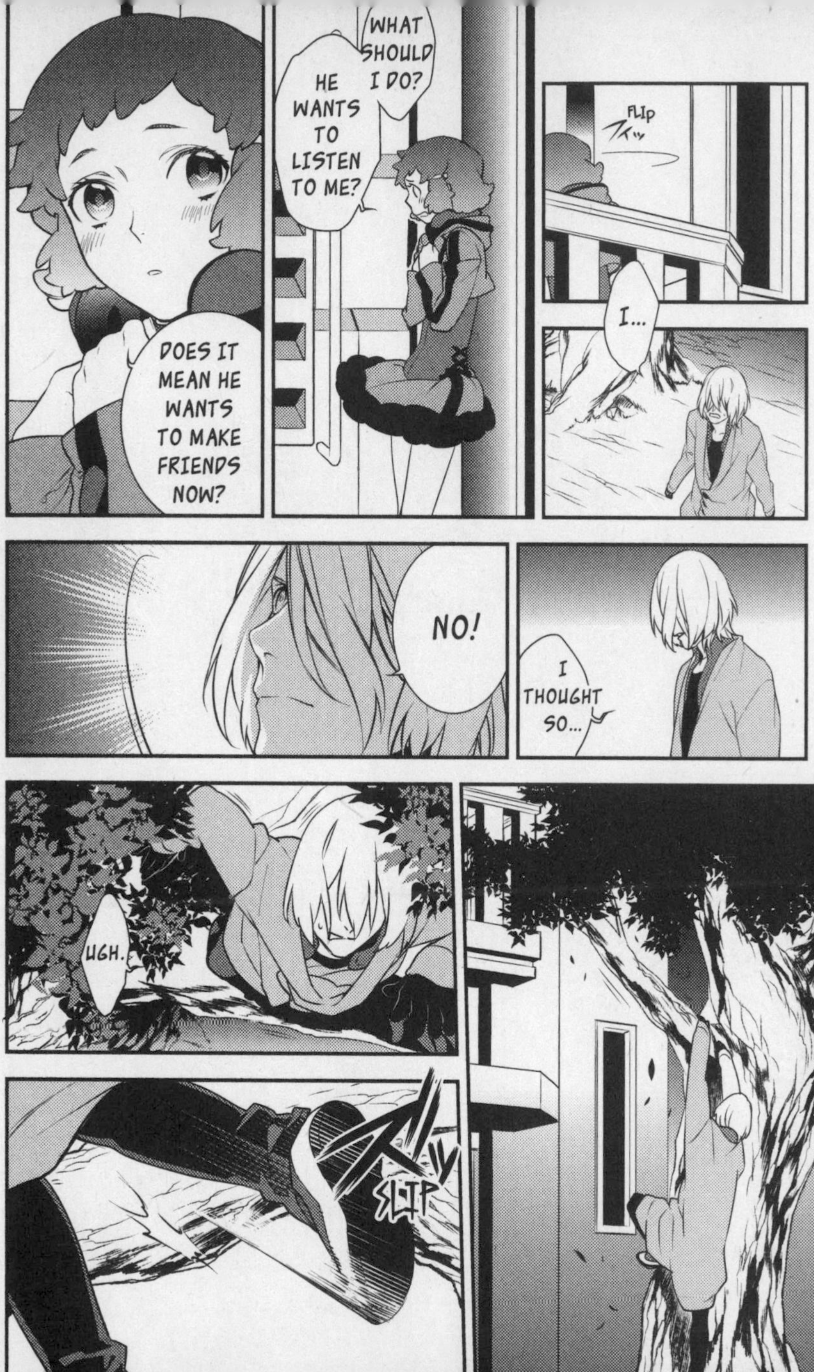
FLIP
フィッ
I...
WHAT SHOULD I DO?
HE WANTS TO LISTEN TO ME?
DOES IT MEAN HE WANTS TO MAKE FRIENDS NOW?
I THOUGHT SO...
NO!
UGH.
SLIP

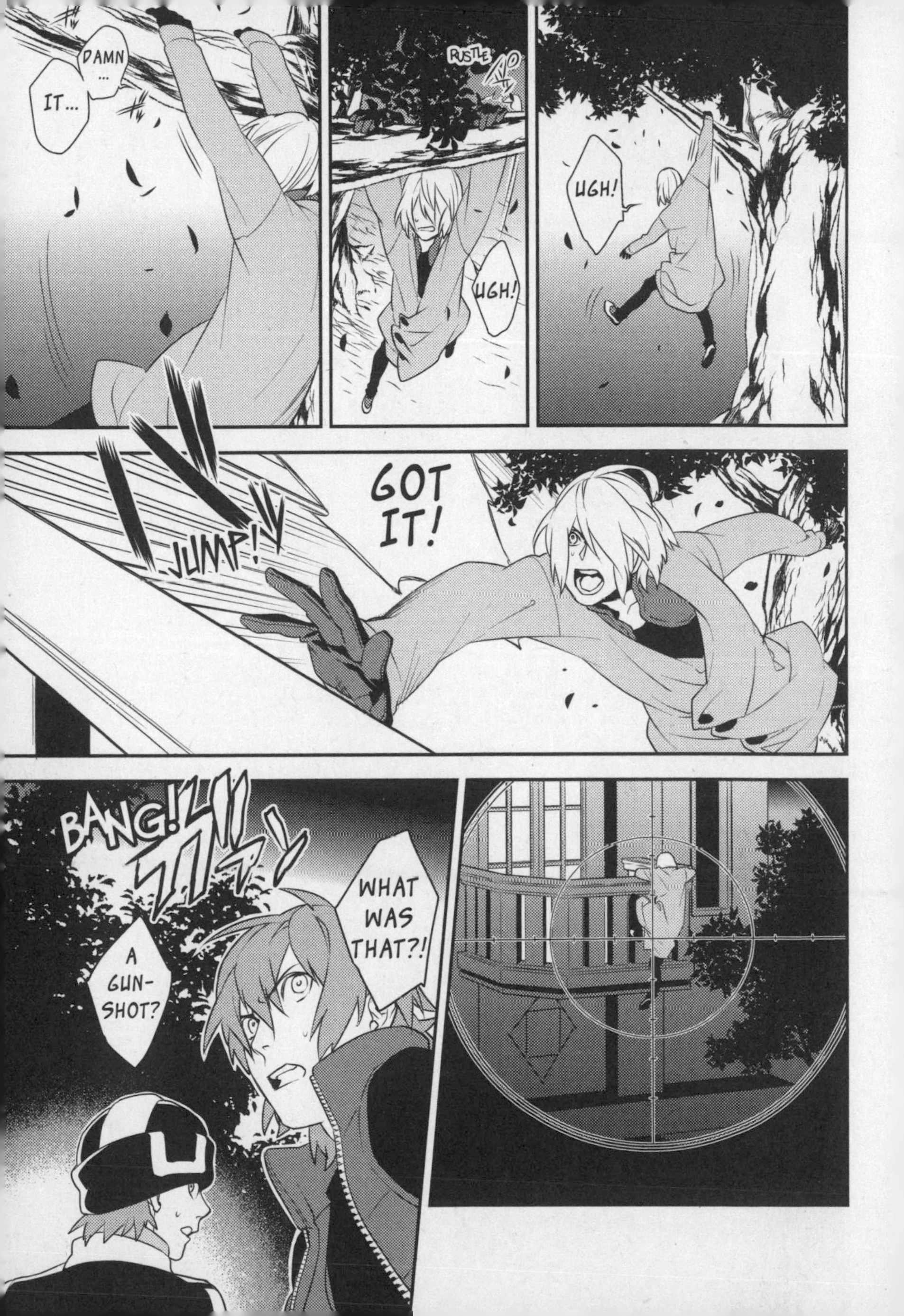
UGH!
RUSTLE
UGH!
DAMN...
IT...
GOT IT!
JUMP!
BANG!!
WHAT WAS THAT?!
A GUN-SHOT?

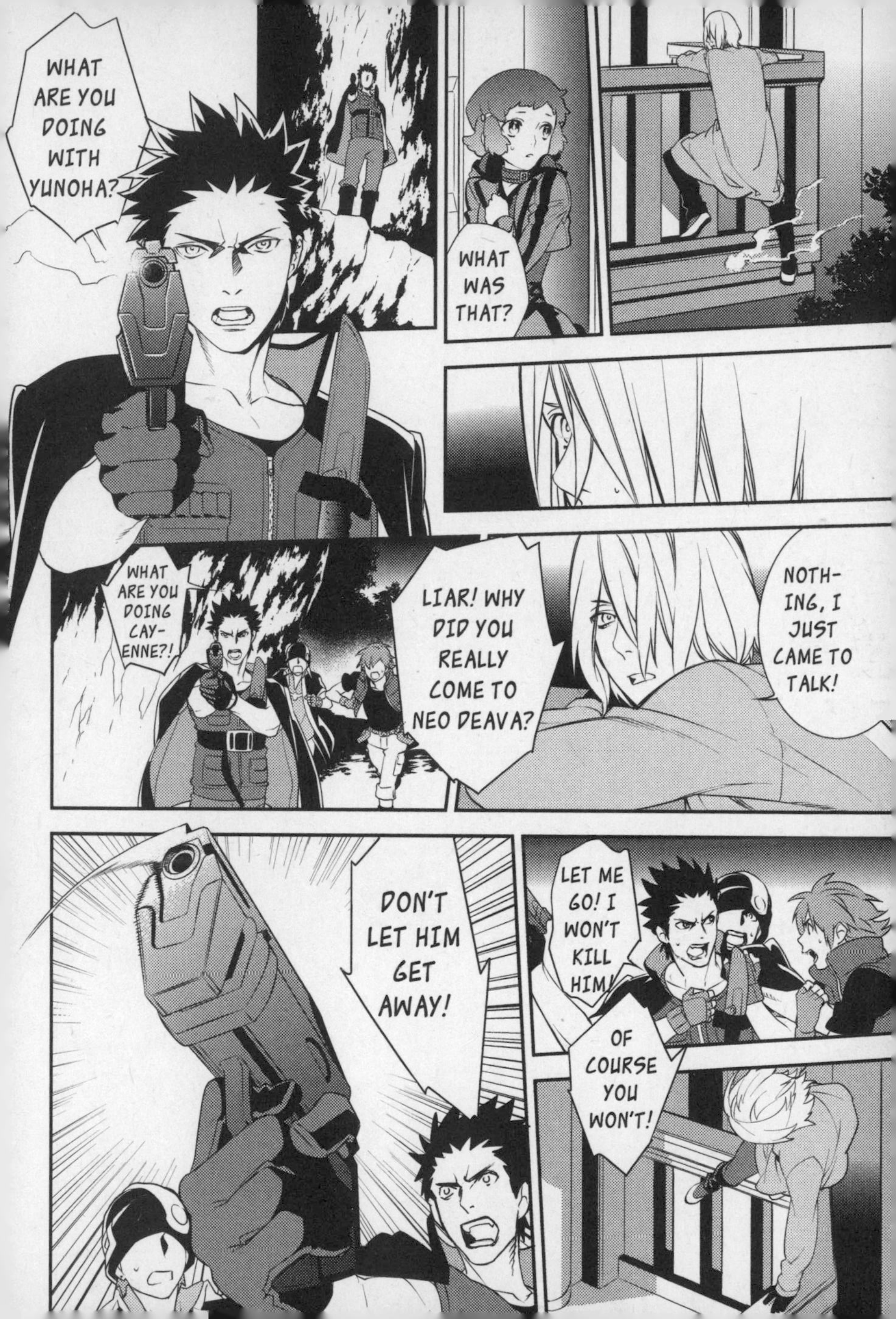
WHAT WAS THAT?
WHAT ARE YOU DOING WITH YUNOHA?
NOTH-ING, I JUST CAME TO TALK!
LIAR! WHY DID YOU REALLY COME TO NEO DEAVA?
WHAT ARE YOU DOING CAY-ENNE?!
LET ME GO! I WON'T KILL HIM!
OF COURSE YOU WON'T!
DON'T LET HIM GET AWAY!

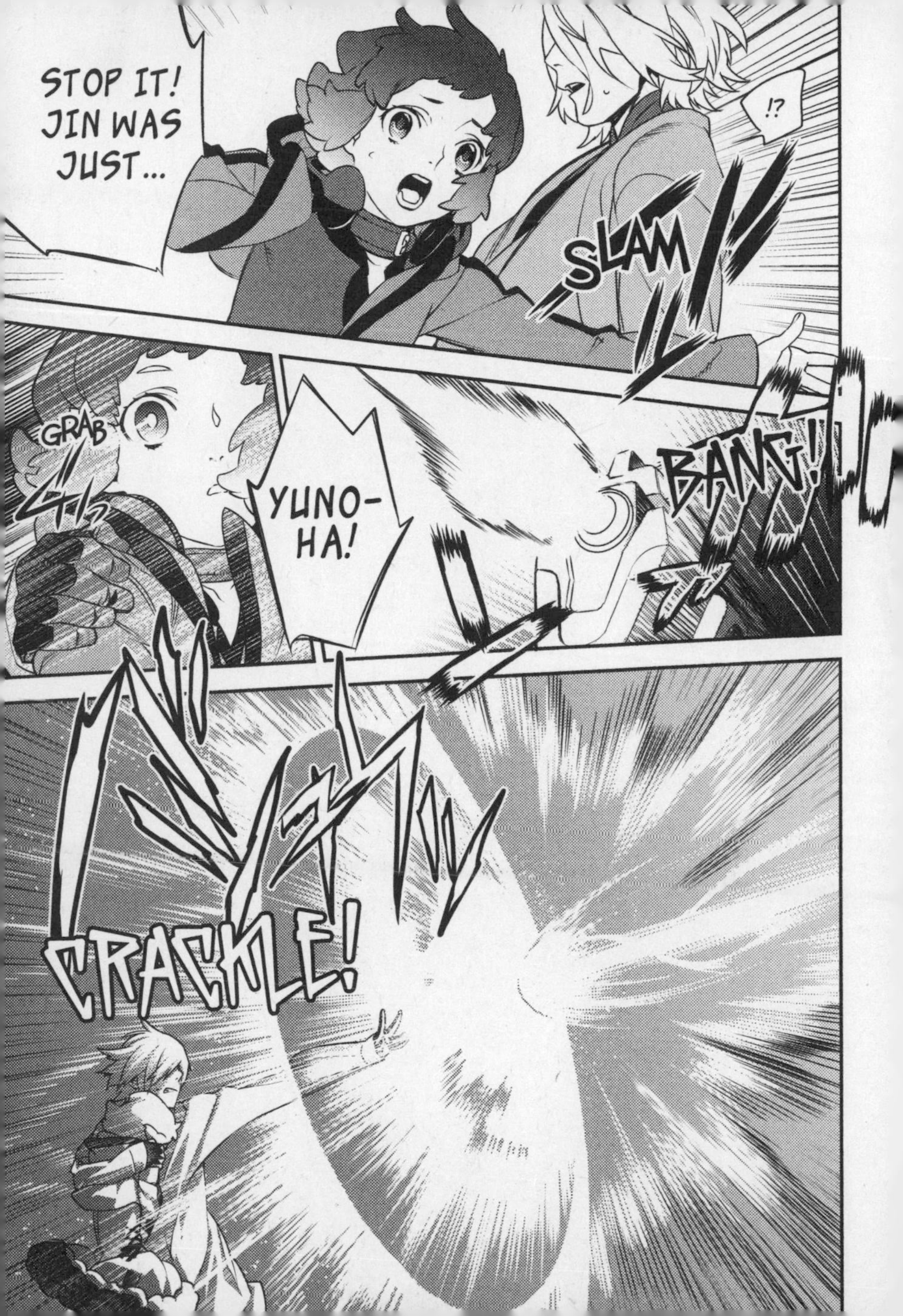
!?
STOP IT! JIN WAS JUST...
SLAM
BANG!
YUNO-HA!
GRAB
CRACKLE!

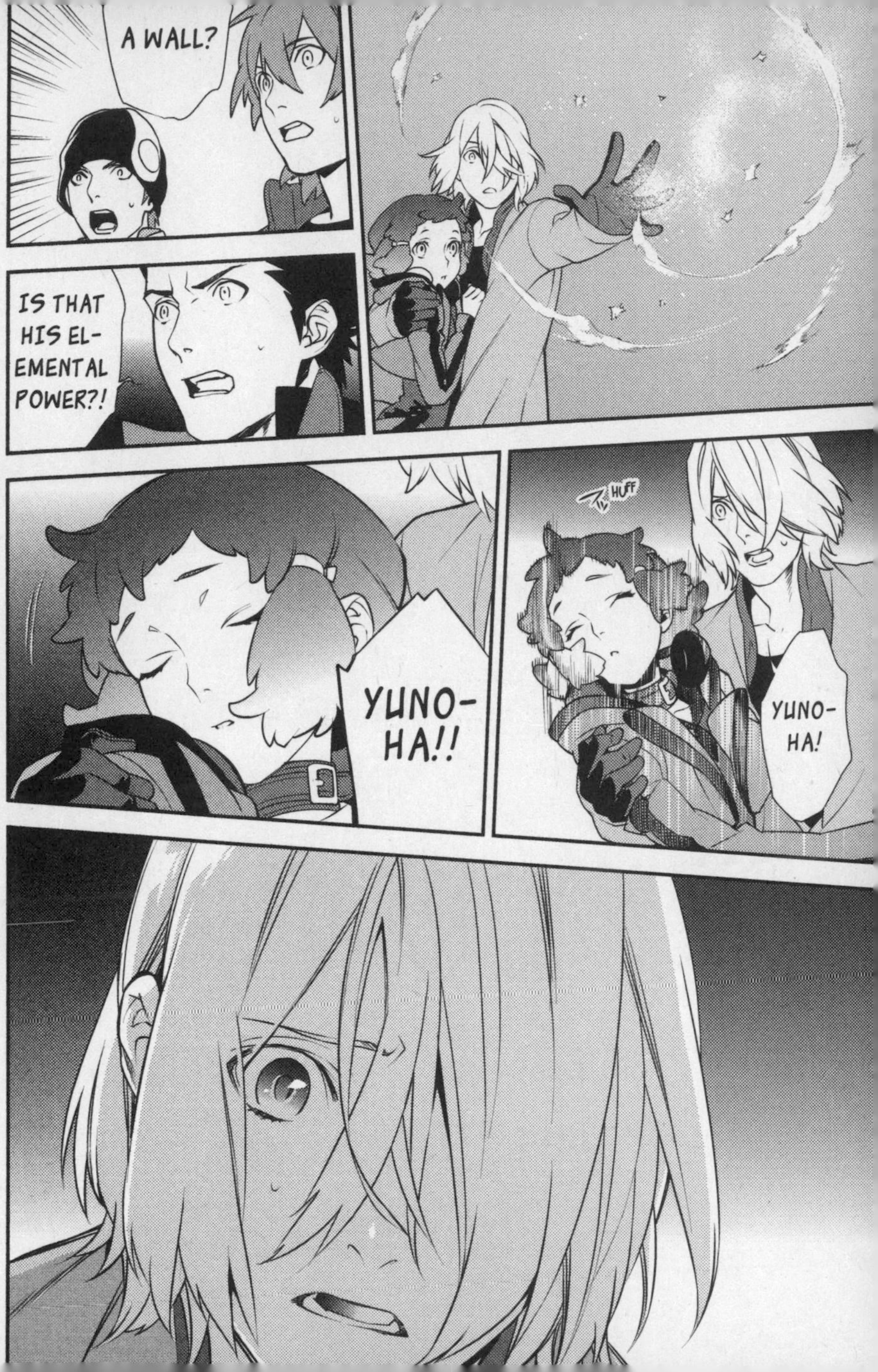
A WALL?
IS THAT HIS EL-EMENTAL POWER?!
HUFF
YUNO-HA!
YUNO-HA!!

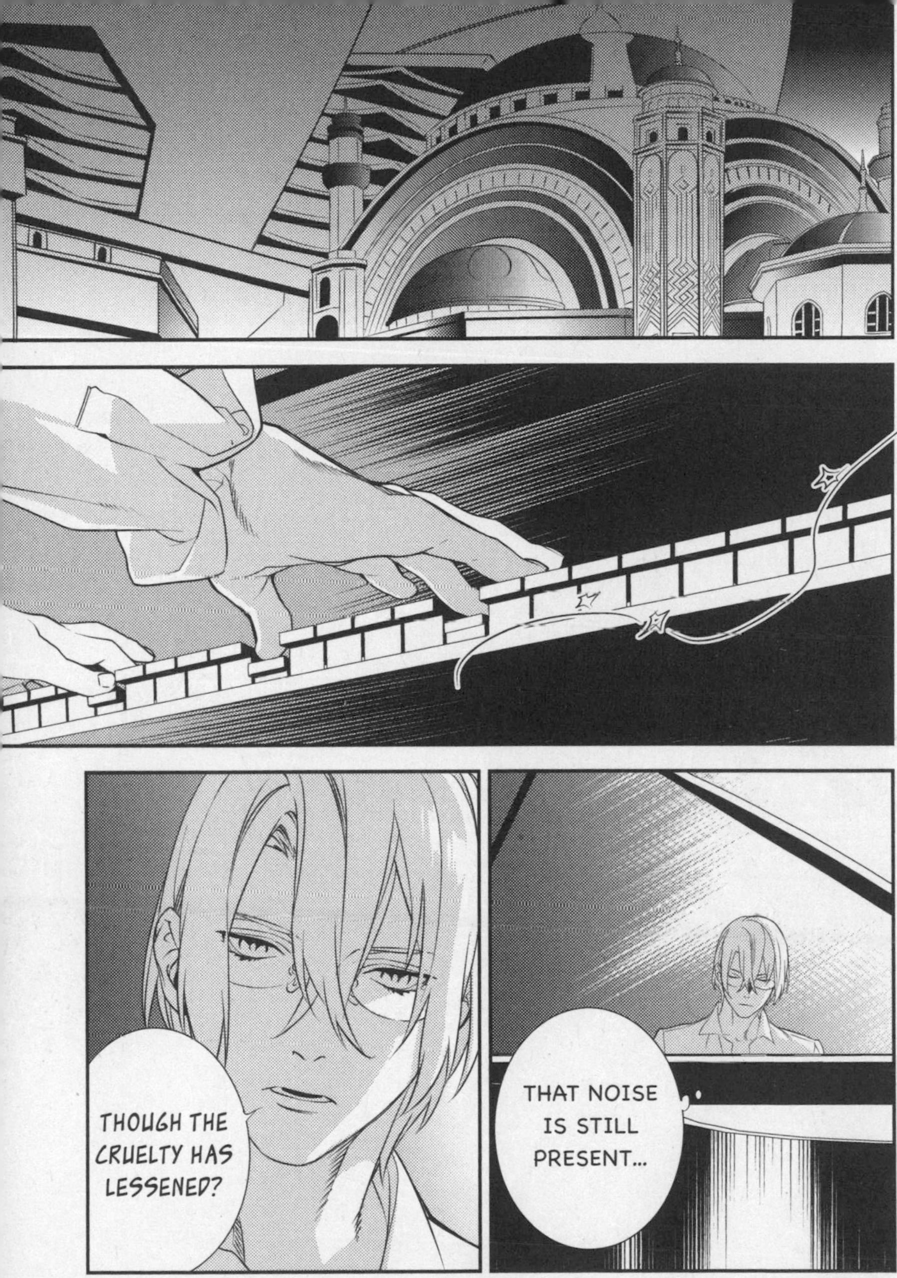
THAT NOISE IS STILL PRESENT...
THOUGH THE CRUELTY HAS LESSENED?

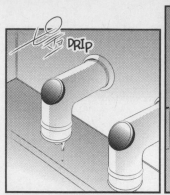

DRIP

HEY

DRIP

JUST WHO
ARE YOU?

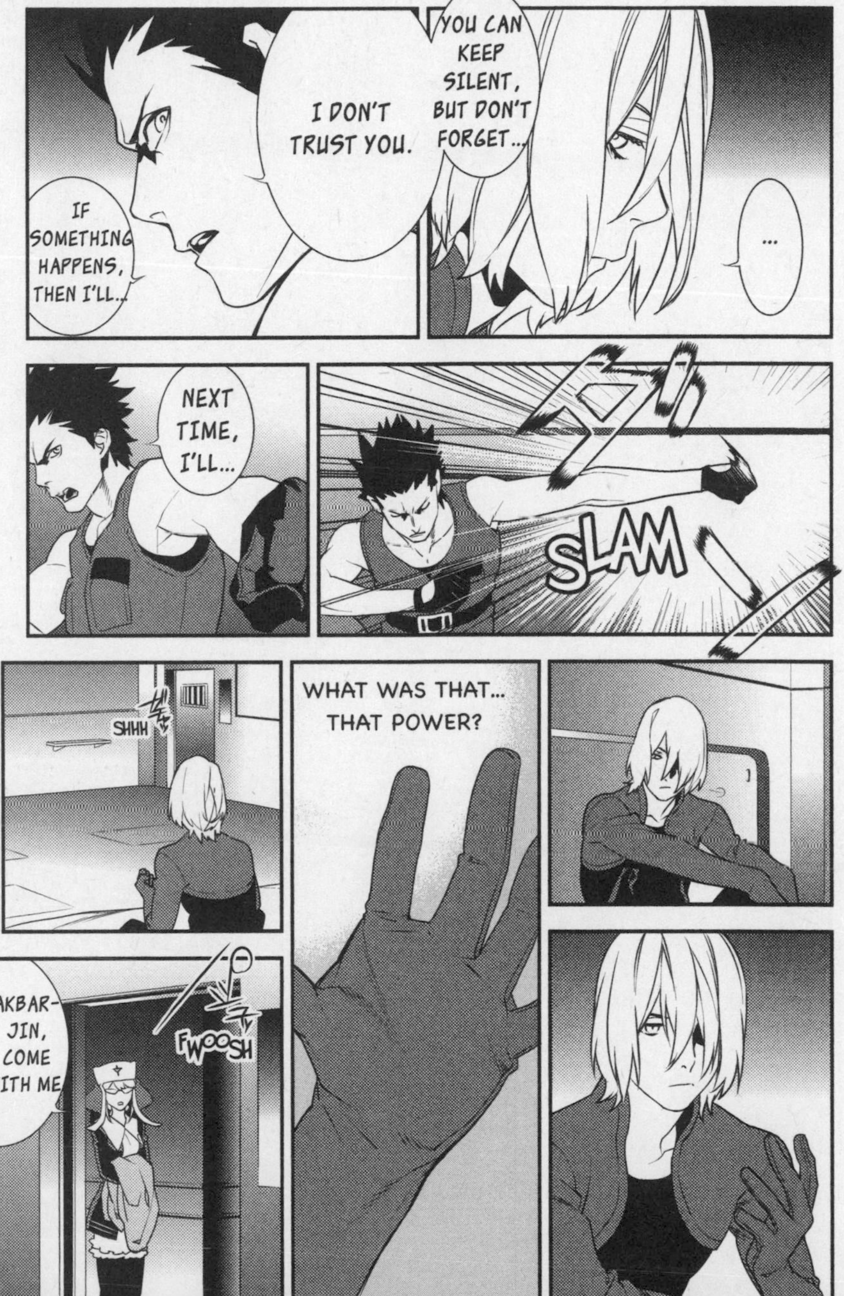
YOU CAN KEEP SILENT, BUT DON'T FORGET...
...
I DON'T TRUST YOU.
IF SOMETHING HAPPENS, THEN I'LL...
SLAM
NEXT TIME, I'LL...
WHAT WAS THAT... THAT POWER?
SHHH
FWOOSH
AKBAR-JIN, COME WITH ME

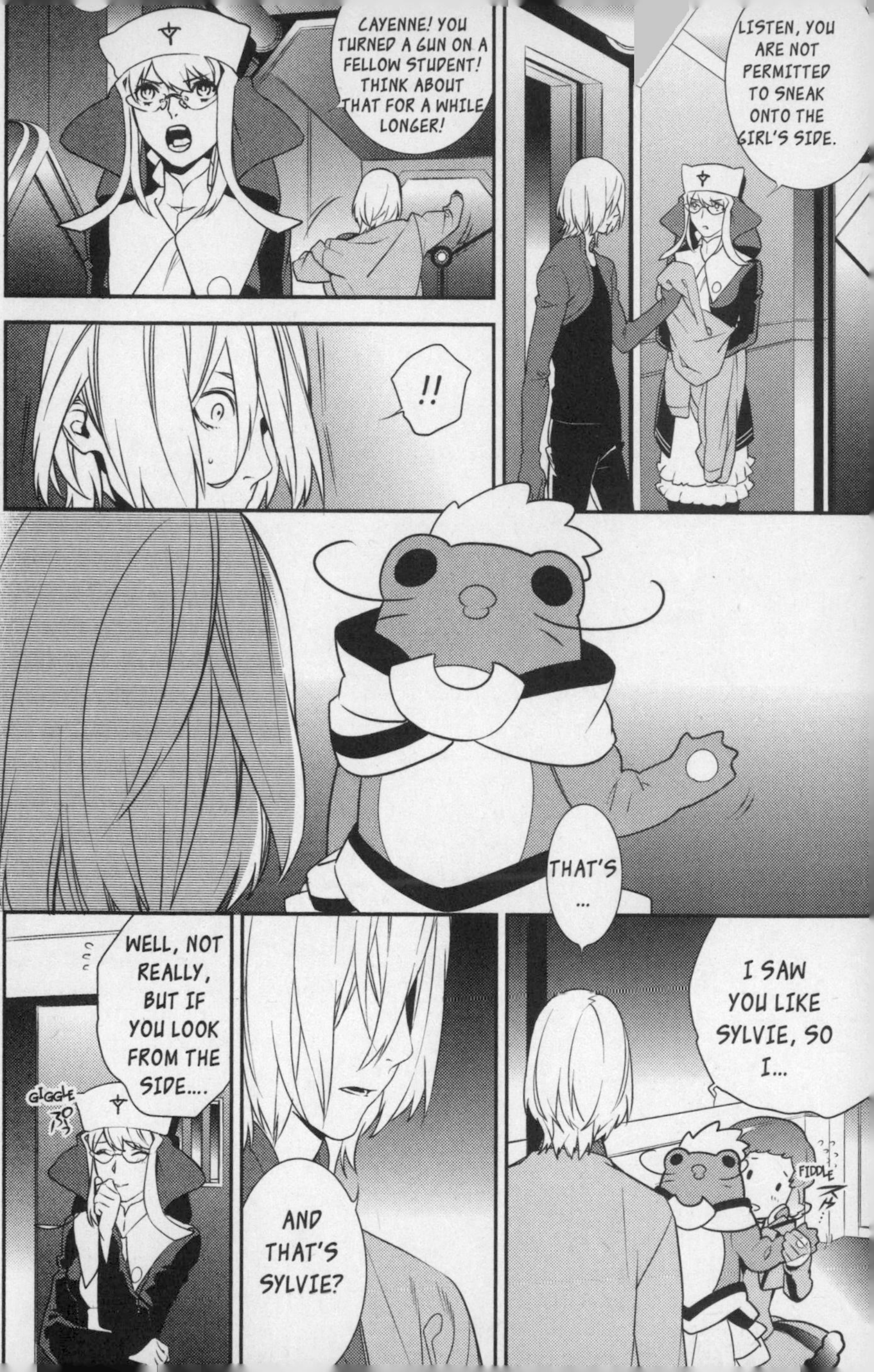

LISTEN, YOU ARE NOT PERMITTED TO SNEAK ONTO THE GIRL'S SIDE.
CAYENNE! YOU TURNED A GUN ON A FELLOW STUDENT! THINK ABOUT THAT FOR A WHILE LONGER!
!!
THAT'S ...
I SAW YOU LIKE SYLVIE, SO I...
FIDDLE
AND THAT'S SYLVIE?
WELL, NOT REALLY, BUT IF YOU LOOK FROM THE SIDE....
GIGGLE

I...
I'M SORRY

COUGH

FWOOSH

UM...

FLIP

WHAT A COLD BOY...

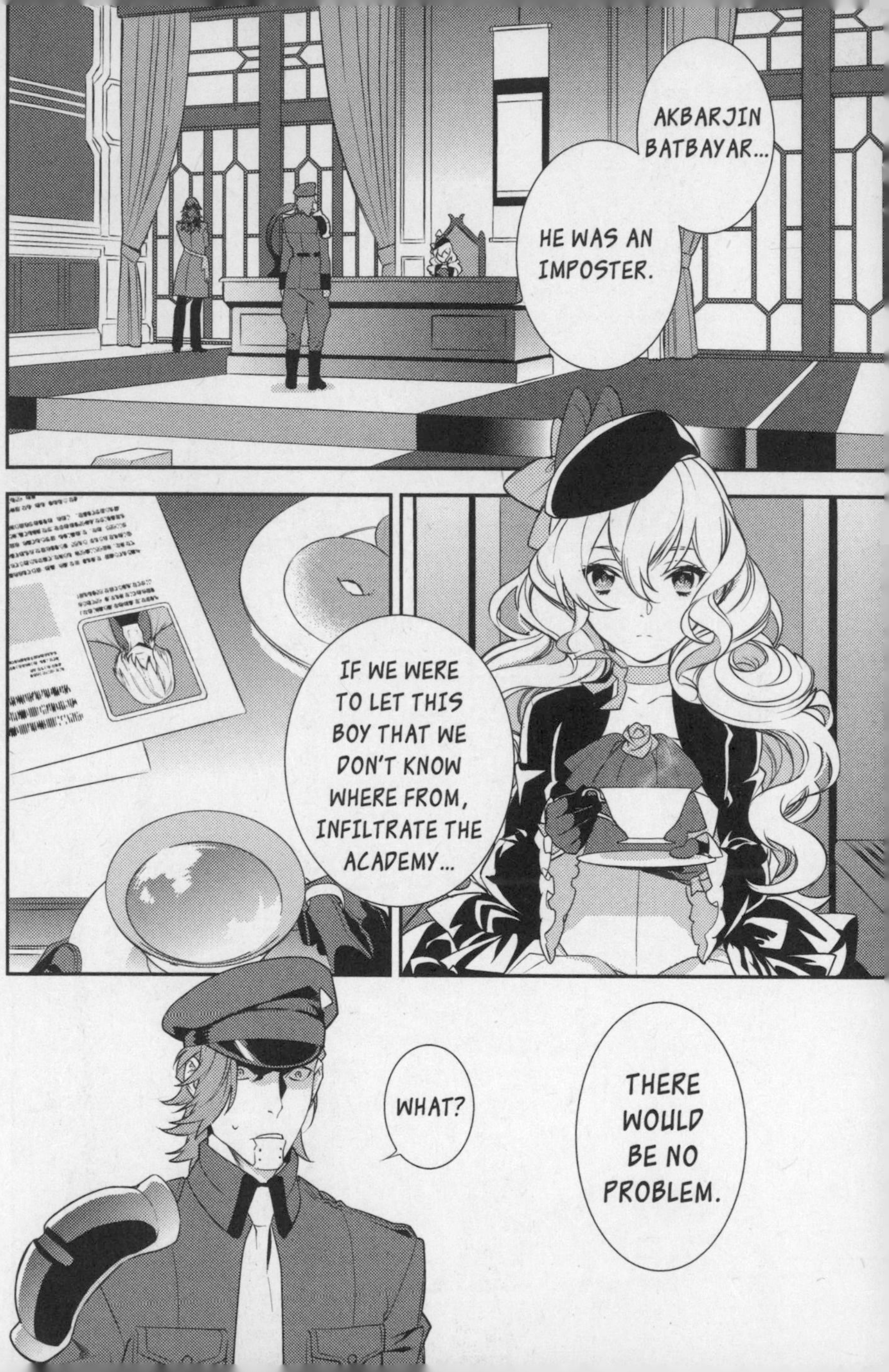
AKBARJIN BATBAYAR...
HE WAS AN IMPOSTER.
IF WE WERE TO LET THIS BOY THAT WE DON'T KNOW WHERE FROM, INFILTRATE THE ACADEMY...
THERE WOULD BE NO PROBLEM.
WHAT?

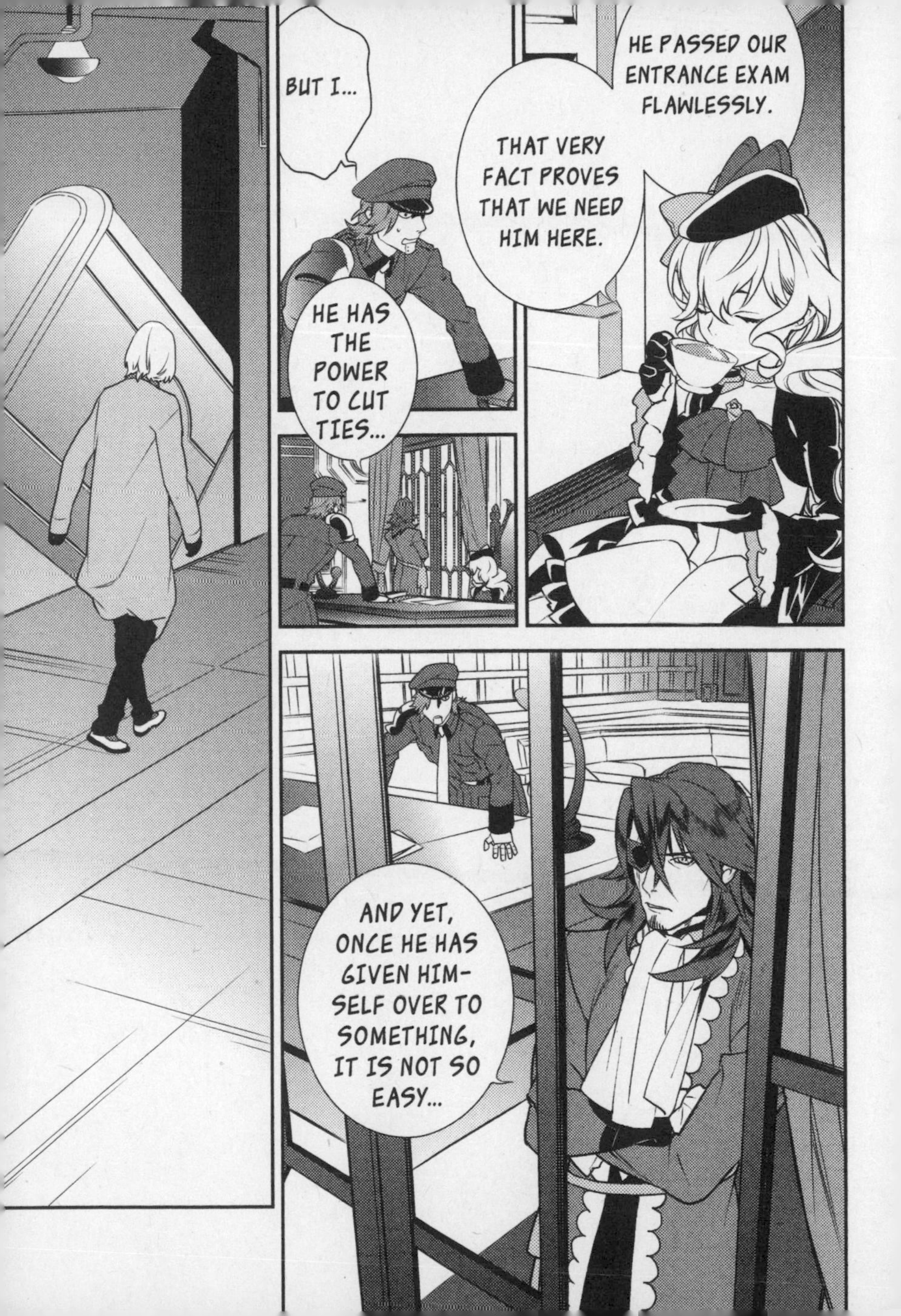
HE PASSED OUR ENTRANCE EXAM FLAWLESSLY.
THAT VERY FACT PROVES THAT WE NEED HIM HERE.
BUT I...
HE HAS THE POWER TO CUT TIES...
AND YET, ONCE HE HAS GIVEN HIM-SELF OVER TO SOMETHING, IT IS NOT SO EASY...

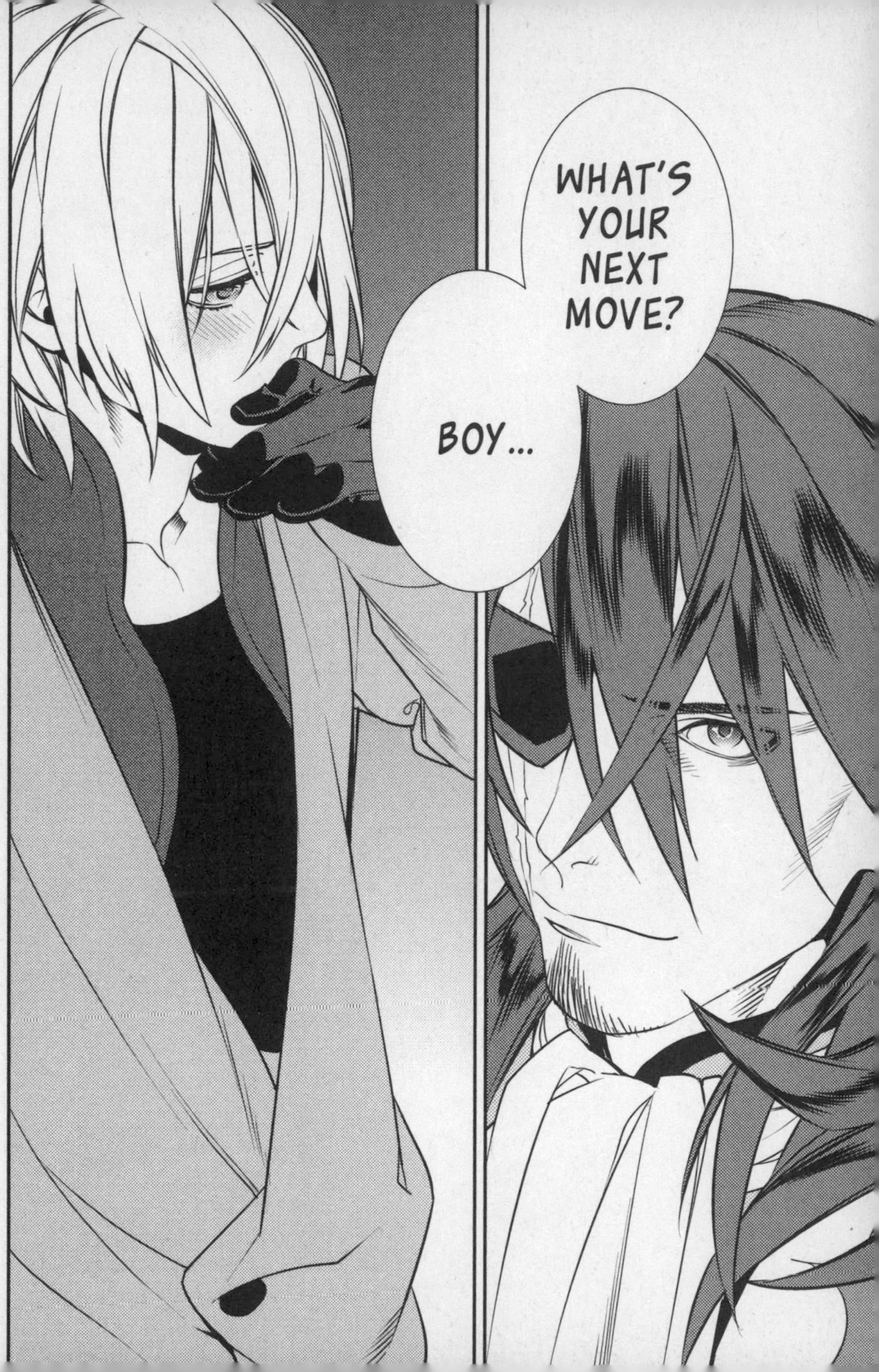
WHAT'S YOUR NEXT MOVE?
BOY...

aquarion evol

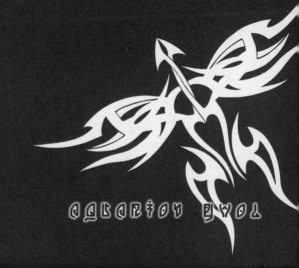

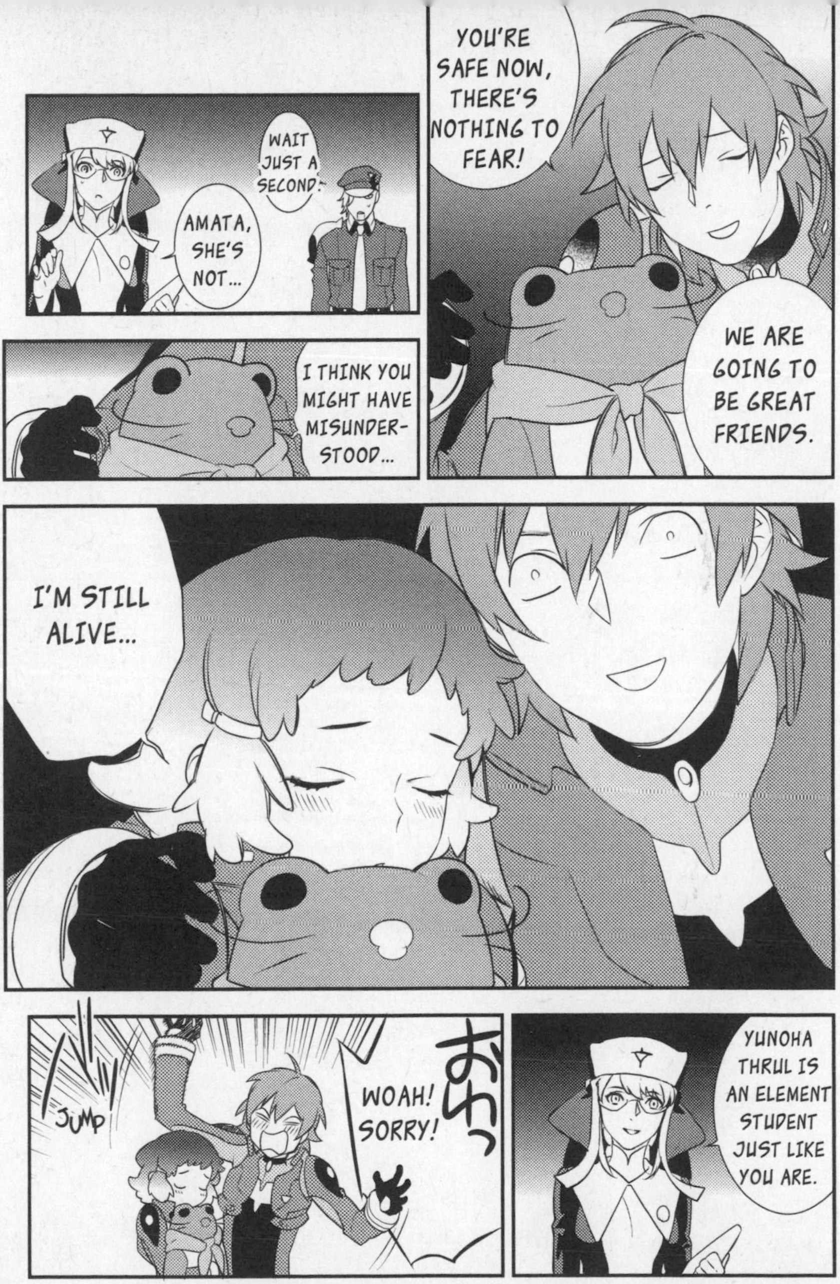
YOU'RE SAFE NOW, THERE'S NOTHING TO FEAR!
WE ARE GOING TO BE GREAT FRIENDS.
WAIT JUST A SECOND.
AMATA, SHE'S NOT...
I THINK YOU MIGHT HAVE MISUNDER-STOOD...
I'M STILL ALIVE...
YUNOHA THRUL IS AN ELEMENT STUDENT JUST LIKE YOU ARE.
おわっ
WOAH! SORRY!
JUMP

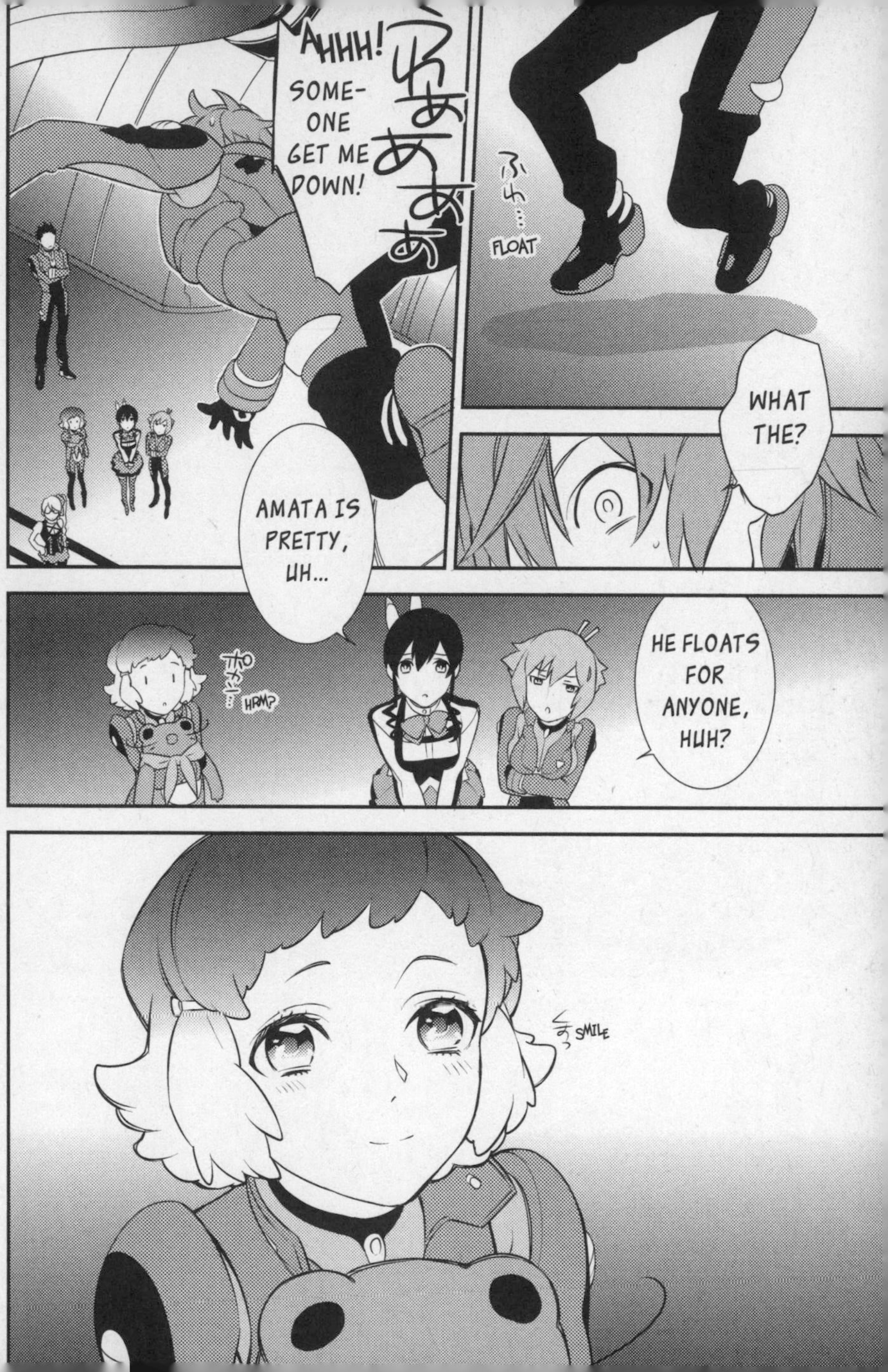
ふわ…
FLOAT
WHAT THE?
AHHH! SOME-ONE GET ME DOWN!
うわあああ
HE FLOATS FOR ANYONE, HUH?
AMATA IS PRETTY, UH...
HRM?
SMILE

aquarion evol

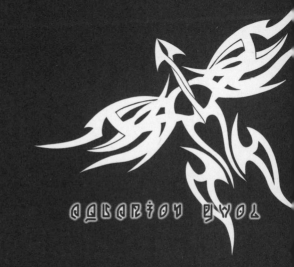

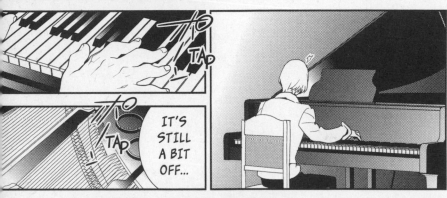

IT'S STILL A BIT OFF...

IT SHOULD BE PERFECTLY IN TIME THOUGH...

THIS IS OUR NEW TRANSFER STUDENT.

#12 THE ONE-EYED STUDENT

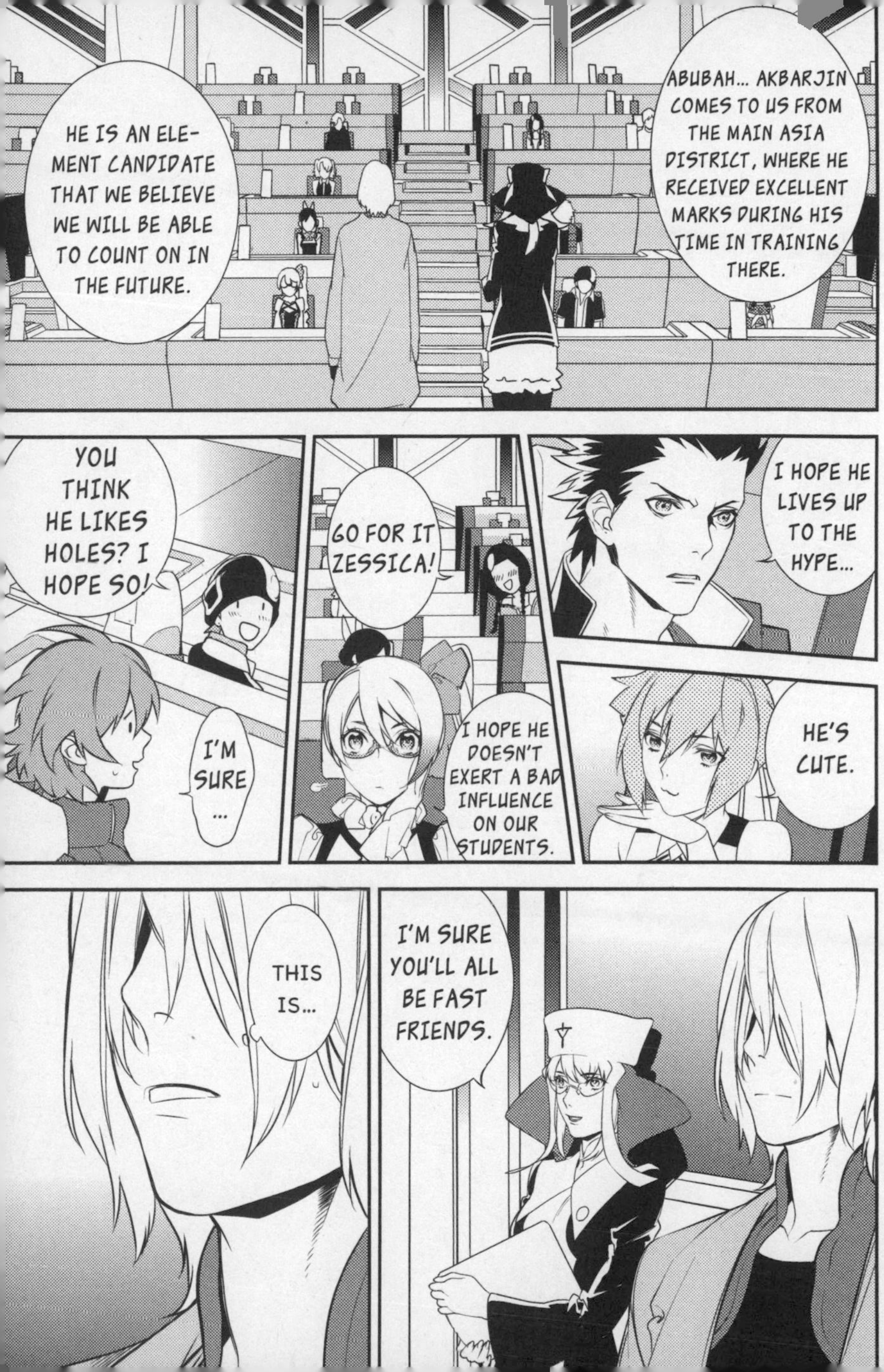
ABUBAH... AKBARJIN COMES TO US FROM THE MAIN ASIA DISTRICT, WHERE HE RECEIVED EXCELLENT MARKS DURING HIS TIME IN TRAINING THERE.
HE IS AN ELEMENT CANDIDATE THAT WE BELIEVE WE WILL BE ABLE TO COUNT ON IN THE FUTURE.
I HOPE HE LIVES UP TO THE HYPE...
HE'S CUTE.
GO FOR IT ZESSICA!
I HOPE HE DOESN'T EXERT A BAD INFLUENCE ON OUR STUDENTS.
YOU THINK HE LIKES HOLES? I HOPE SO!
I'M SURE ...
I'M SURE YOU'LL ALL BE FAST FRIENDS.
THIS IS...

RARE....

RARE IGURA...

I JUST REMEMBERED....

THAT I AM A TRANSFER STUDENT TOO...

IS HE YOUR TYPE, YUNOHA?

I.... UH...

YOU WANT TO STEAL THE ANGEL?

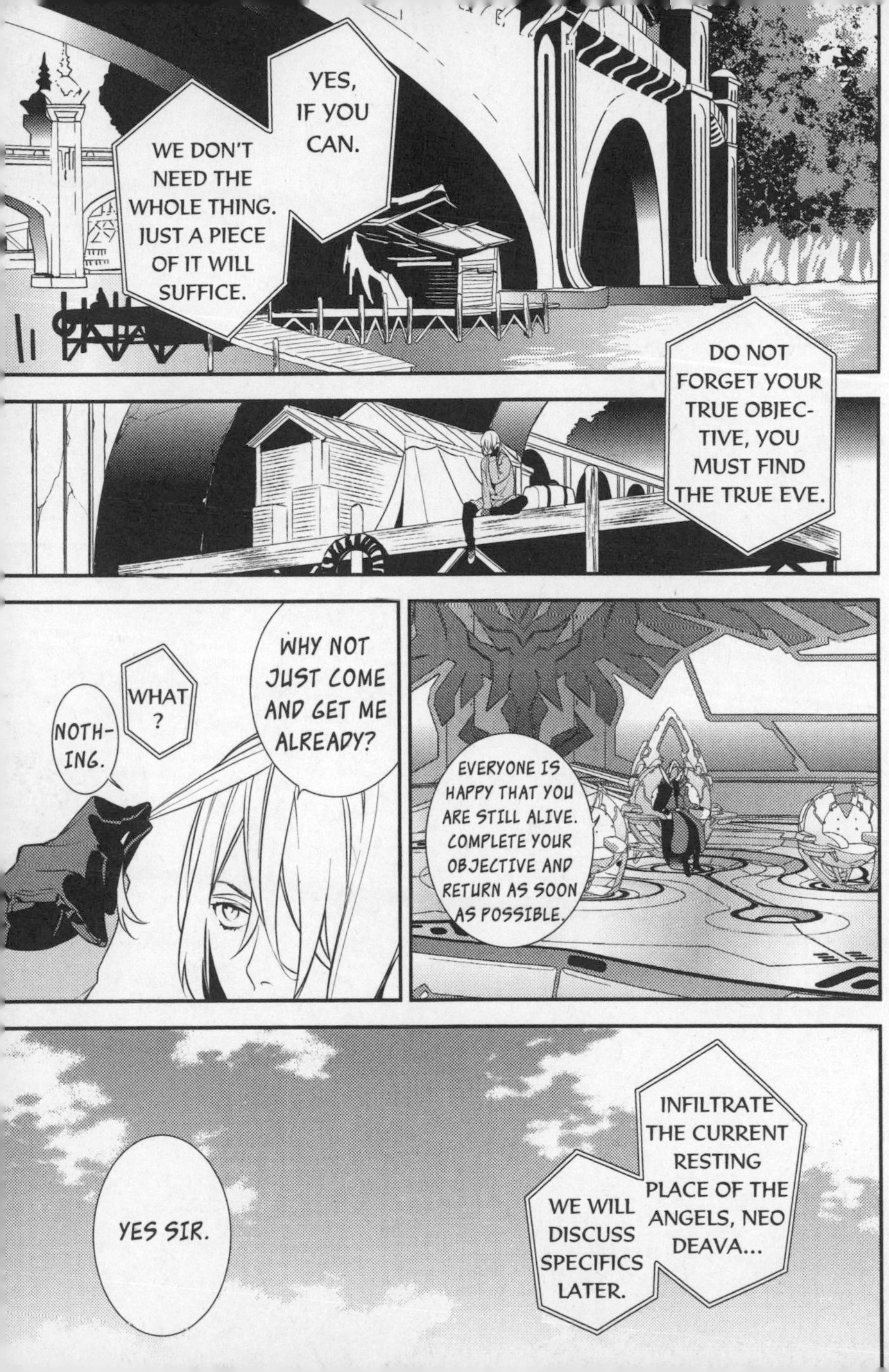
YES, IF YOU CAN.
WE DON'T NEED THE WHOLE THING. JUST A PIECE OF IT WILL SUFFICE.
DO NOT FORGET YOUR TRUE OBJEC-TIVE, YOU MUST FIND THE TRUE EVE.
EVERYONE IS HAPPY THAT YOU ARE STILL ALIVE. COMPLETE YOUR OBJECTIVE AND RETURN AS SOON AS POSSIBLE.
WHY NOT JUST COME AND GET ME ALREADY?
WHAT?
NOTH-ING.
INFILTRATE THE CURRENT RESTING PLACE OF THE ANGELS, NEO DEAVA...
WE WILL DISCUSS SPECIFICS LATER.
YES SIR.

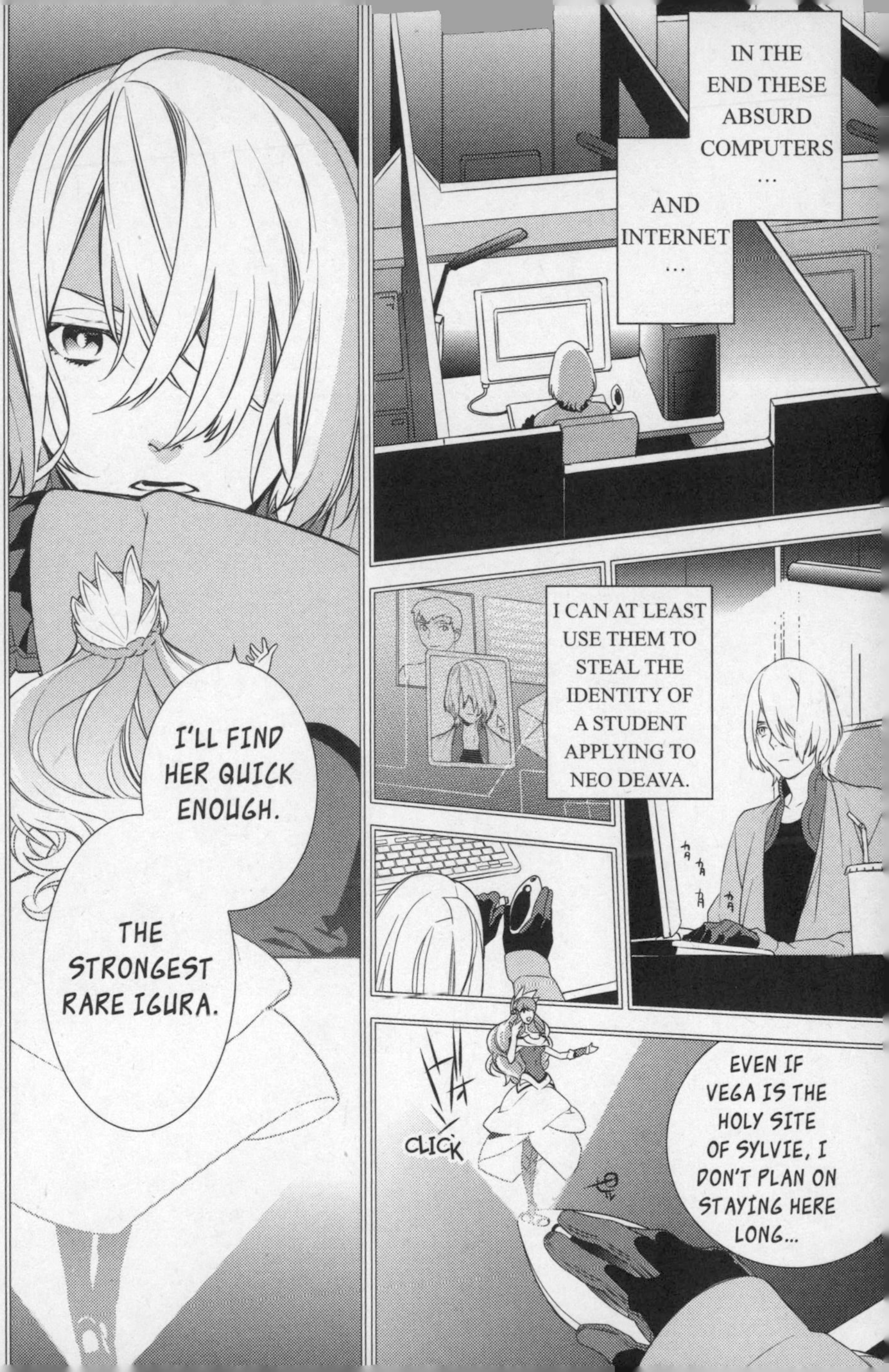
IN THE END THESE ABSURD COMPUTERS …
AND INTERNET …
I CAN AT LEAST USE THEM TO STEAL THE IDENTITY OF A STUDENT APPLYING TO NEO DEAVA.
CLICK
EVEN IF VEGA IS THE HOLY SITE OF SYLVIE, I DON'T PLAN ON STAYING HERE LONG...
I'LL FIND HER QUICK ENOUGH.
THE STRONGEST RARE IGURA.

HEY, WHAT ARE YOUR HOBBIES?!

CLATTER

NO! JUST LET HIM TALK.

WAS YOUR SCHOOL CO-ED?

WHAT KIND OF MUSIC DO YOU LIKE?

HE'S MEEEEAN!

SHUFFLE

WHAT THE HELL?

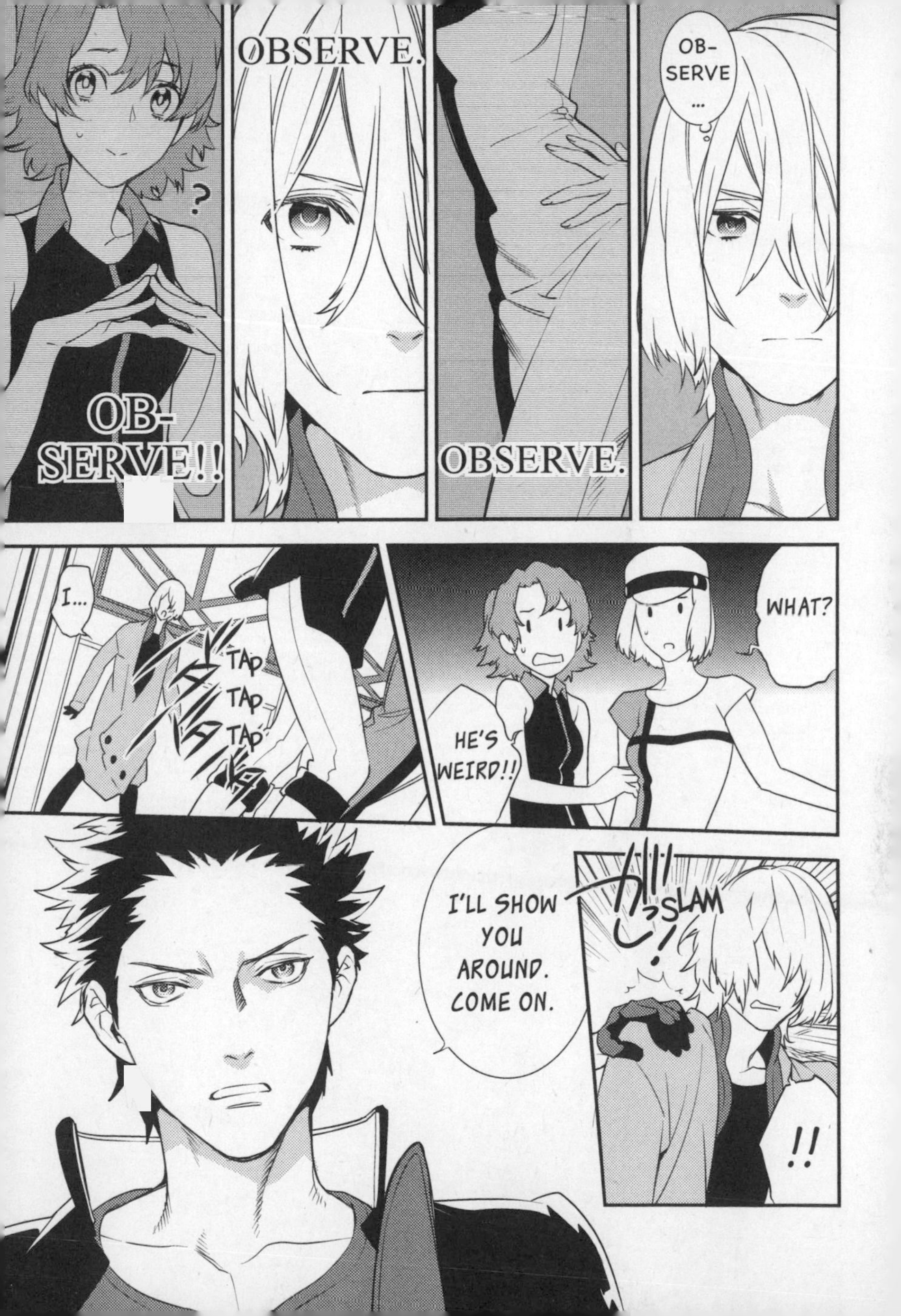
OB-
SERVE
...
OBSERVE.
OBSERVE.
?
OB-
SERVE!!
WHAT?
HE'S WEIRD!!
I...
TAP
TAP
TAP
SLAM
!!
I'LL SHOW YOU AROUND. COME ON.

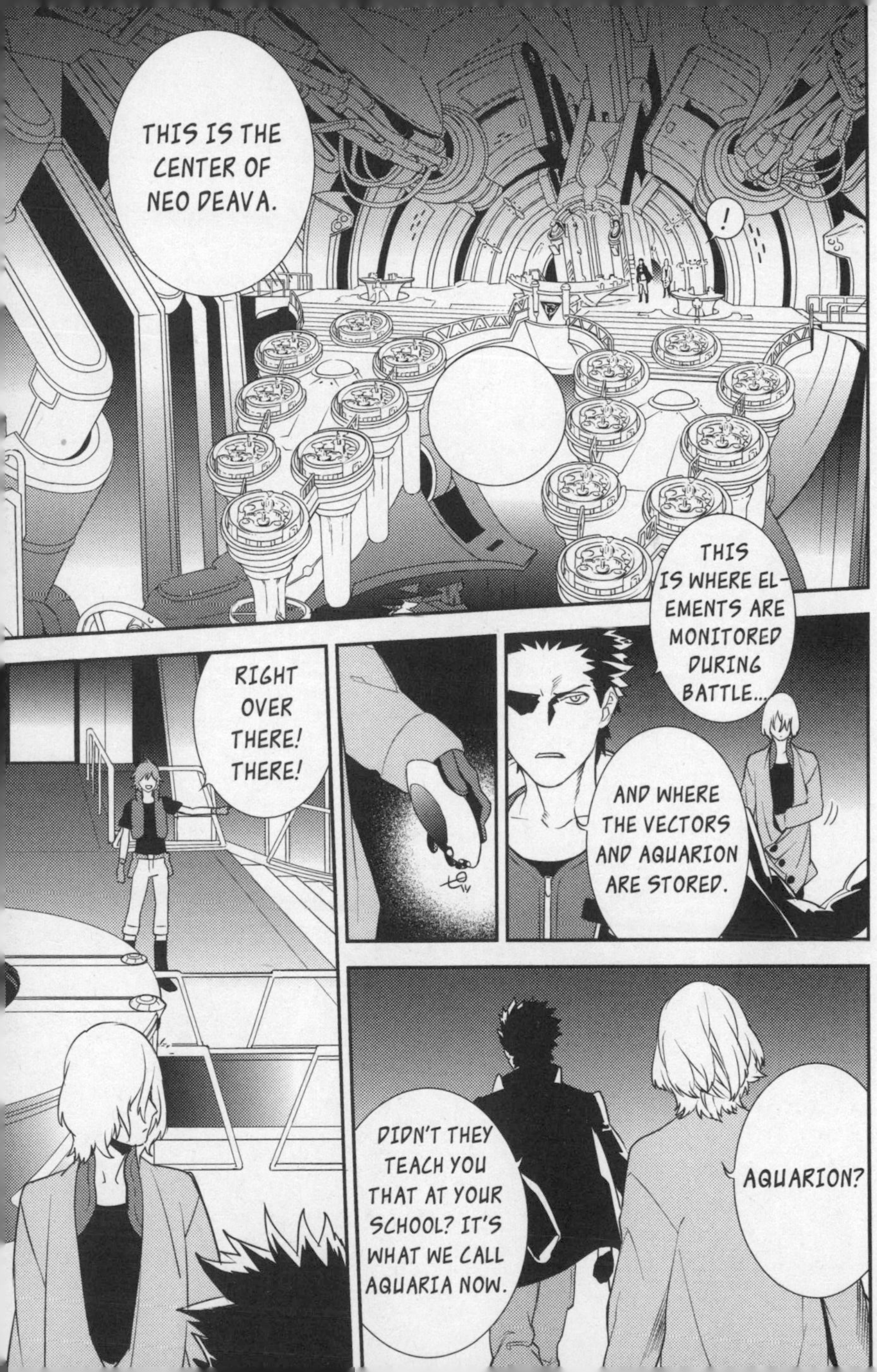
THIS IS THE CENTER OF NEO DEAVA.
!
THIS IS WHERE EL- EMENTS ARE MONITORED DURING BATTLE...
AND WHERE THE VECTORS AND AQUARION ARE STORED.
AQUARION?
DIDN'T THEY TEACH YOU THAT AT YOUR SCHOOL? IT'S WHAT WE CALL AQUARIA NOW.
RIGHT OVER THERE! THERE!

THE ME-
CHANICAL
ANGEL!

YOU BAS-TARD!...

NO FIGHT-ING!

YEAH, HE'S ANNOY-ING.

LIKE I'D EVEN BOTHER WITH THIS GUY!

I AM BEING NICE.

IF YOU'RE GOING TO EXPLAIN STUFF TO HIM, BE NICE ABOUT IT!

NO!!

BUT IT IS NOW, ISN'T IT?!

IT WASN'T LIKE THAT!

BECAUSE YOU WON'T LEAVE MY SISTER ALONE!

YOU TRIED TO FIGHT ME!

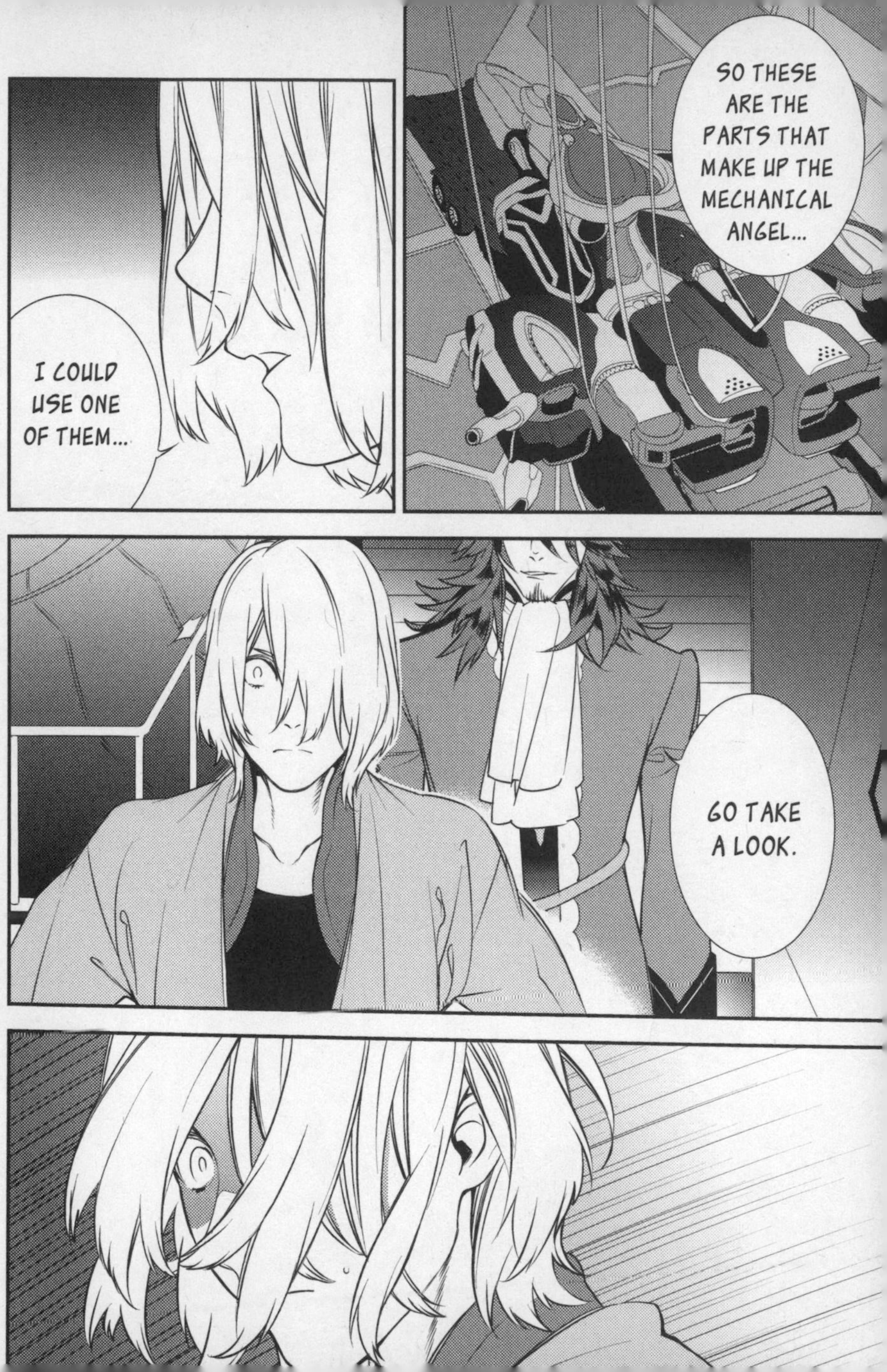
SO THESE ARE THE PARTS THAT MAKE UP THE MECHANICAL ANGEL...
I COULD USE ONE OF THEM...
GO TAKE A LOOK.

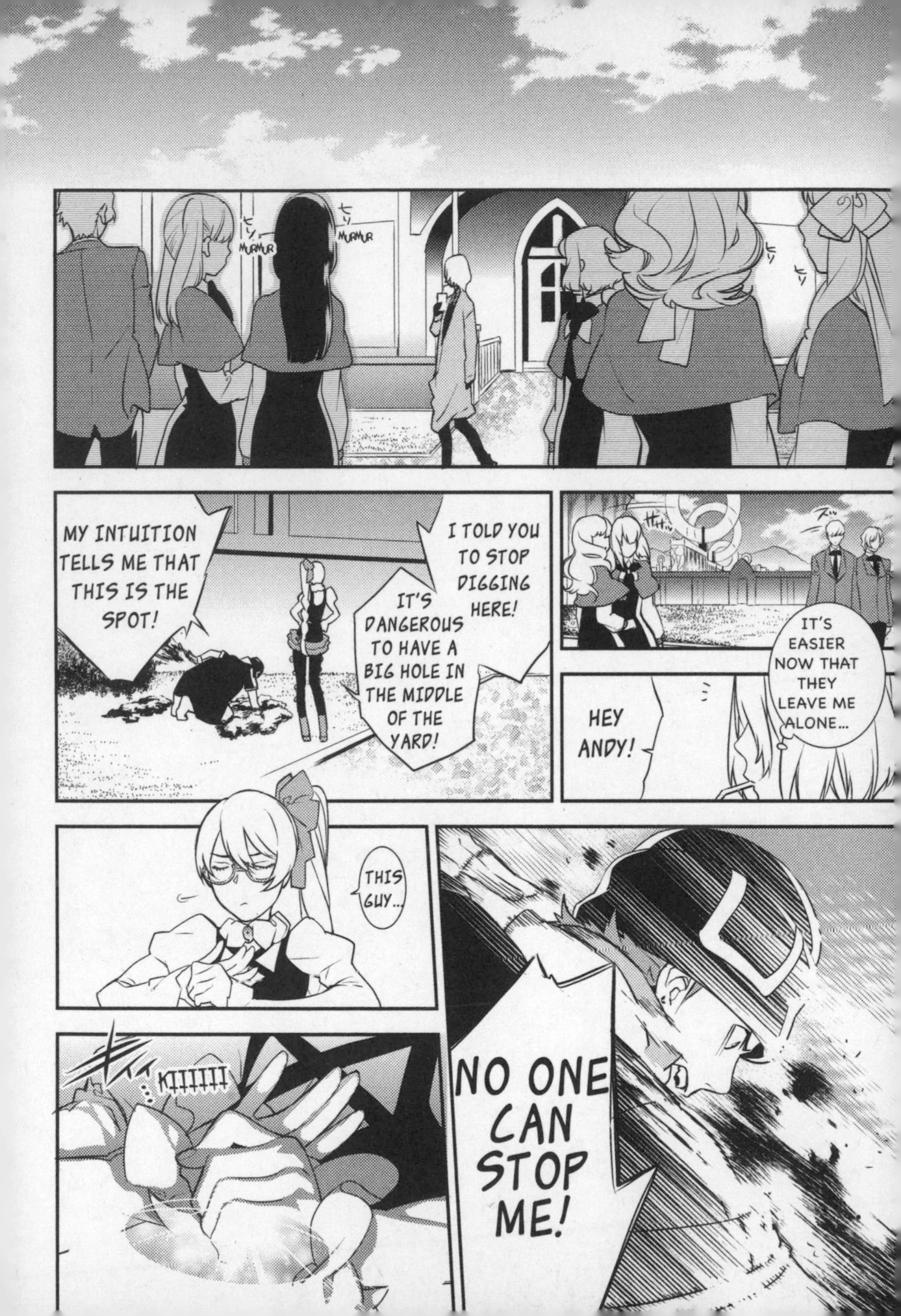
MURMUR
MURMUR
MY INTUITION TELLS ME THAT THIS IS THE SPOT!
I TOLD YOU TO STOP DIGGING HERE!
IT'S DANGEROUS TO HAVE A BIG HOLE IN THE MIDDLE OF THE YARD!
IT'S EASIER NOW THAT THEY LEAVE ME ALONE...
HEY ANDY!
THIS GUY...
KIIIIII
NO ONE CAN STOP ME!

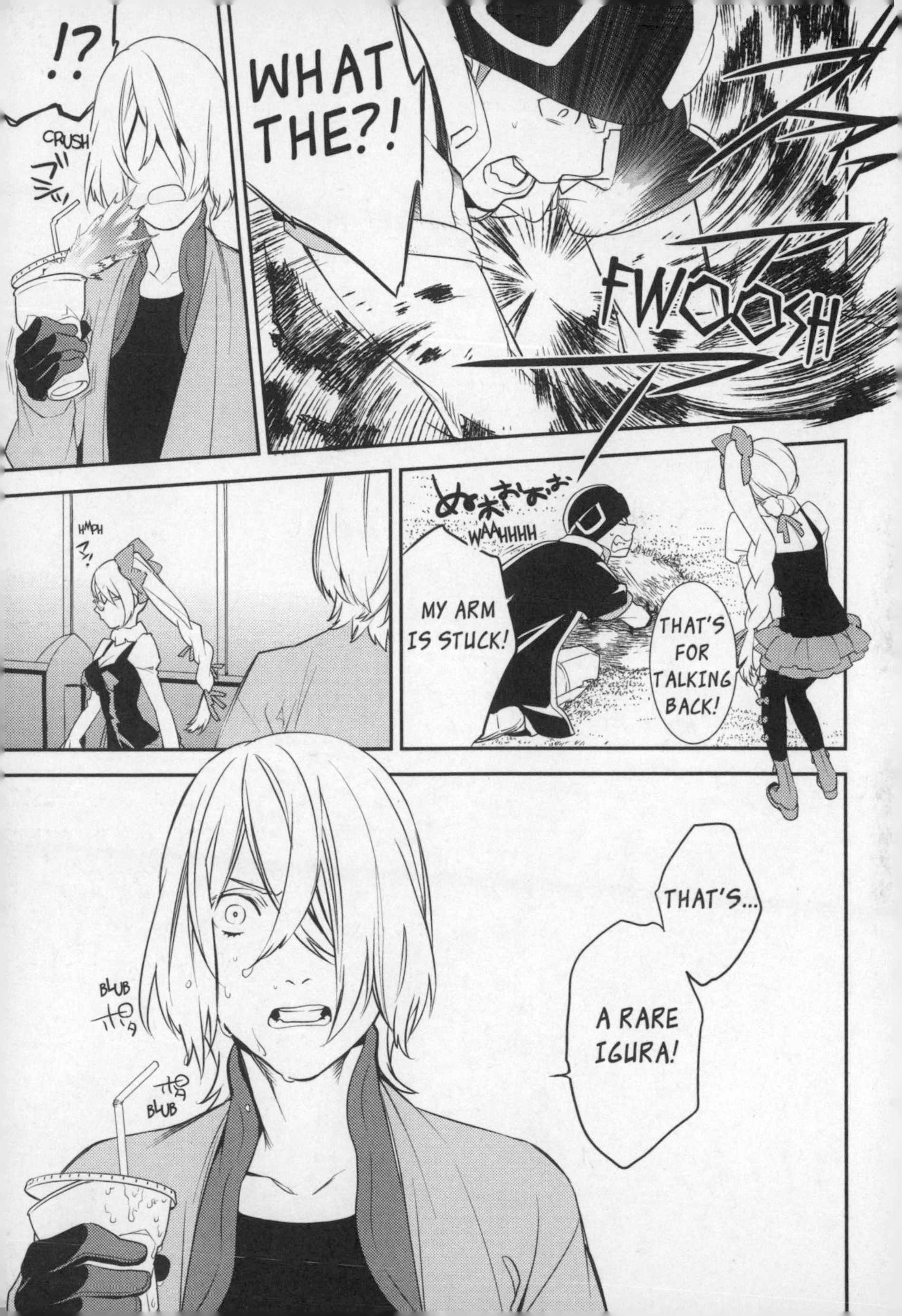
WHAT THE?!
FWOOSH
!?
CRUSH
WAAHHHH
MY ARM IS STUCK!
THAT'S FOR TALKING BACK!
HMPH
THAT'S...
A RARE IGURA!
BLUB
BLUB

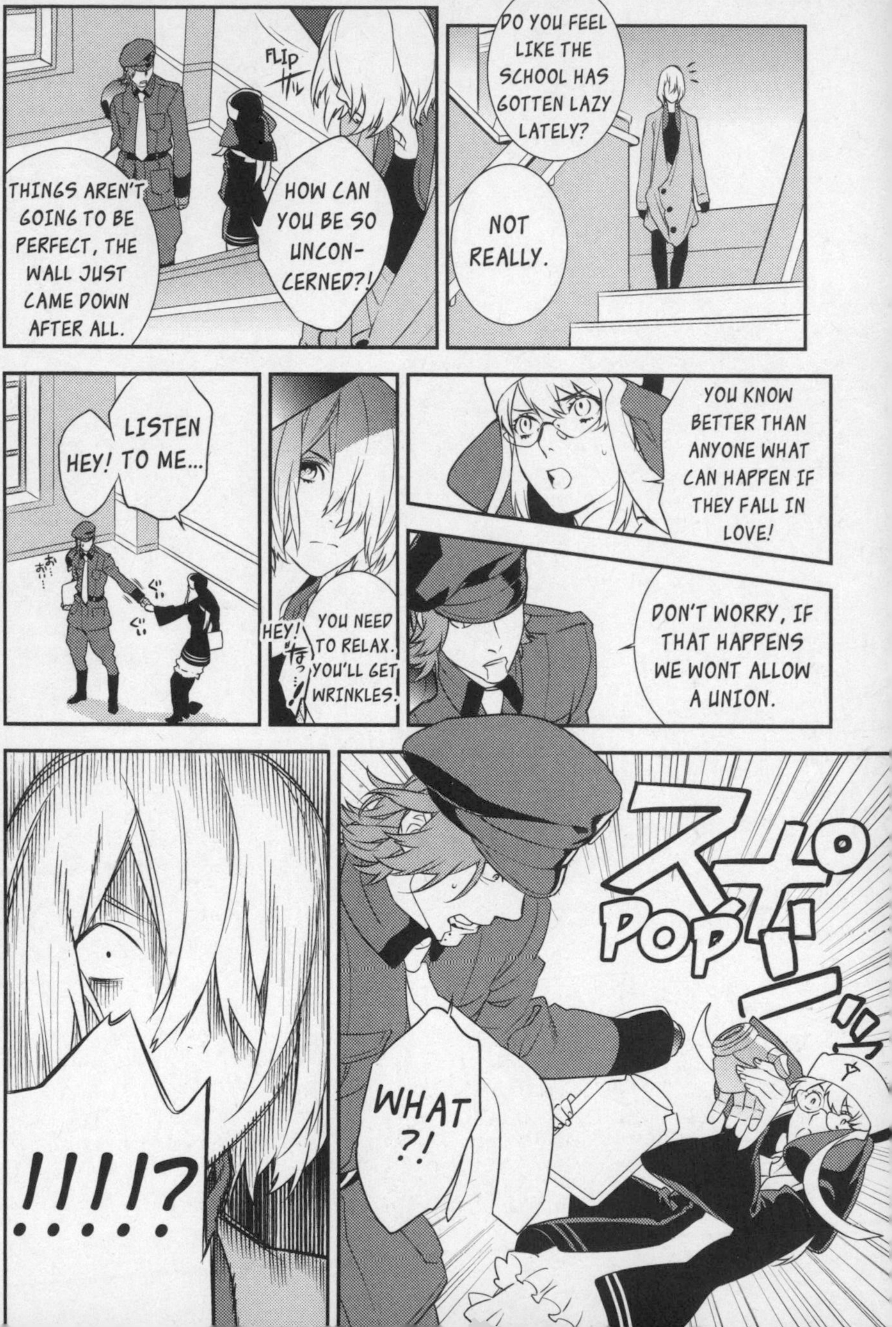
DO YOU FEEL LIKE THE SCHOOL HAS GOTTEN LAZY LATELY?
NOT REALLY.
FLIP
HOW CAN YOU BE SO UNCON-CERNED?!
THINGS AREN'T GOING TO BE PERFECT, THE WALL JUST CAME DOWN AFTER ALL.
YOU KNOW BETTER THAN ANYONE WHAT CAN HAPPEN IF THEY FALL IN LOVE!
DON'T WORRY, IF THAT HAPPENS WE WONT ALLOW A UNION.
YOU NEED TO RELAX. YOU'LL GET WRINKLES.
HEY!
LISTEN TO ME...
HEY!
POP
WHAT?!
!!!!?

I'D NEVER SURVIVE THE ORDEAL!

I CAN'T DO IT.

HEY, HEY!

PUT IT BACK ON!

YIKES

RARE IGURA ARE CRAZY!

SHE RIPPED HIS HAND OFF!

AHH!

TAP TAP TAP

THERE'S ONLY TWO MELON PASTRIES LEFT!

HEY, I SAW IT FIRST!

THEY'RE GONNA SELL OUT!

LOOK, LOOK!

I CAN'T DO IT...

NONE OF THEM ARE ANYTHING LIKE SYLVIE...

RARE IGURA.... WOMEN?

ZIP

SWAY

FWISH

WHO'S THAT?!

YOU!!

CRACK

SWISH

CLANG

DON'T LET HIM OUT! LOCK HIM IN!

YOU PERV!

THE NEW KID?

UM...

WAIT JUST A SECOND!

WHAT SHOULD WE DO WITH YOU?

CRU-CIFY HIM!

CRACK

CRACK

NOW THEN

RIP HIS SKIN OFF!

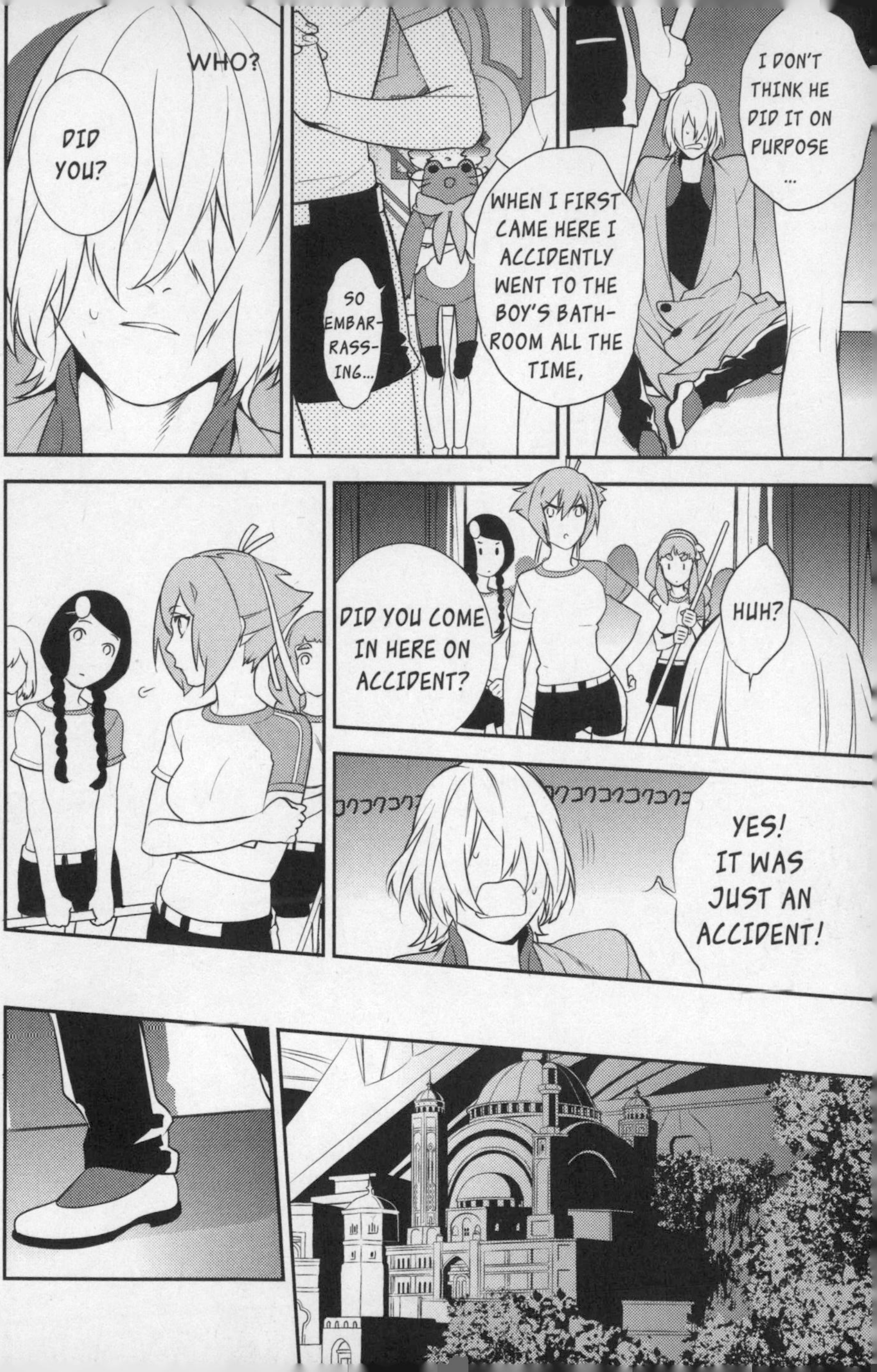
I DON'T THINK HE DID IT ON PURPOSE ...
WHEN I FIRST CAME HERE I ACCIDENTLY WENT TO THE BOY'S BATHROOM ALL THE TIME,
SO EMBARRASSING...
WHO?
DID YOU?
HUH?
DID YOU COME IN HERE ON ACCIDENT?
YES! IT WAS JUST AN ACCIDENT!

IT HAD TO BE JIN...

SMACK

HE'S CONSTI-PATED?

HUH?

SLAM

HUM?

H.. HOLES ?

YEAH, HOLES!

SHOCK

CLATTER

HEY, DO YOU LIKE HOLES?!

I WANT TO GO HOME...

#13 WAVERING SOUNDS

I KNOW! THAT SHOULD NEVER HAPPEN! I DON'T REALLY GET IT, BUT IT'S NUTS.

I KNOW! IT'S CRAZY, ISN'T IT?

I KNOW... THAT'S SO FUNNY!

A SECRET CODE?

I CAN'T UNDERSTAND THE POINT OF THE CONVERSATION... RARE IGURA'S ARE STRANGE.

!

MIND IF WE SIT HERE?

SLUMP

YOU OKAY? YOU LOOK LIKE YOU ARE ABOUT TO VANISH.

YES. I'M FINE...

UH... SURE?

WHAT'S UP WITH JIN?

JIN?

HUH?

YEAH, HIS NAME IS LONG AND HARD TO REMEMBER, SO ANDY...

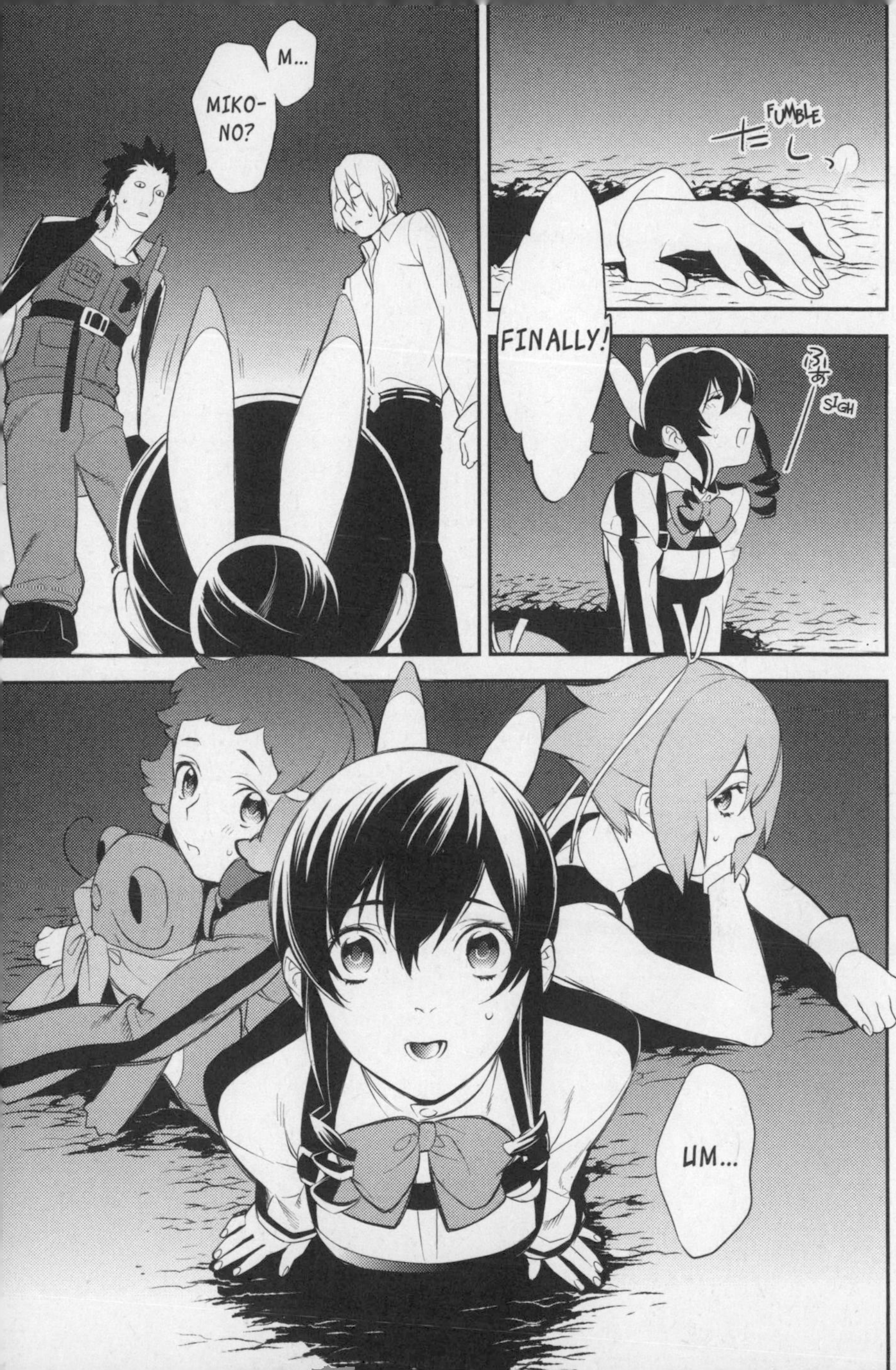
FUMBLE
FINALLY!
SIGH
M...
MIKO-NO?
UM...

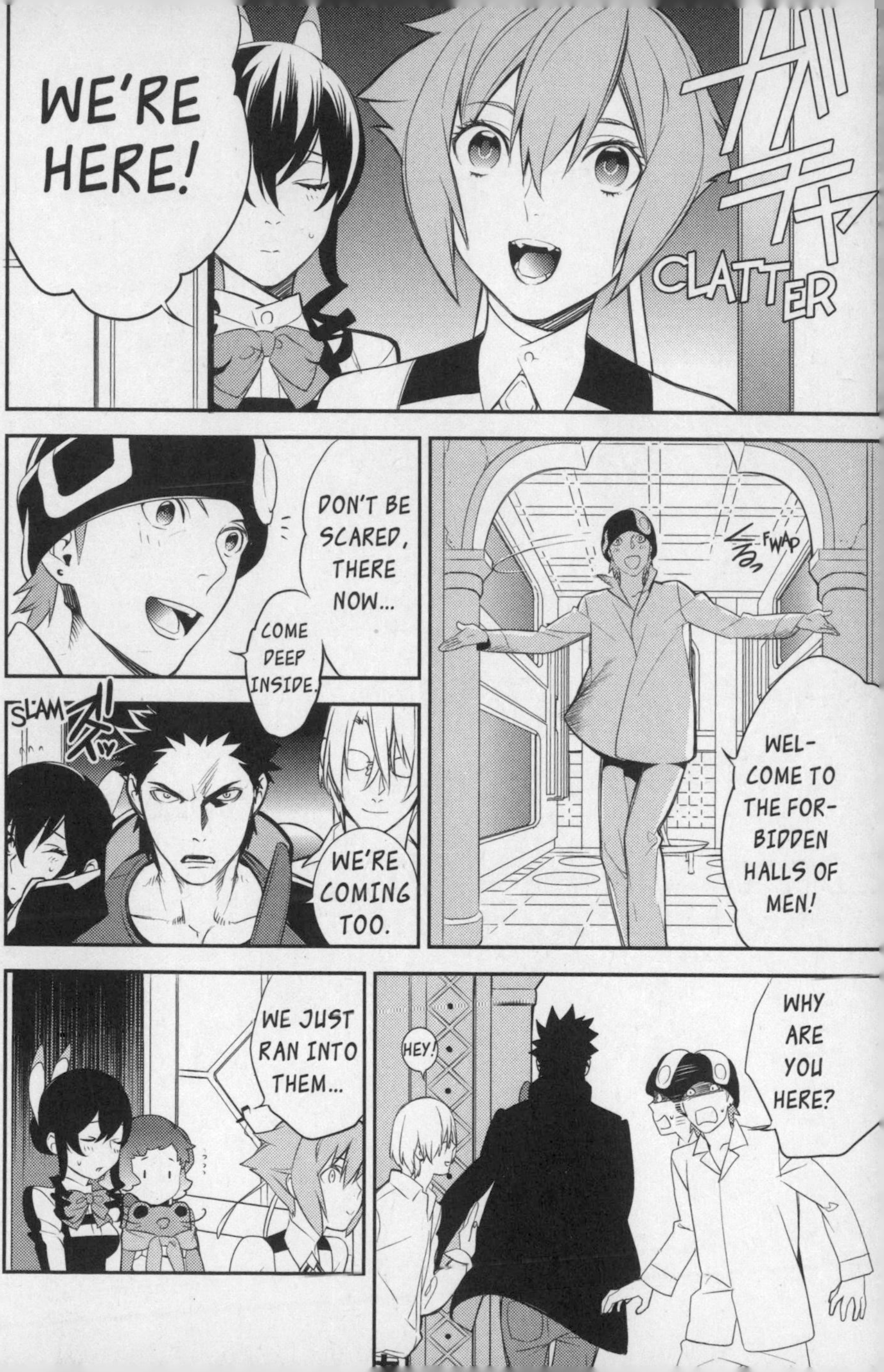

ガチャ
CLATTER
WE'RE HERE!
FWAP
WEL-COME TO THE FOR-BIDDEN HALLS OF MEN!
DON'T BE SCARED, THERE NOW...
COME DEEP INSIDE.
SLAM
WE'RE COMING TOO.
WHY ARE YOU HERE?
HEY!
WE JUST RAN INTO THEM...

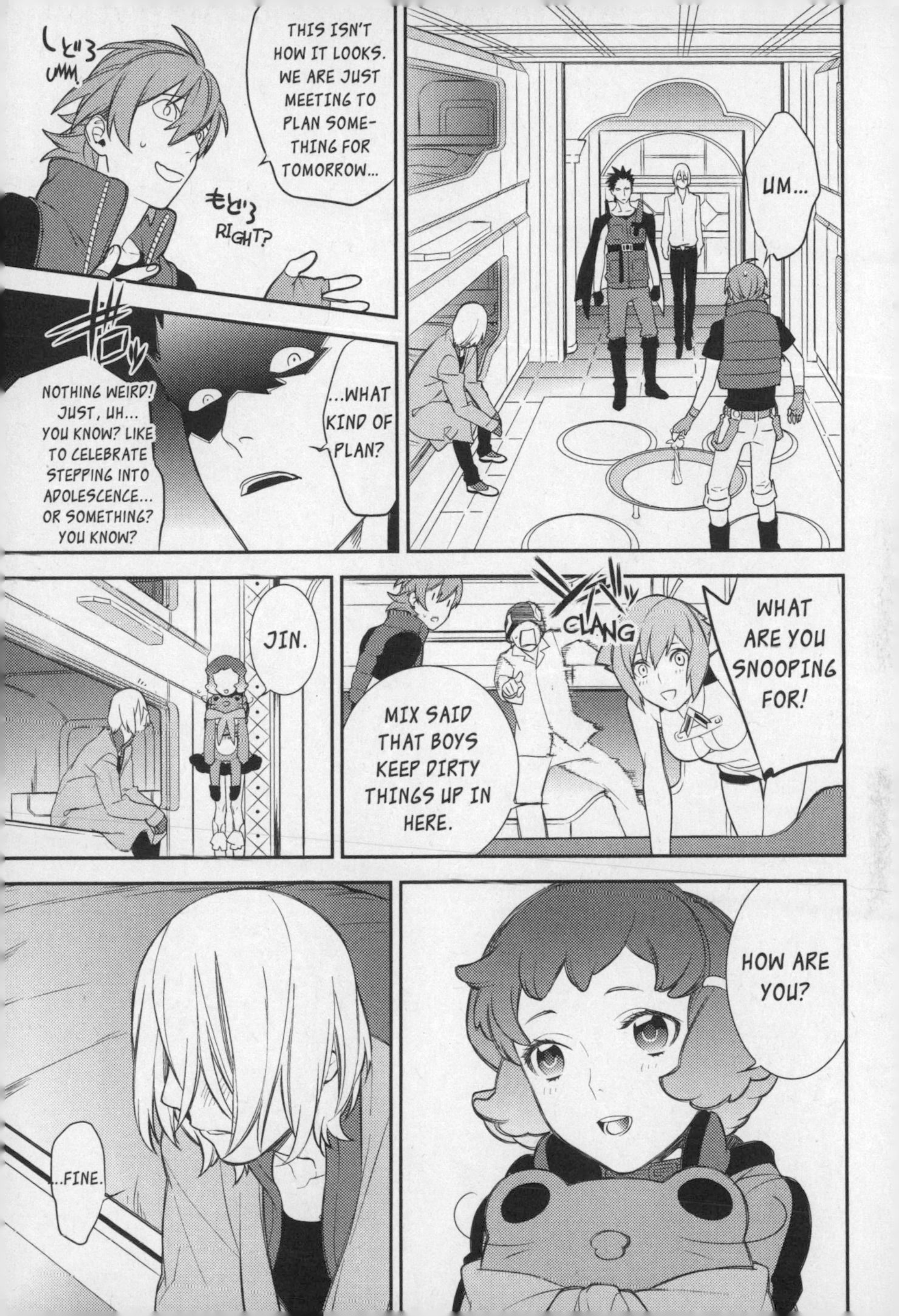
UM...
THIS ISN'T HOW IT LOOKS. WE ARE JUST MEETING TO PLAN SOMETHING FOR TOMORROW...
しどろ
UMM,
もどろ
RIGHT?
...WHAT KIND OF PLAN?
NOTHING WEIRD! JUST, UH... YOU KNOW? LIKE TO CELEBRATE STEPPING INTO ADOLESCENCE... OR SOMETHING? YOU KNOW?
WHAT ARE YOU SNOOPING FOR!
CLANG
MIX SAID THAT BOYS KEEP DIRTY THINGS UP IN HERE.
JIN.
HOW ARE YOU?
...FINE.

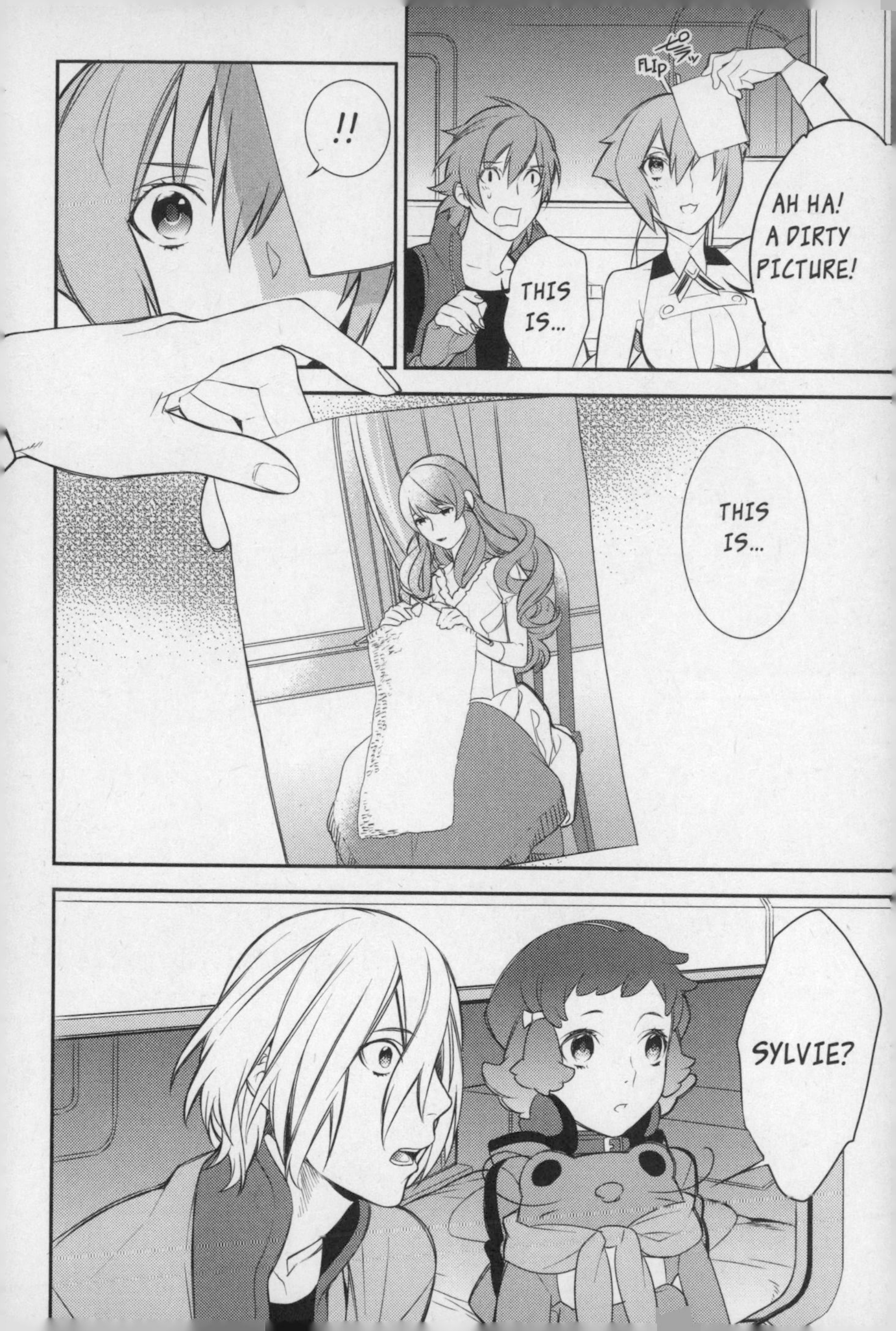
FLIP
AH HA! A DIRTY PICTURE!
THIS IS...
!!
THIS IS...
SYLVIE?

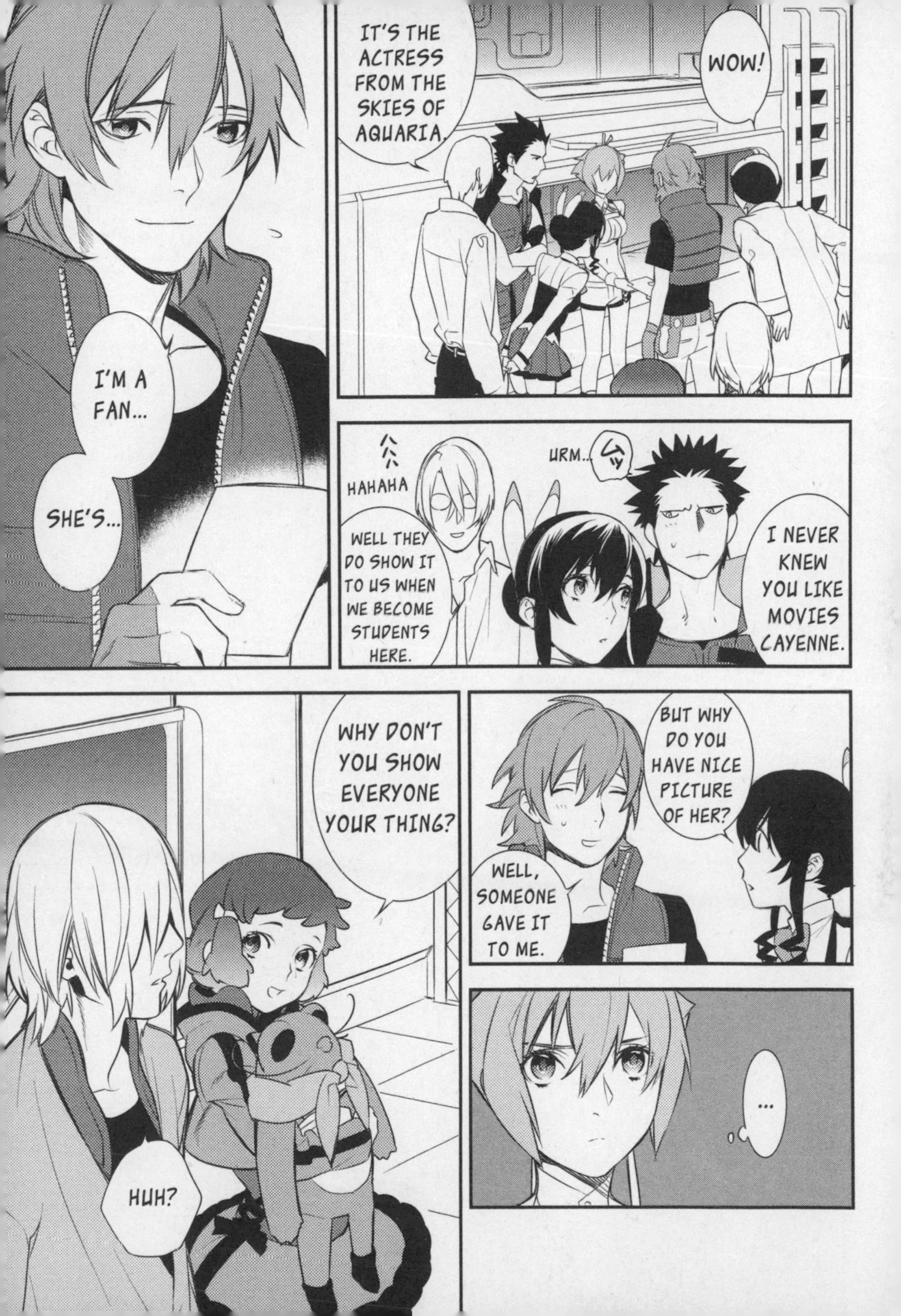
WOW!
IT'S THE ACTRESS FROM THE SKIES OF AQUARIA.
I NEVER KNEW YOU LIKE MOVIES CAYENNE.
URM...
ムッ
HAHAHA
WELL THEY DO SHOW IT TO US WHEN WE BECOME STUDENTS HERE.
I'M A FAN...
SHE'S...
BUT WHY DO YOU HAVE NICE PICTURE OF HER?
WELL, SOMEONE GAVE IT TO ME.
...
WHY DON'T YOU SHOW EVERYONE YOUR THING?
HUH?

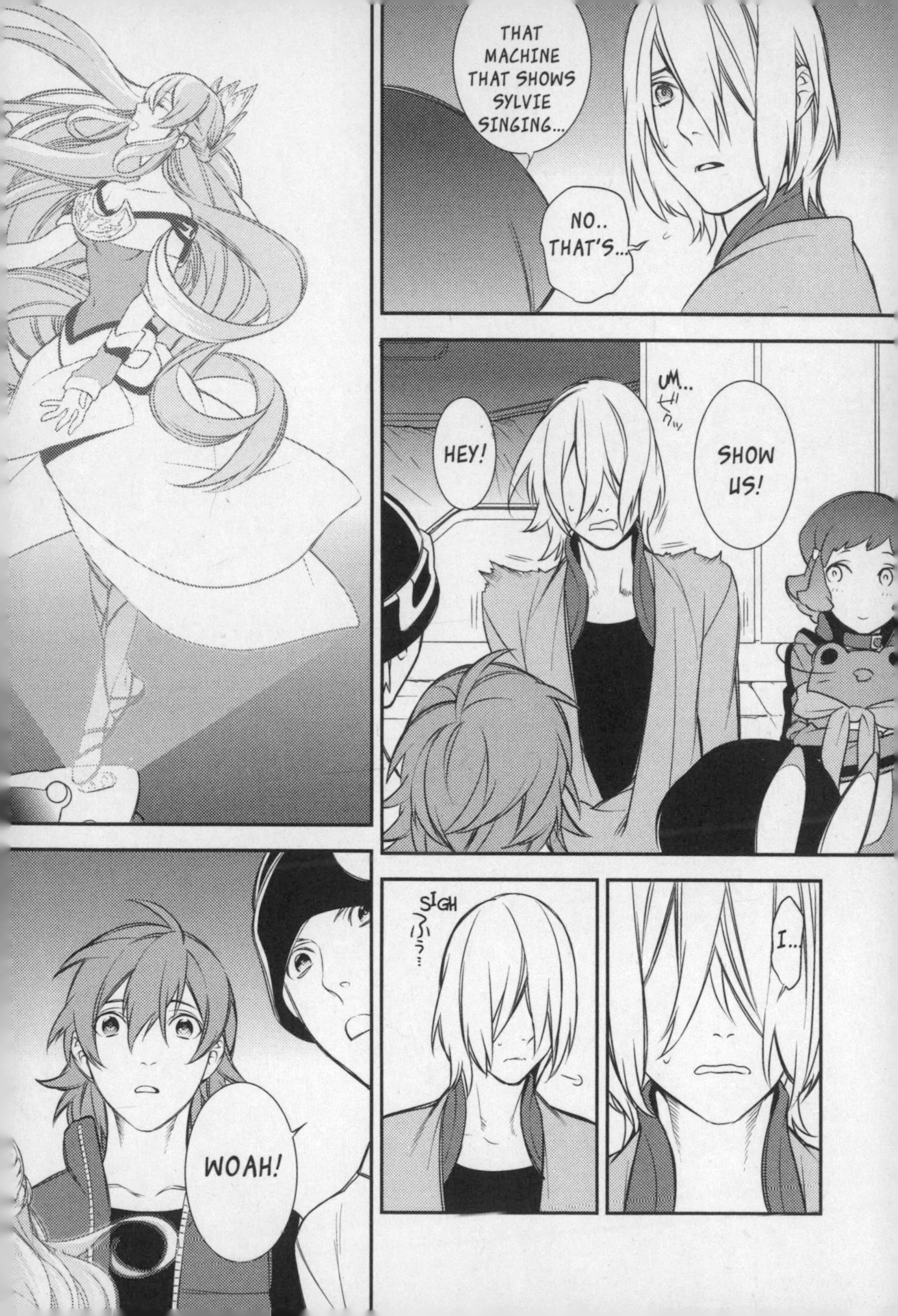
THAT MACHINE THAT SHOWS SYLVIE SINGING...
NO.. THAT'S...
UM...
SHOW US!
HEY!
I...
SIGH
WOAH!

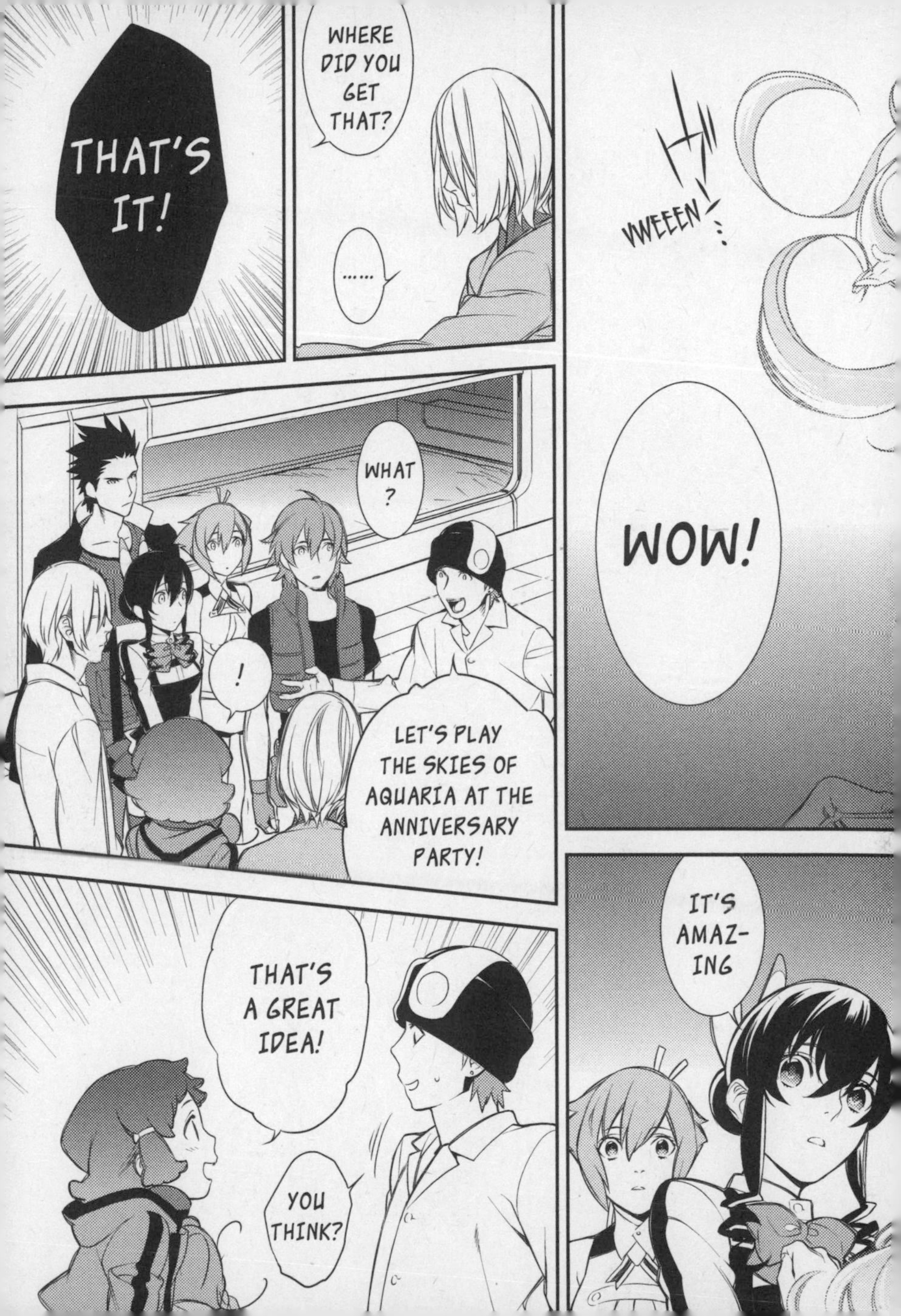
VWEEEN
WOW!
WHERE DID YOU GET THAT?
......
THAT'S IT!
WHAT?
!
LET'S PLAY THE SKIES OF AQUARIA AT THE ANNIVERSARY PARTY!
IT'S AMAZ-ING
THAT'S A GREAT IDEA!
YOU THINK?

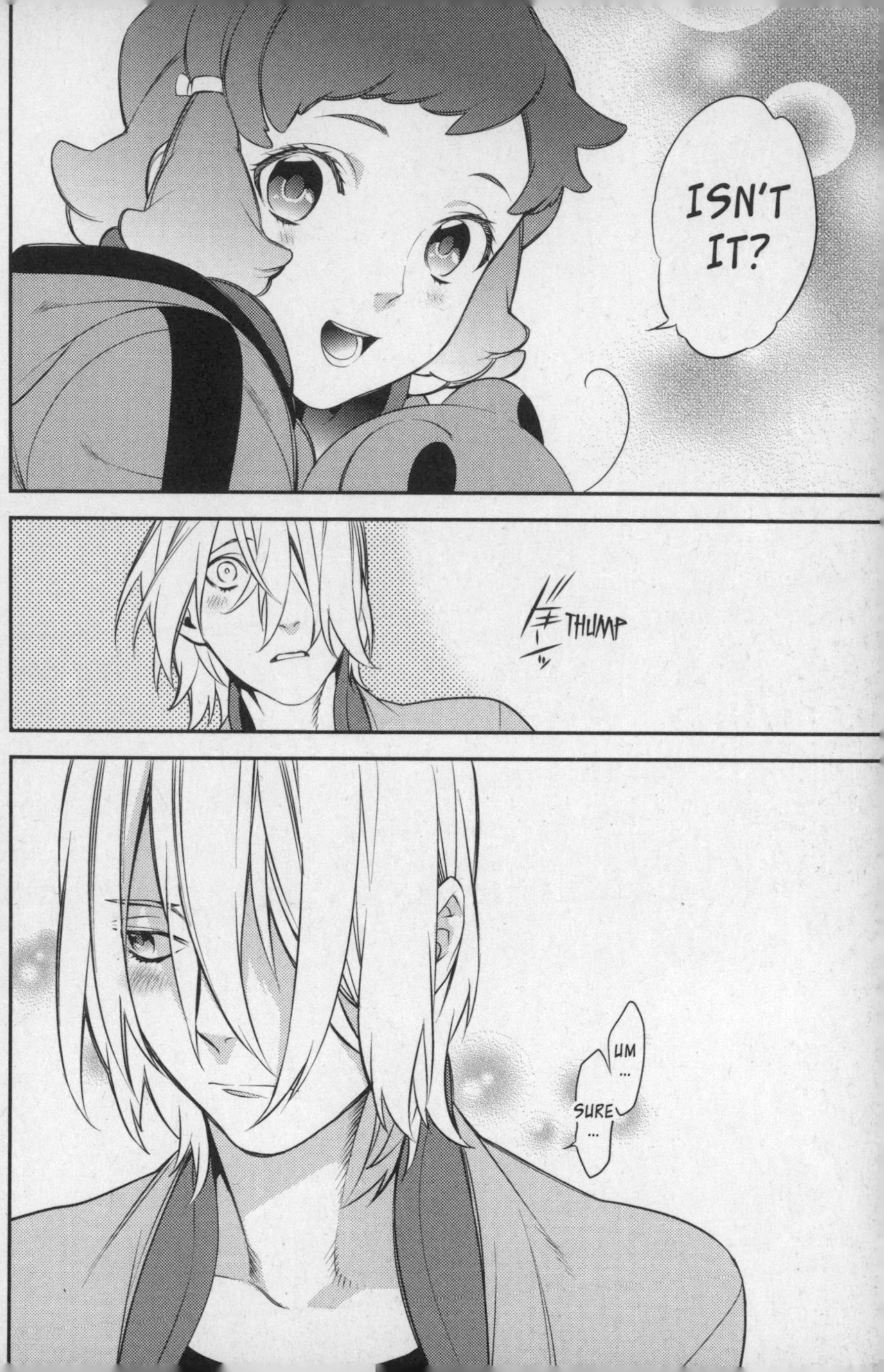
ISN'T IT?
THUMP
UM ...
SURE ...

#15 THE RED THREAD OF DESTINY

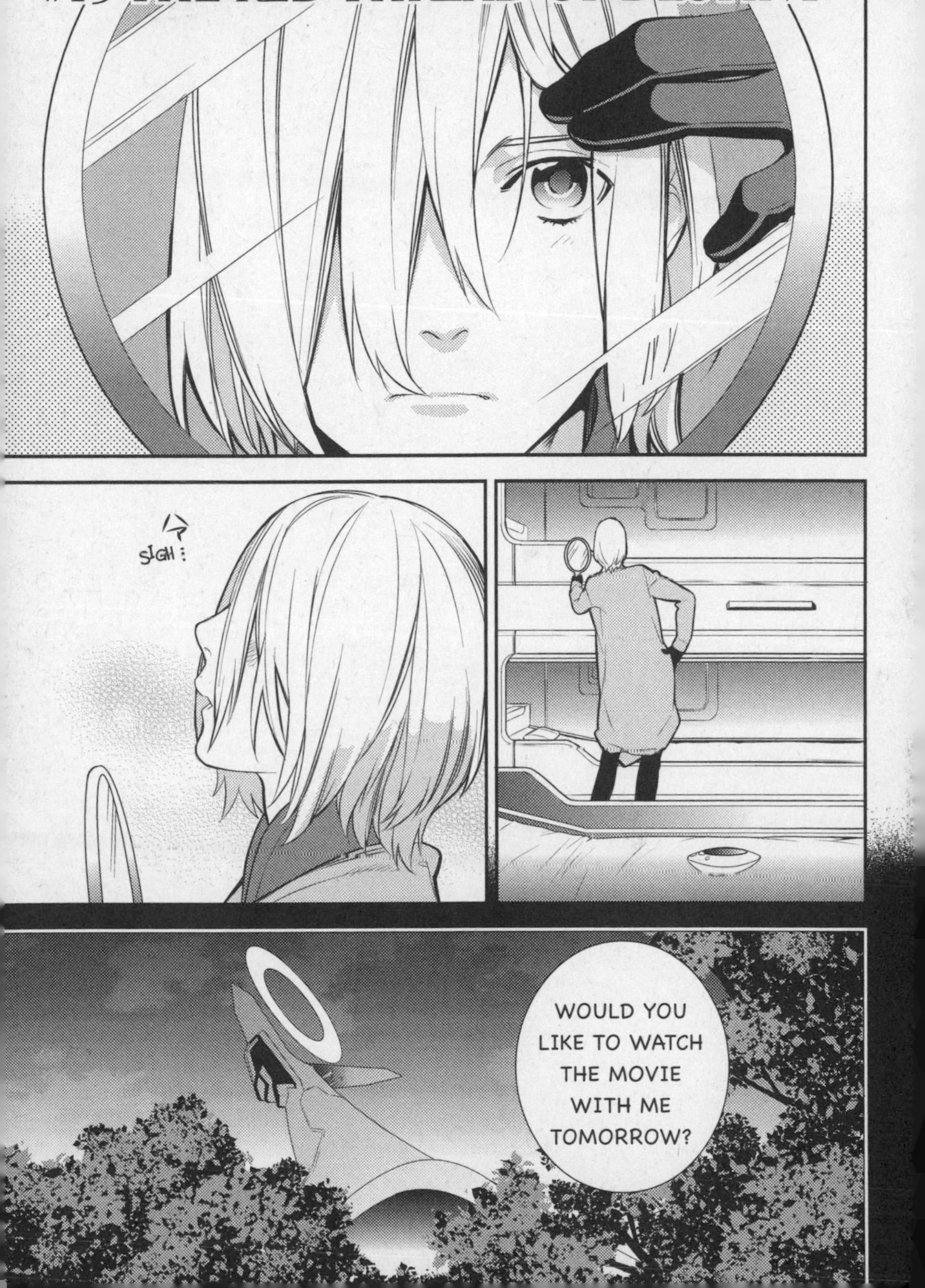
SIGH
WOULD YOU LIKE TO WATCH THE MOVIE WITH ME TOMORROW?

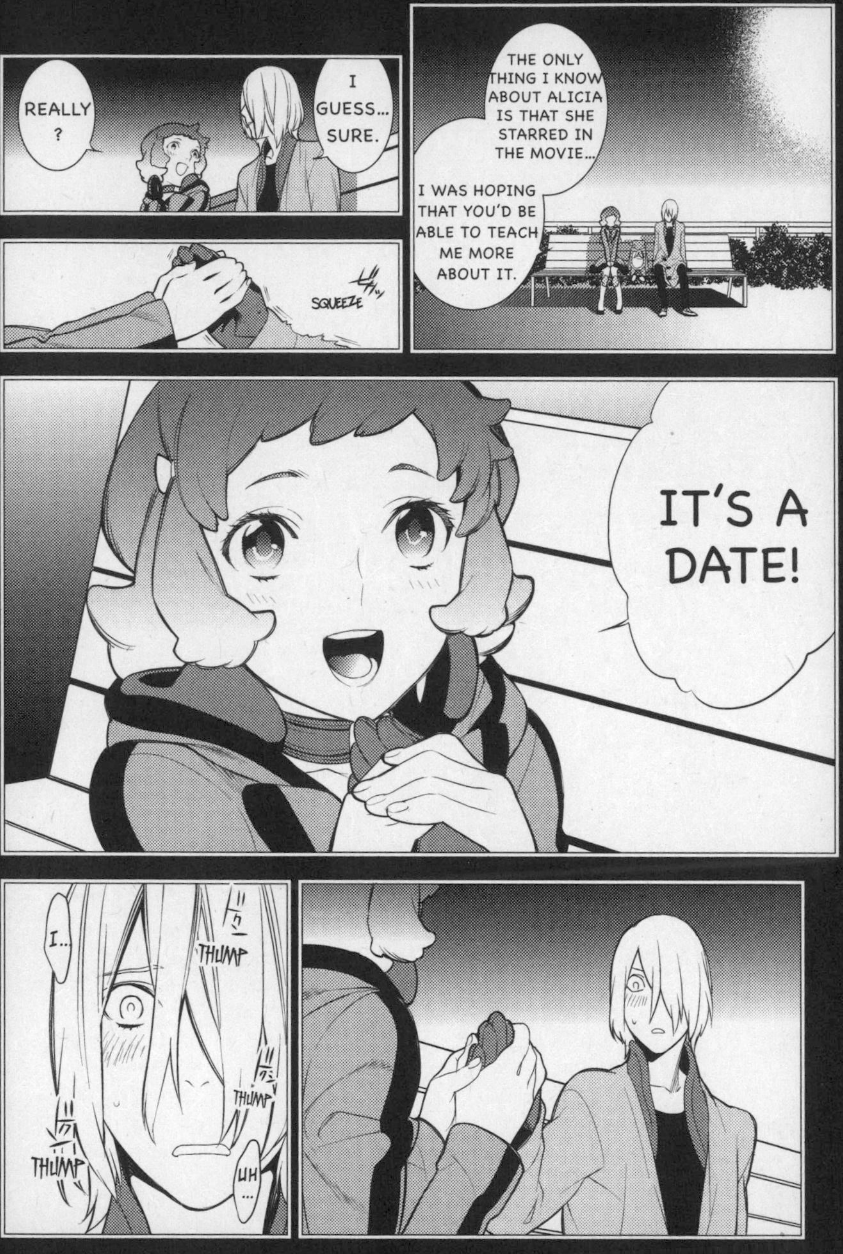
THE ONLY THING I KNOW ABOUT ALICIA IS THAT SHE STARRED IN THE MOVIE...
I WAS HOPING THAT YOU'D BE ABLE TO TEACH ME MORE ABOUT IT.
I GUESS... SURE.
REALLY?
SQUEEZE
IT'S A DATE!
THUMP
THUMP
THUMP
I...
UH...

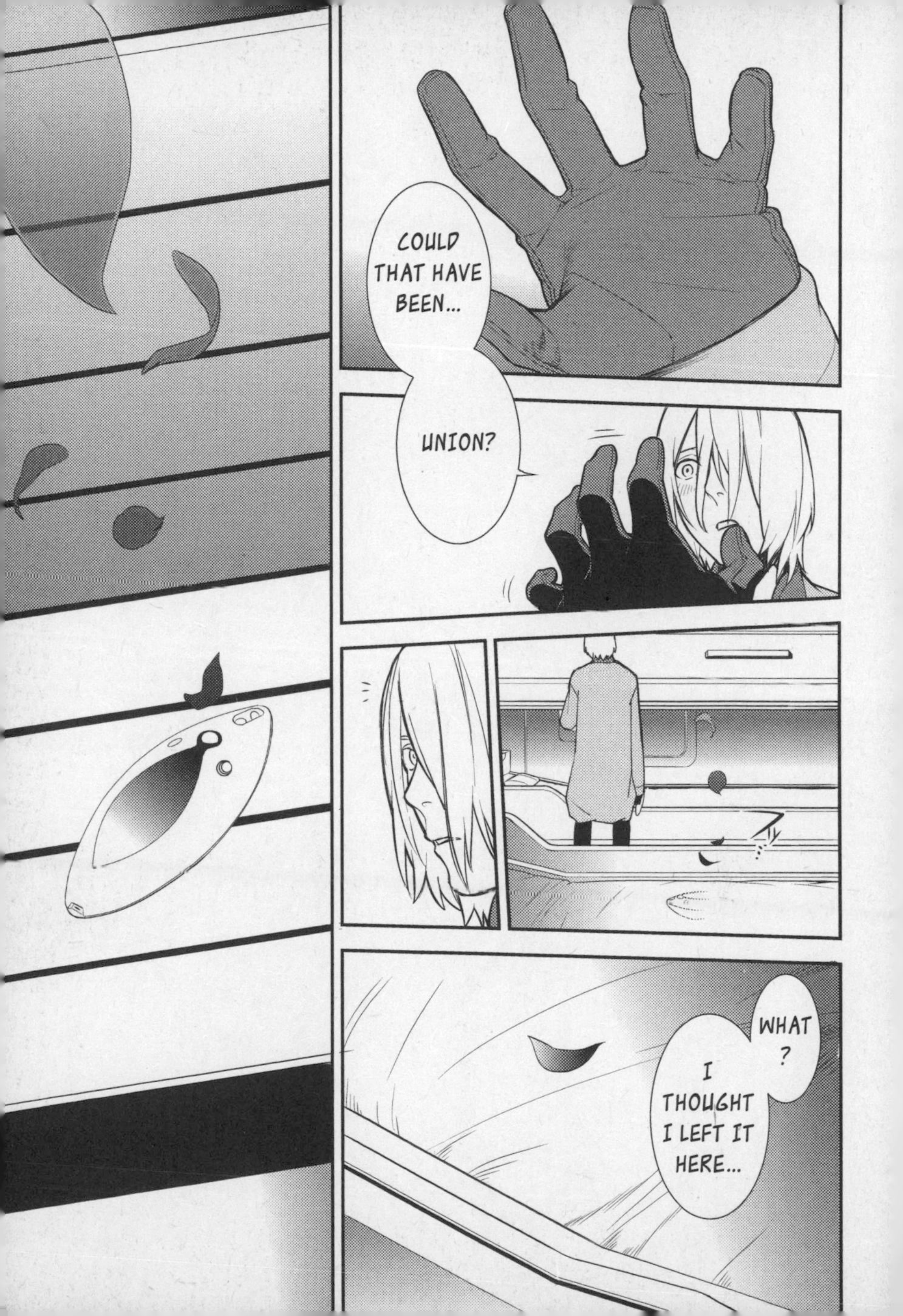
COULD THAT HAVE BEEN...
UNION?
WHAT?
I THOUGHT I LEFT IT HERE...

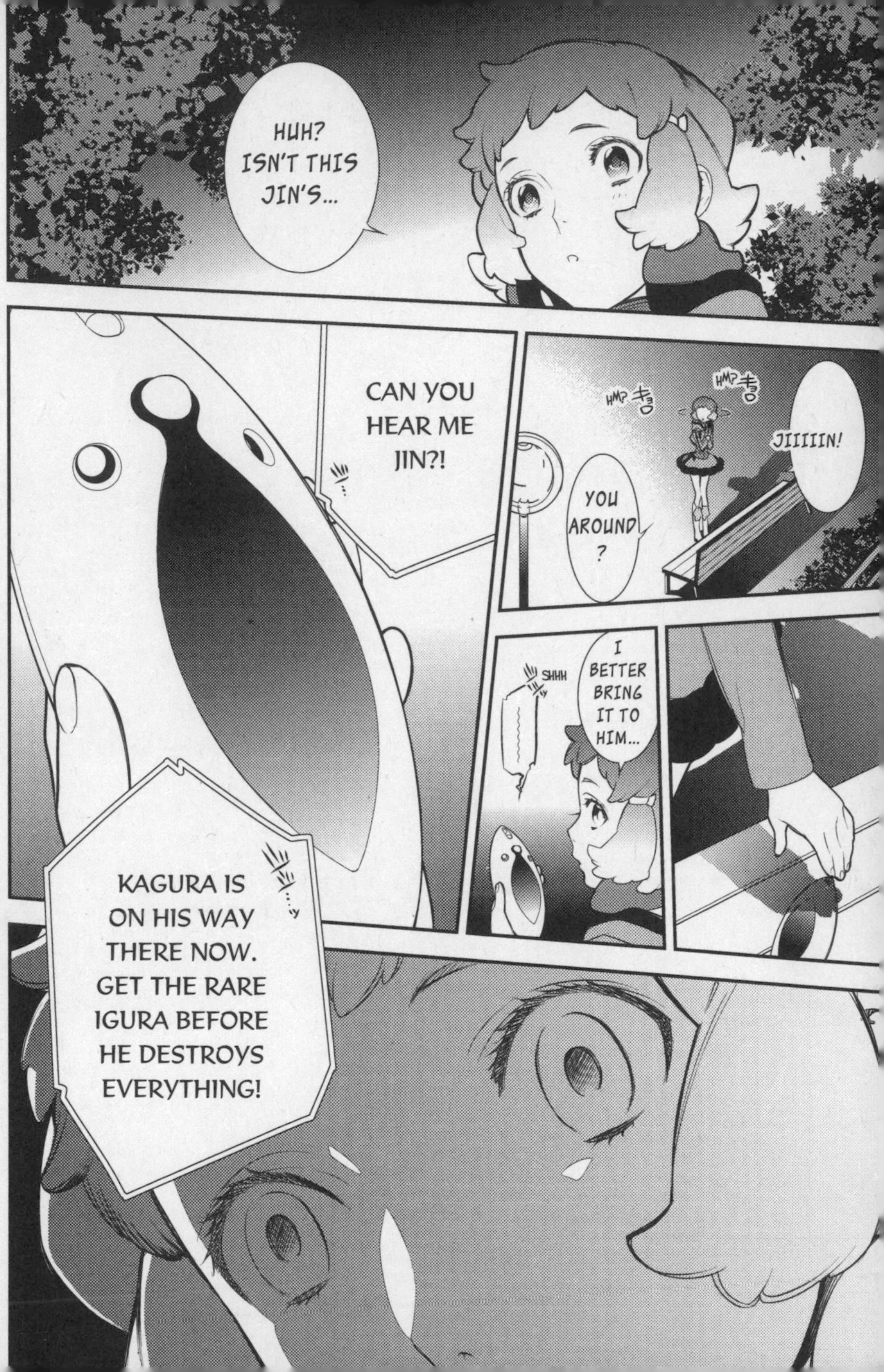
HUH? ISN'T THIS JIN'S...
JIIIIIN!
HM?
HM?
YOU AROUND?
SHHH
I BETTER BRING IT TO HIM...
CAN YOU HEAR ME JIN?!
KAGURA IS ON HIS WAY THERE NOW. GET THE RARE IGURA BEFORE HE DESTROYS EVERYTHING!

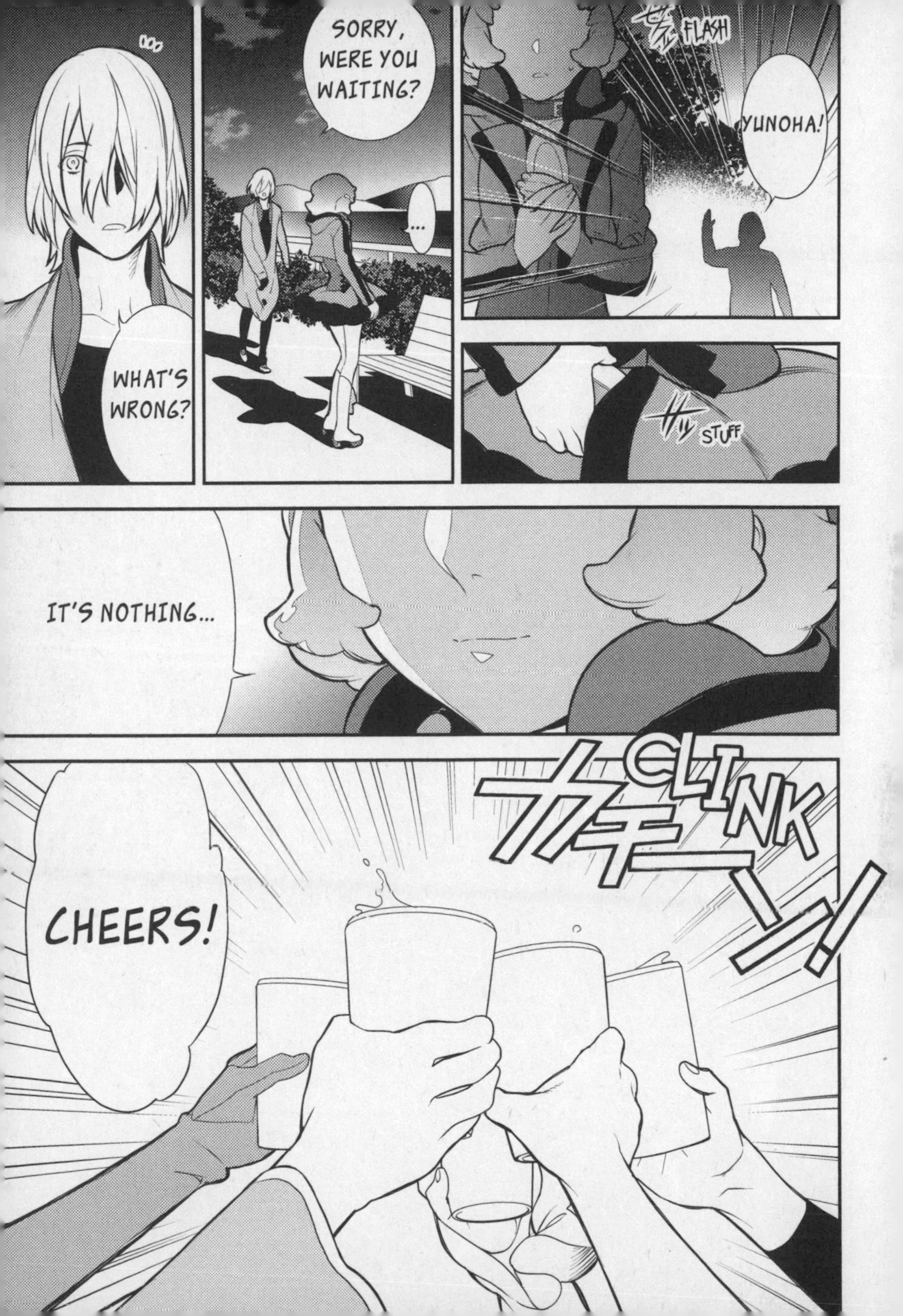
FLASH
YUNOHA!
STUFF
SORRY, WERE YOU WAITING?
...
WHAT'S WRONG?
IT'S NOTHING...
CLINK
CHEERS!

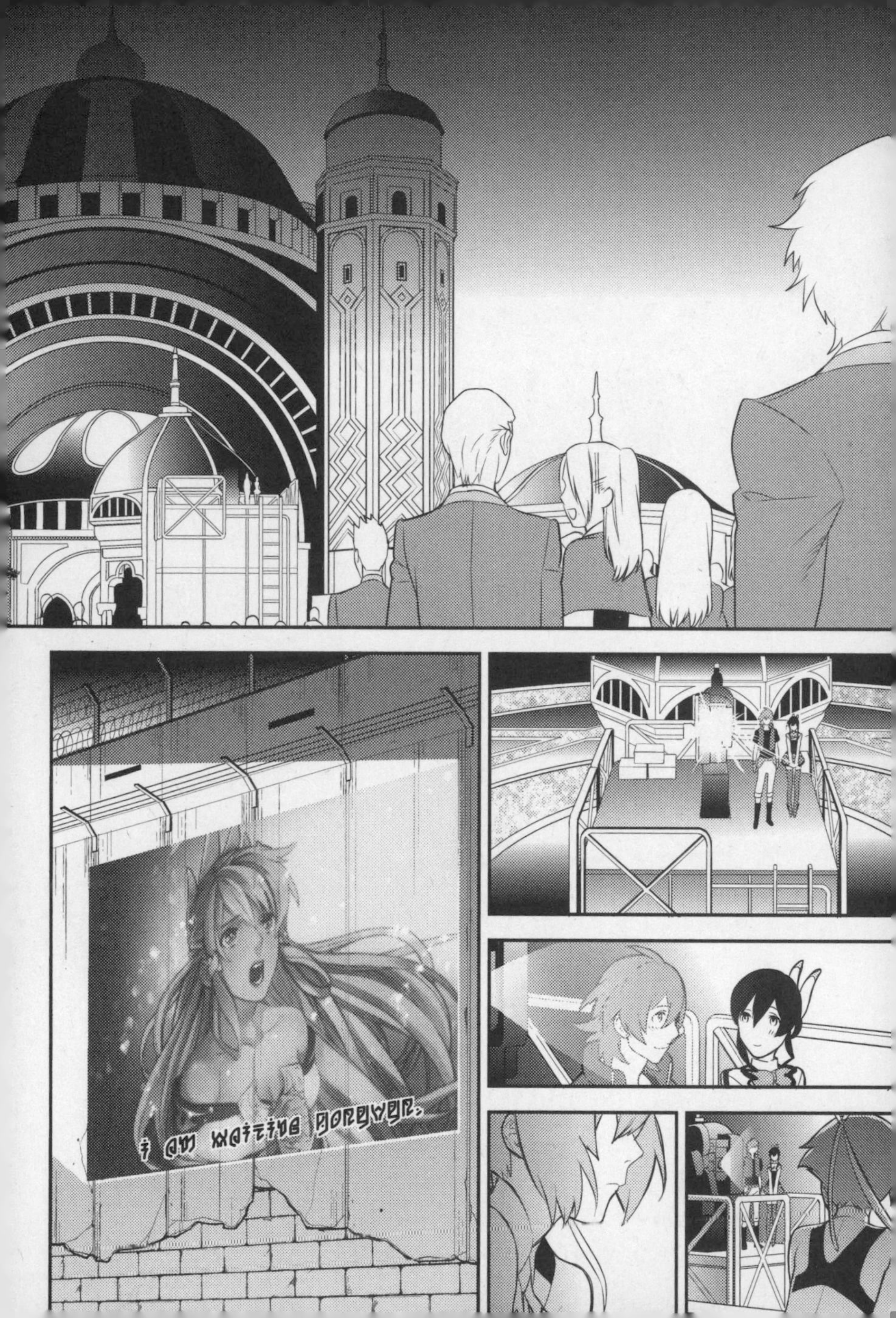
I am waiting forever.

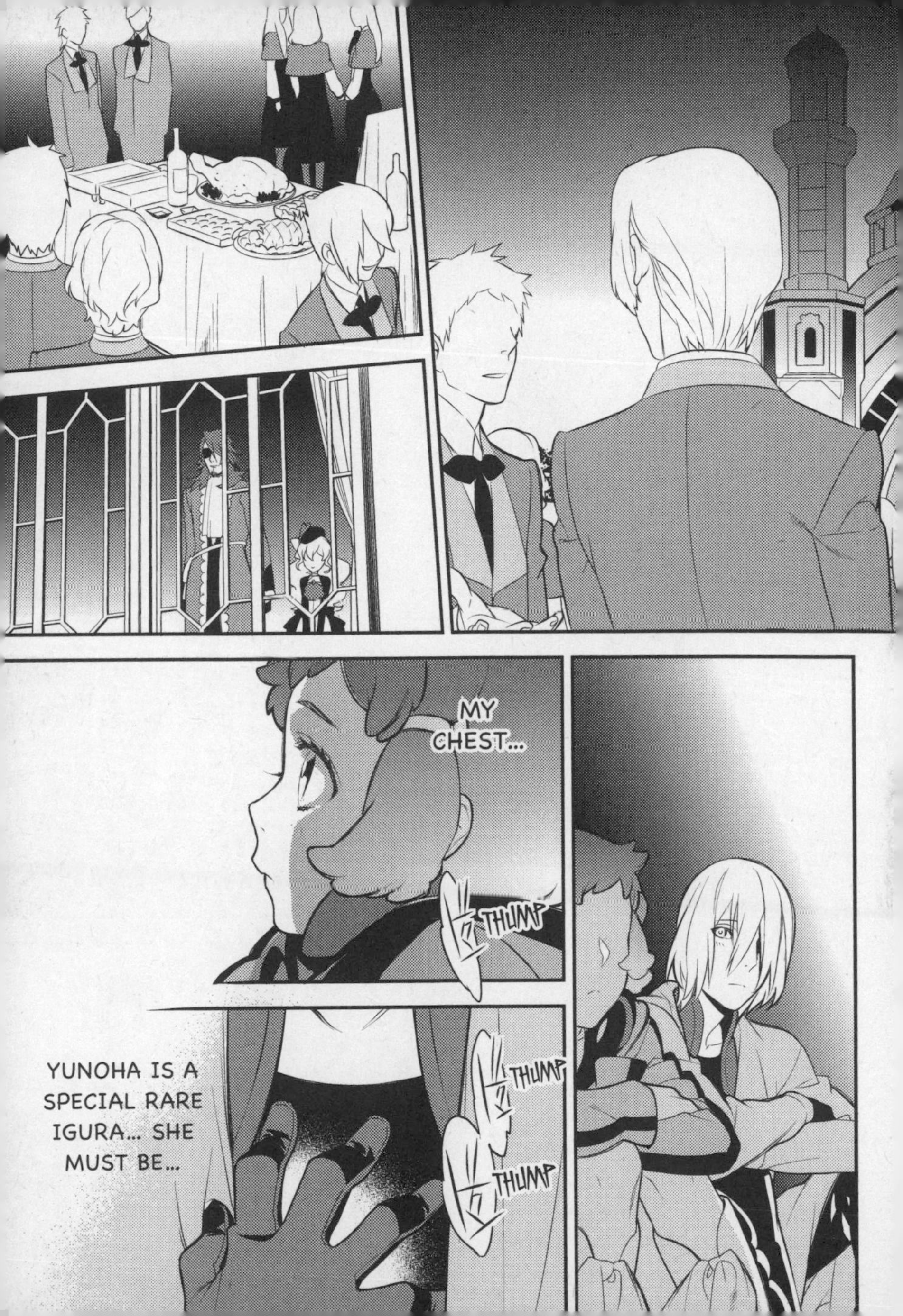
MY CHEST...
THUMP
THUMP
YUNOHA IS A SPECIAL RARE IGURA... SHE MUST BE...
THUMP

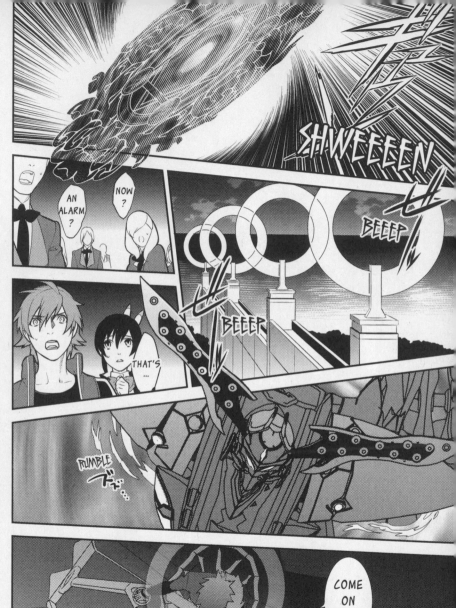

SHWEEEEN

AN ALARM?

NOW?

BEEEP

BEEEP

THAT'S...

RUMBLE
ブドド...

COME ON OUT...

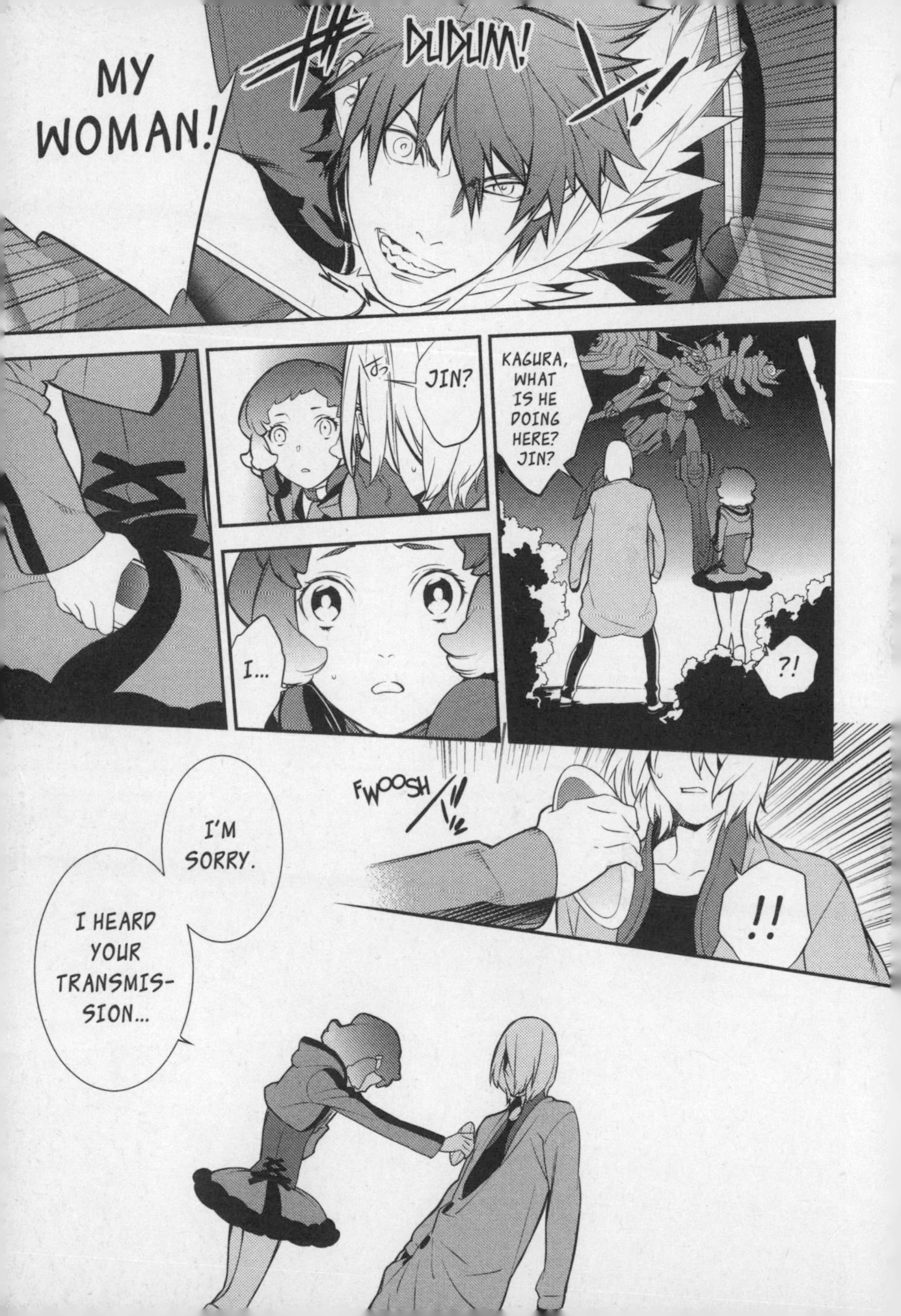
DUDUM!
MY WOMAN!
KAGURA, WHAT IS HE DOING HERE? JIN?
?!
JIN?
I...
!!
FWOOSH
I'M SORRY.
I HEARD YOUR TRANSMIS-SION...

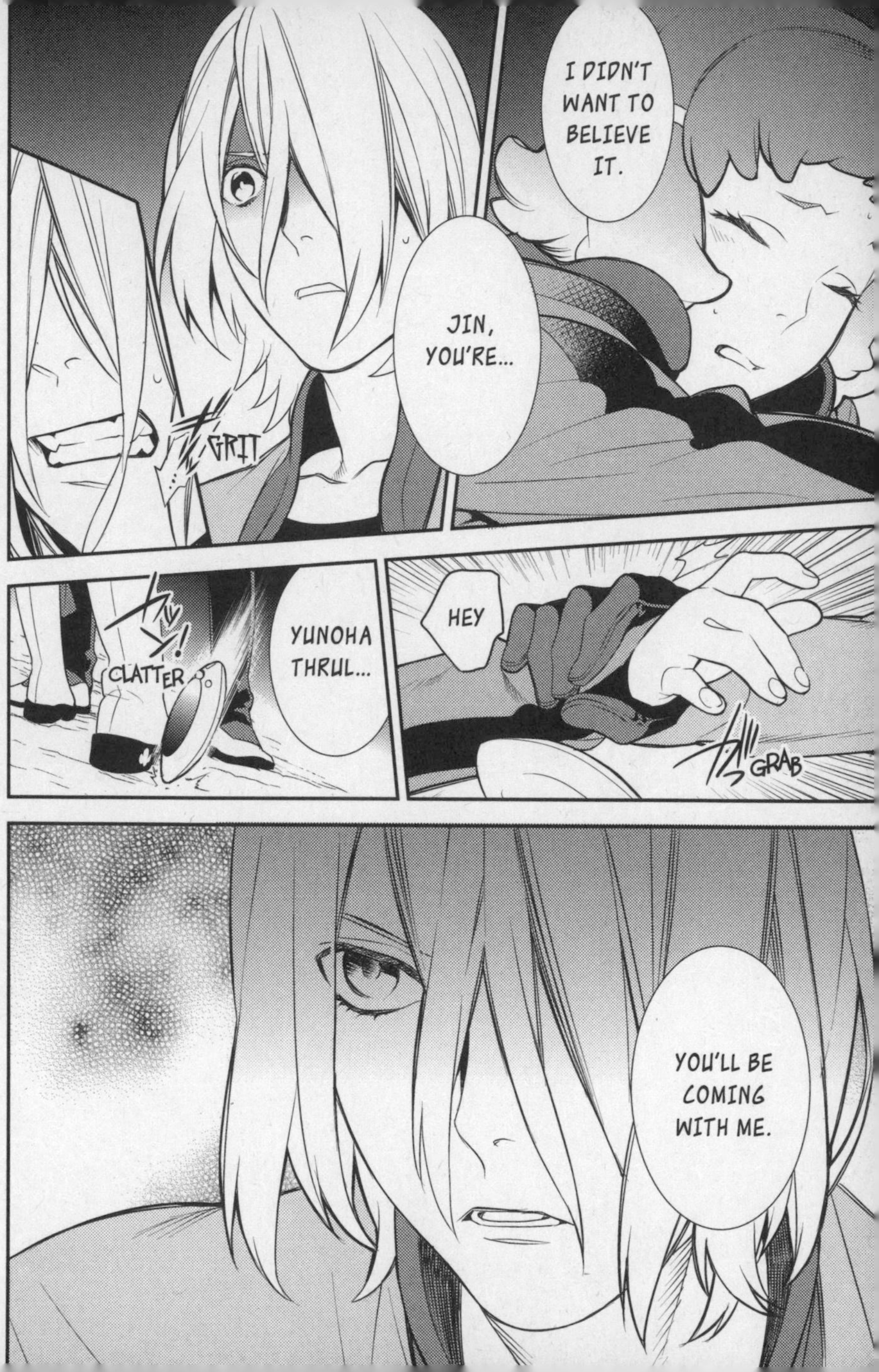
I DIDN'T WANT TO BELIEVE IT.
JIN, YOU'RE...
GRIT
HEY
GRAB
YUNOHA THRUL...
CLATTER
YOU'LL BE COMING WITH ME.

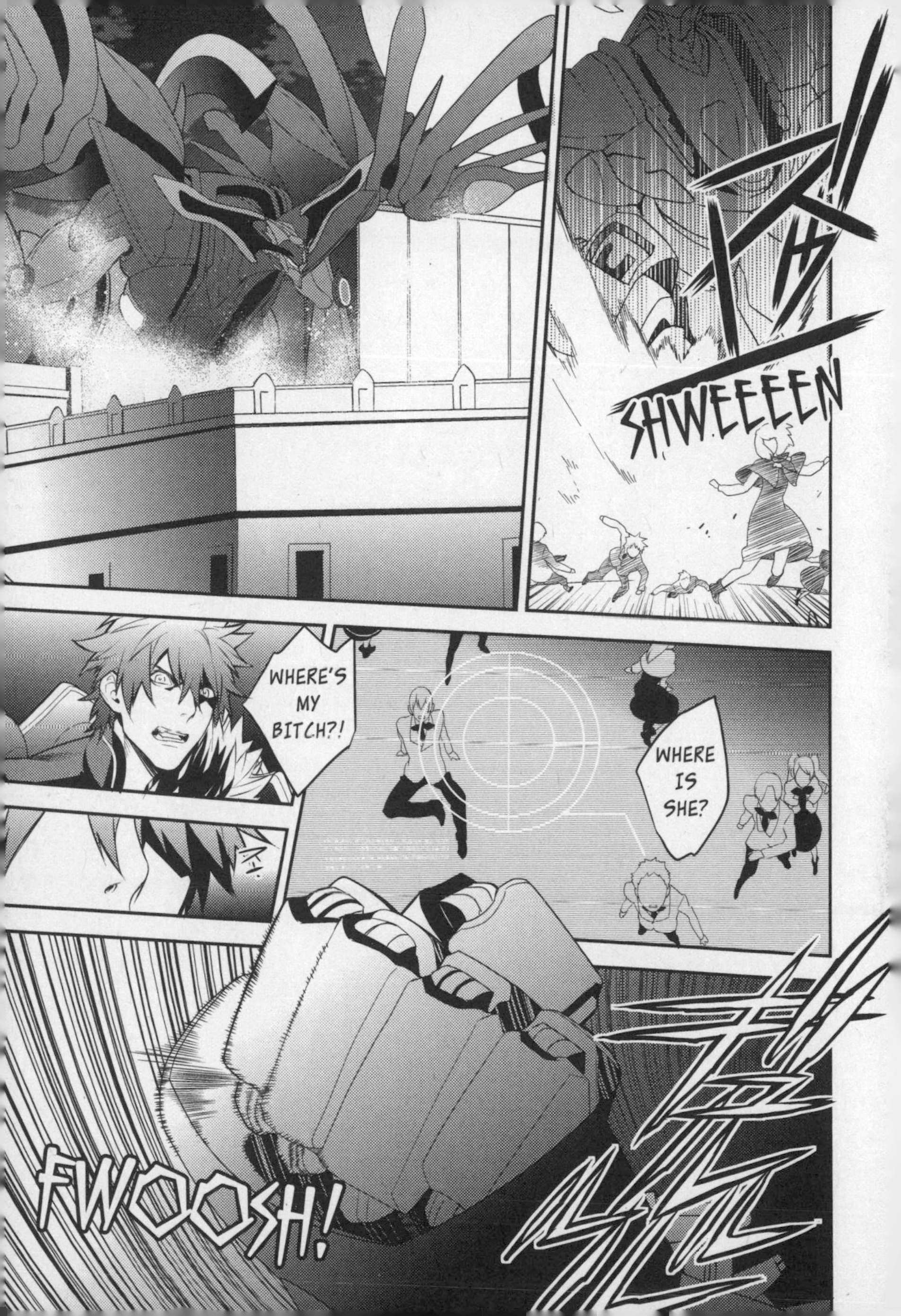
SHWEEEEN
WHERE IS SHE?
WHERE'S MY BITCH?!
FWOOSH!

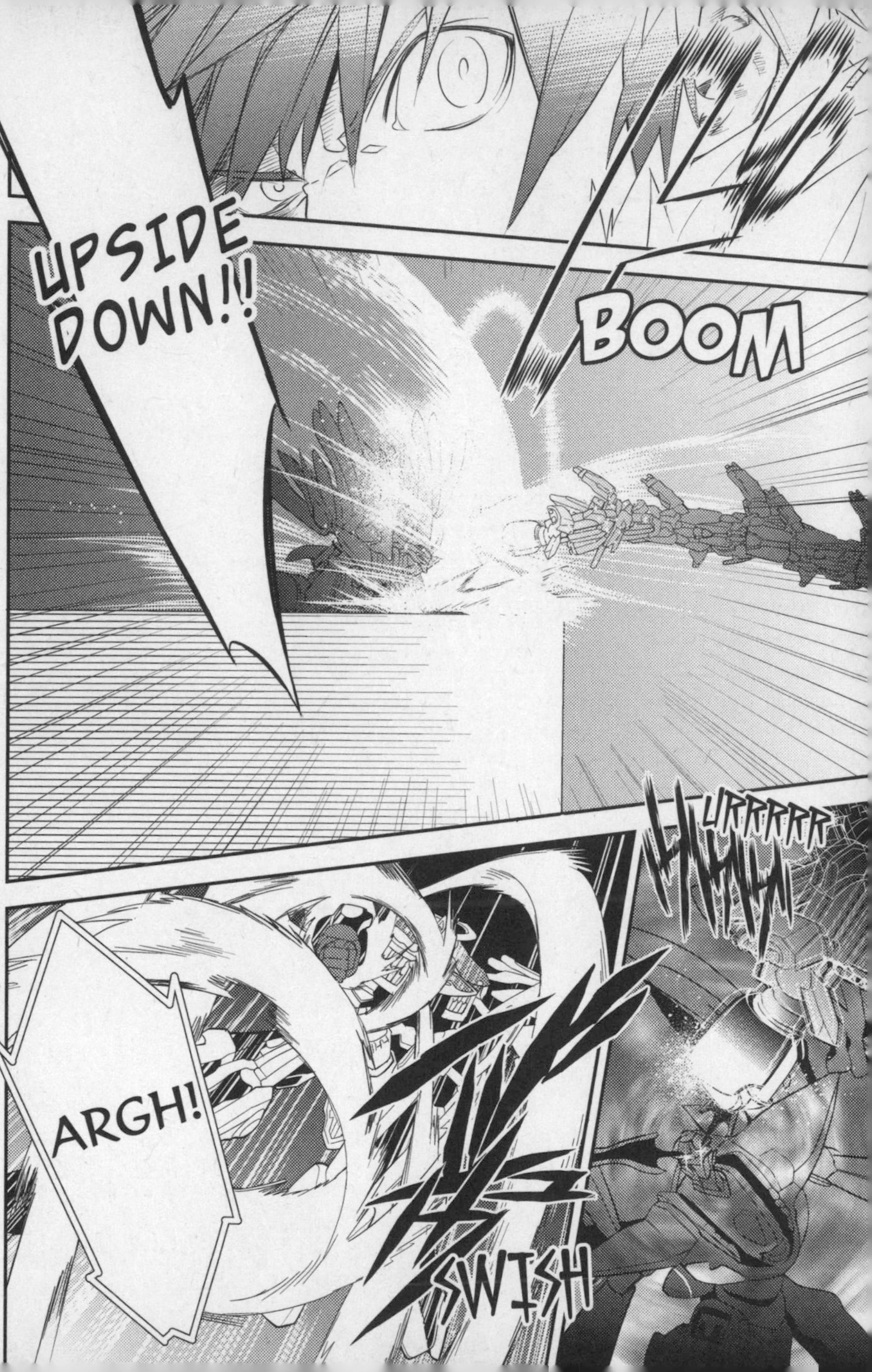
UPSIDE DOWN!!
BOOM
URRRRRR
SWISH
ARGH!

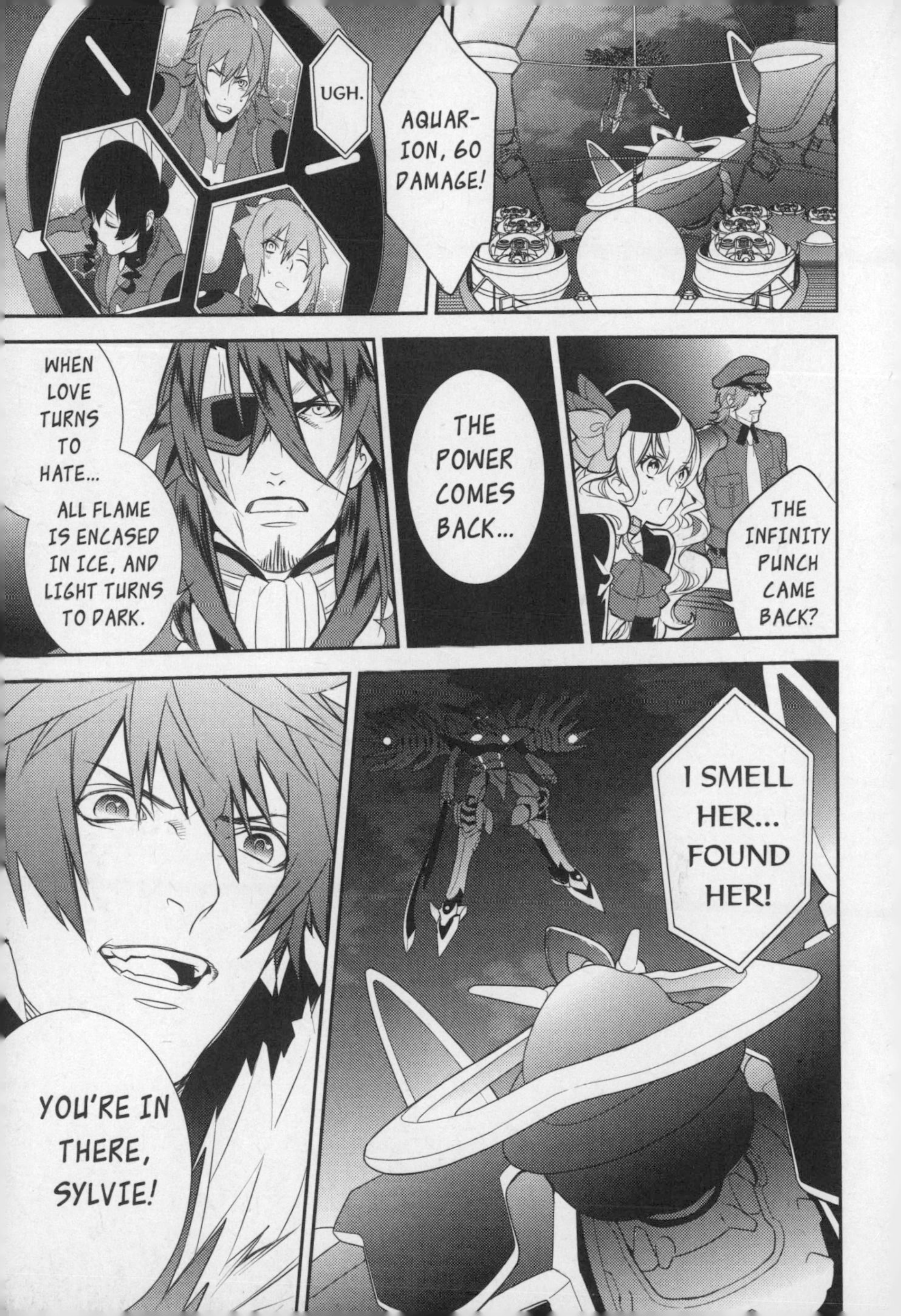
AQUARION, 60 DAMAGE!
UGH.
THE INFINITY PUNCH CAME BACK?
THE POWER COMES BACK...
WHEN LOVE TURNS TO HATE...
ALL FLAME IS ENCASED IN ICE, AND LIGHT TURNS TO DARK.
I SMELL HER... FOUND HER!
YOU'RE IN THERE, SYLVIE!

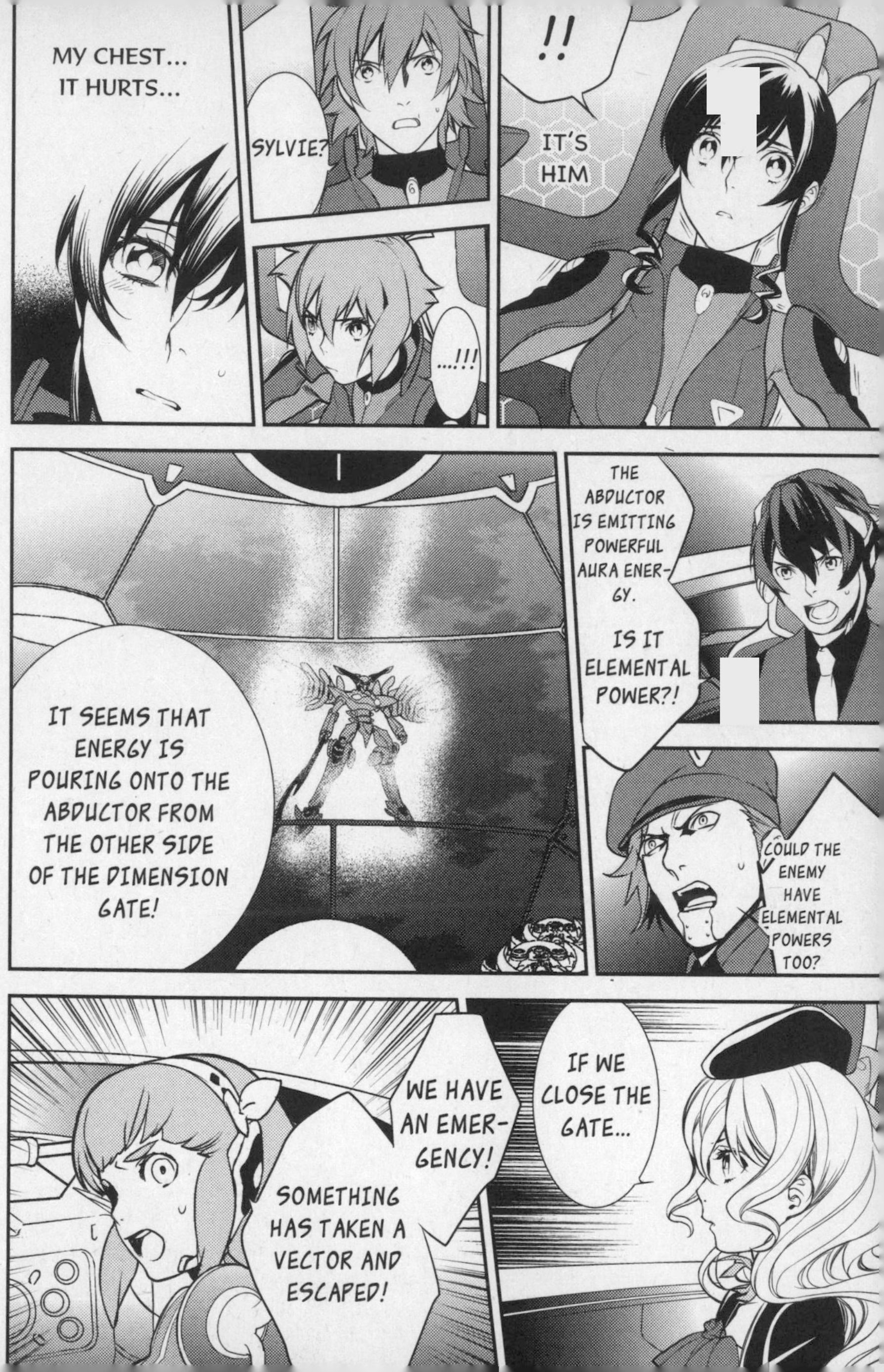
!!
IT'S HIM
SYLVIE?
...!!!
MY CHEST... IT HURTS...
THE ABDUCTOR IS EMITTING POWERFUL AURA ENERGY.
IS IT ELEMENTAL POWER?!
COULD THE ENEMY HAVE ELEMENTAL POWERS TOO?
IT SEEMS THAT ENERGY IS POURING ONTO THE ABDUCTOR FROM THE OTHER SIDE OF THE DIMENSION GATE!
IF WE CLOSE THE GATE...
WE HAVE AN EMERGENCY!
SOMETHING HAS TAKEN A VECTOR AND ESCAPED!

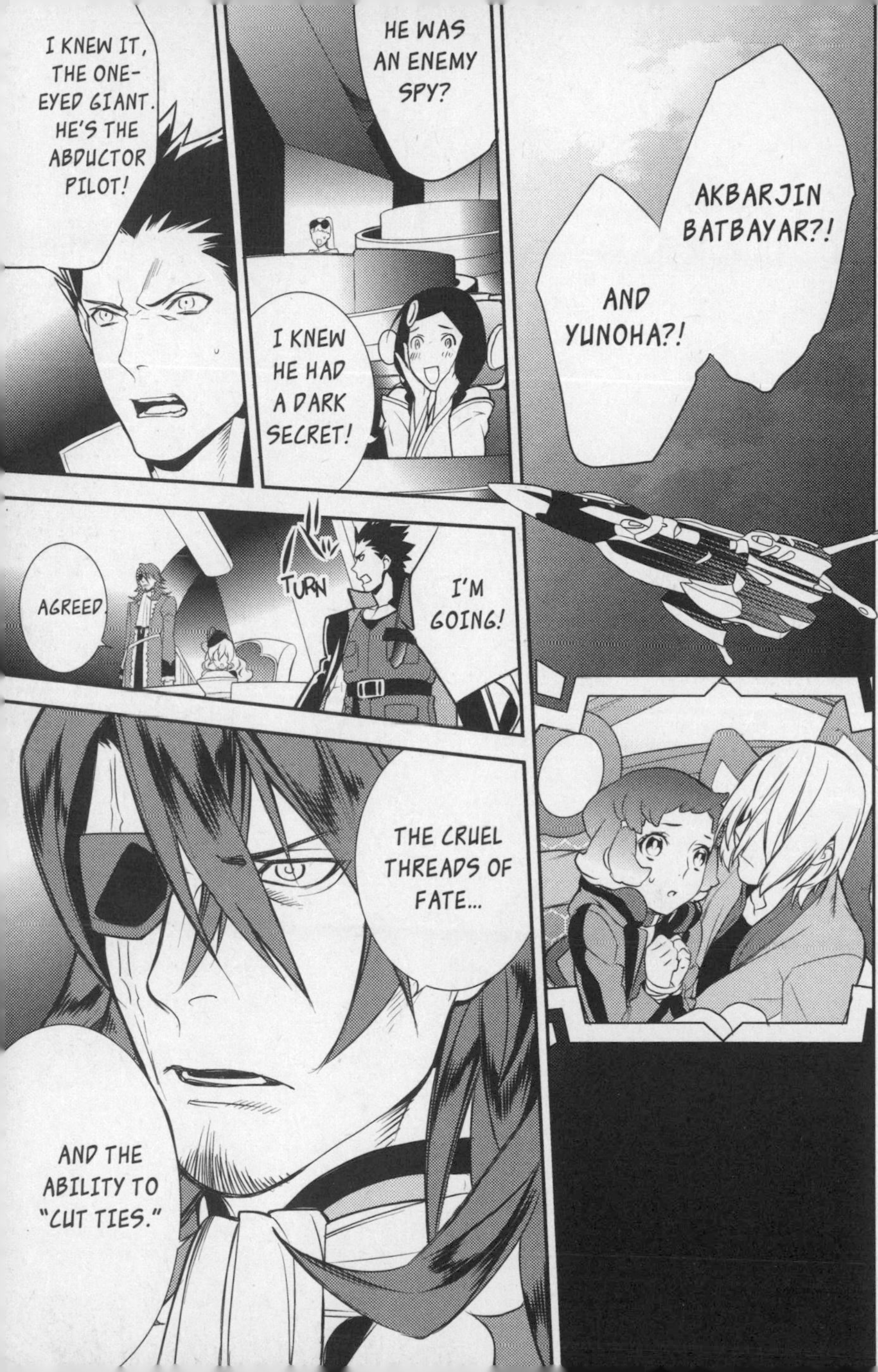
AKBARJIN BATBAYAR?!
AND YUNOHA?!
HE WAS AN ENEMY SPY?
I KNEW HE HAD A DARK SECRET!
I KNEW IT, THE ONE-EYED GIANT. HE'S THE ABDUCTOR PILOT!
I'M GOING!
TURN
AGREED.
THE CRUEL THREADS OF FATE...
AND THE ABILITY TO "CUT TIES."

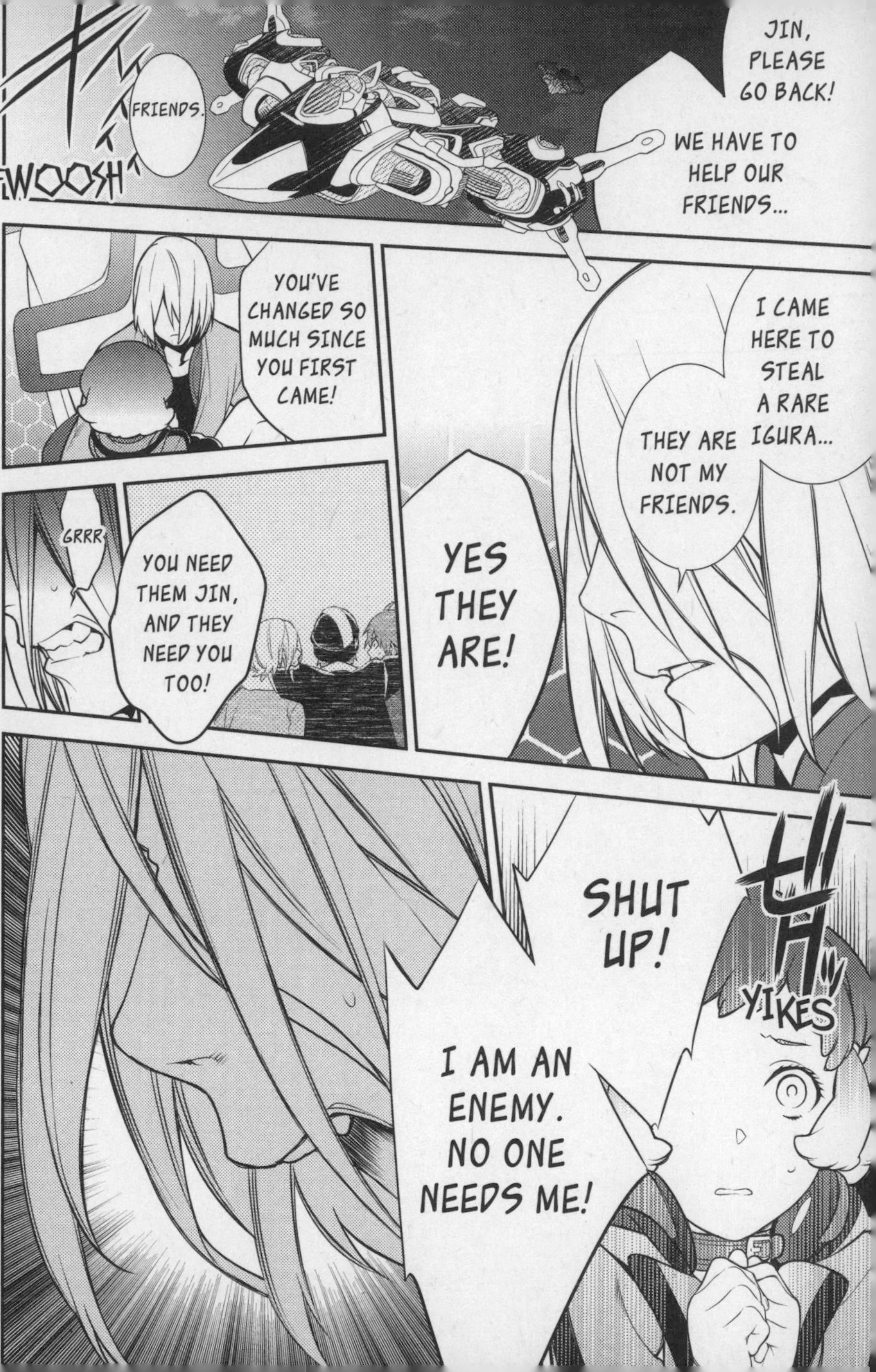
JIN, PLEASE GO BACK!
WE HAVE TO HELP OUR FRIENDS...
FRIENDS.
FWOOSH
I CAME HERE TO STEAL A RARE IGURA...
THEY ARE NOT MY FRIENDS.
YES THEY ARE!
YOU'VE CHANGED SO MUCH SINCE YOU FIRST CAME!
YOU NEED THEM JIN, AND THEY NEED YOU TOO!
GRRR
SHUT UP!
YIKES
I AM AN ENEMY. NO ONE NEEDS ME!

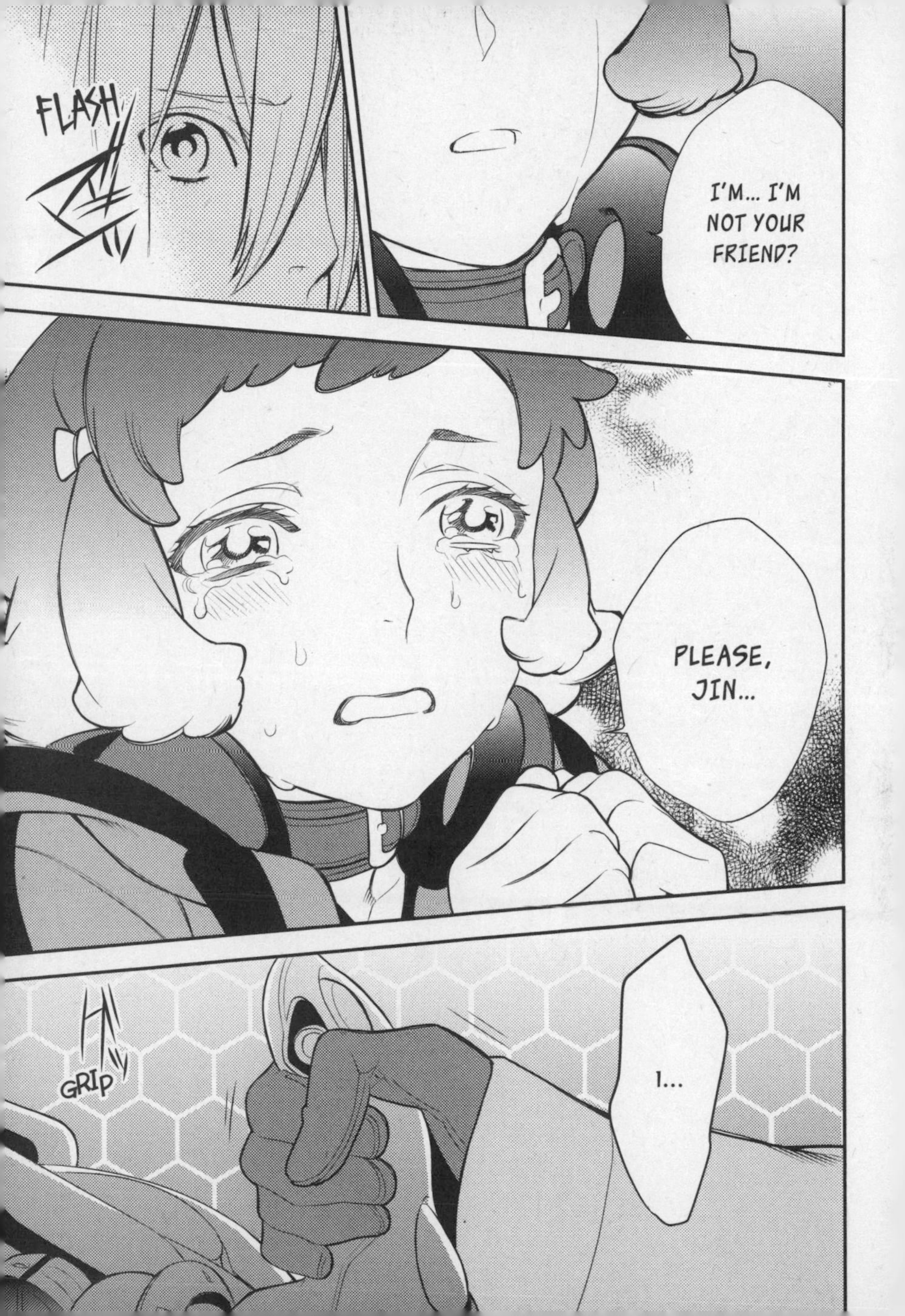
I'M... I'M NOT YOUR FRIEND?
FLASH
PLEASE, JIN...
I...
GRIP

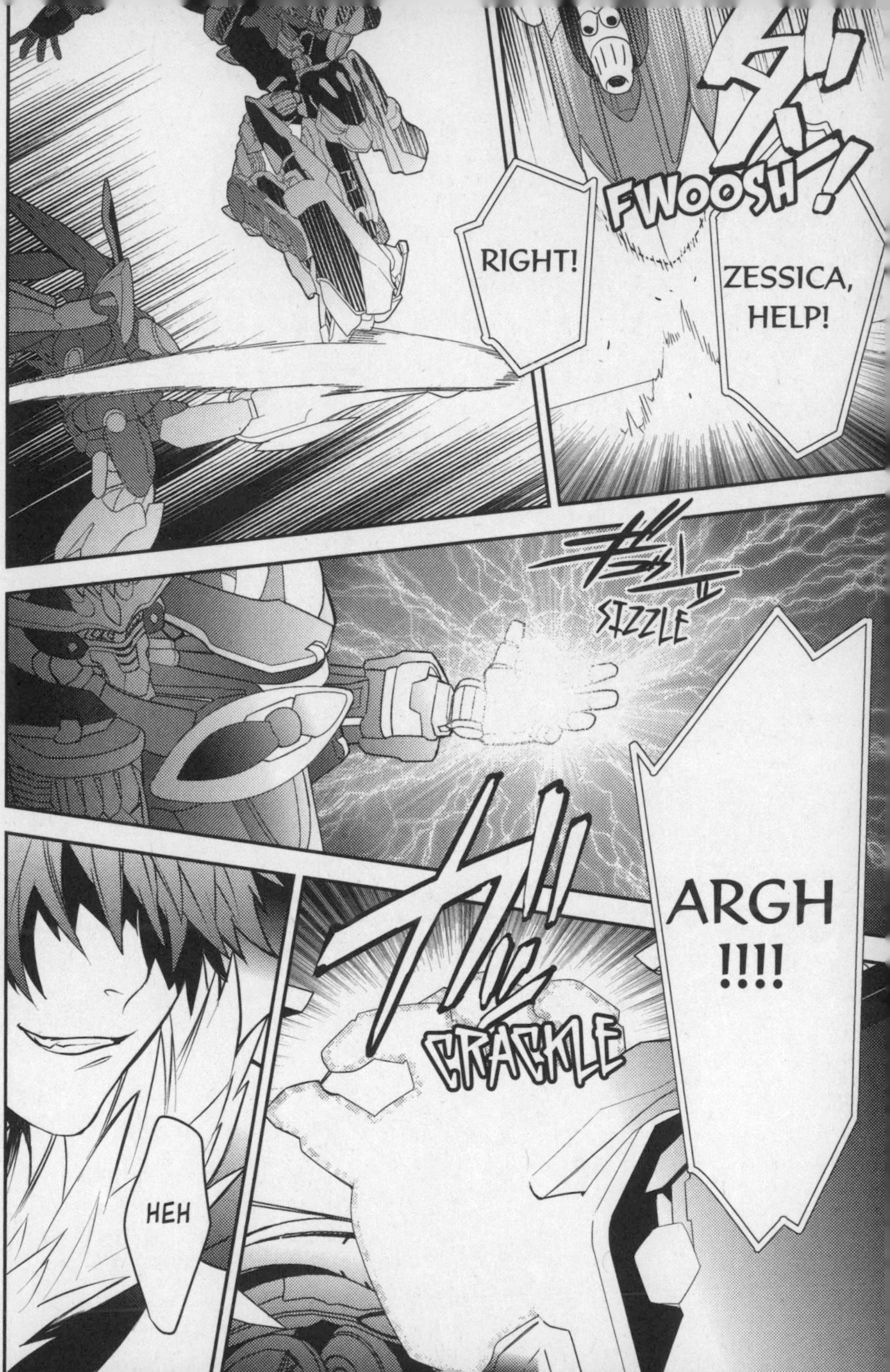
ZESSICA, HELP!
FWOOSH!
RIGHT!
SIZZLE
ARGH !!!!
CRACKLE
HEH

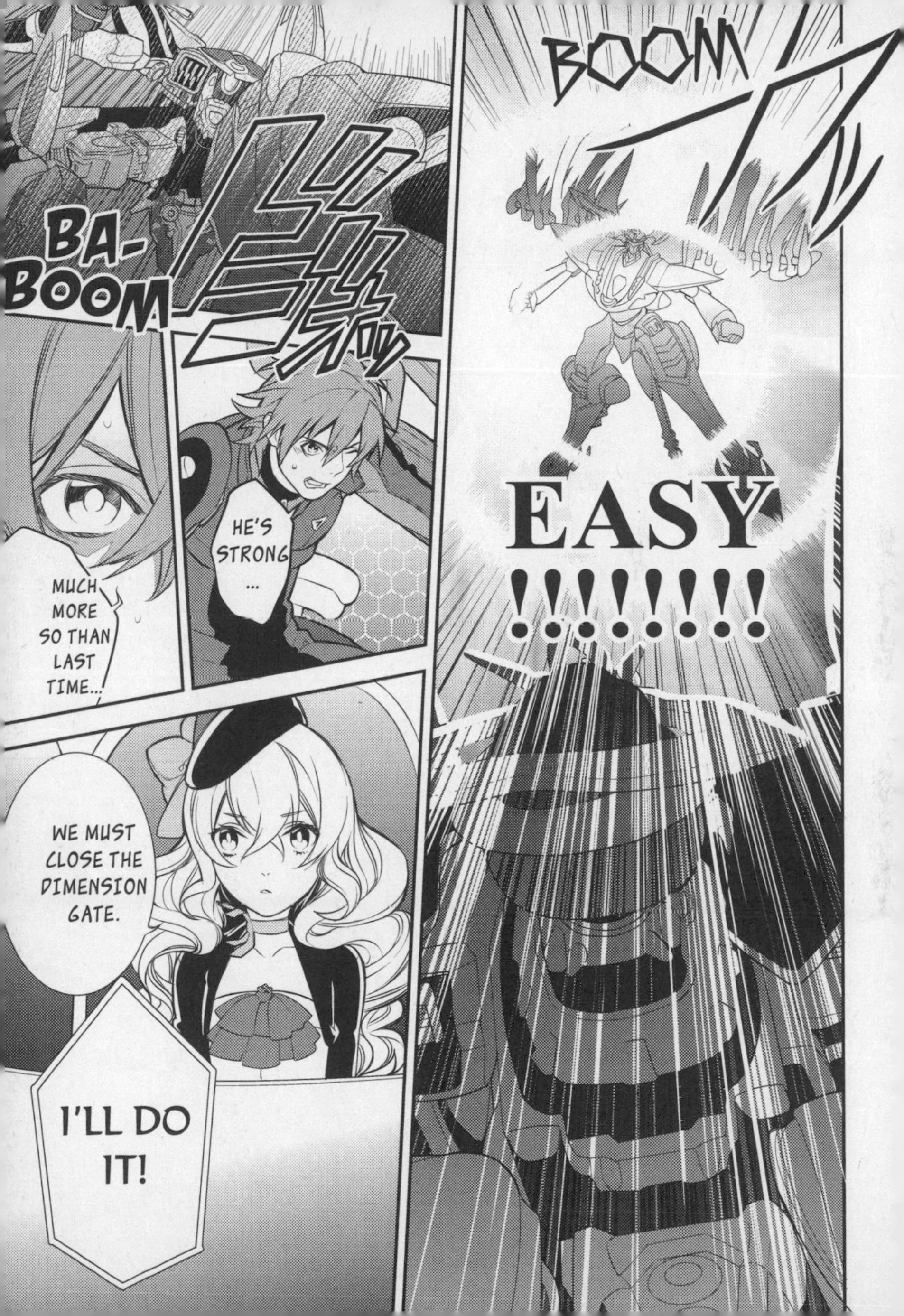
BOOM
EASY !!!!!!!!
BA-BOOM
HE'S STRONG ...
MUCH MORE SO THAN LAST TIME...
WE MUST CLOSE THE DIMENSION GATE.
I'LL DO IT!

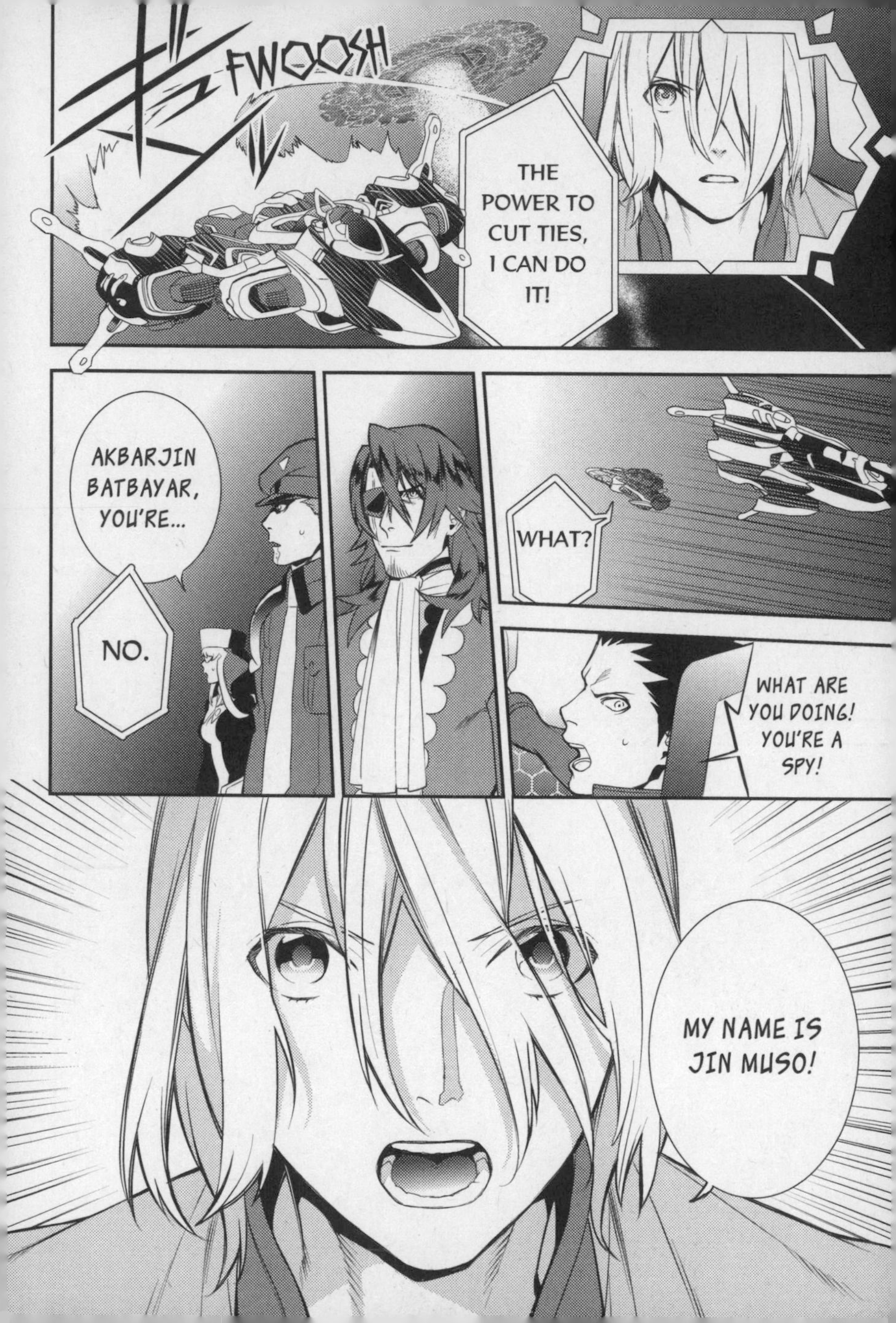
THE POWER TO CUT TIES, I CAN DO IT!
FWOOSH
WHAT?
WHAT ARE YOU DOING! YOU'RE A SPY!
AKBARJIN BATBAYAR, YOU'RE...
NO.
MY NAME IS JIN MUSO!

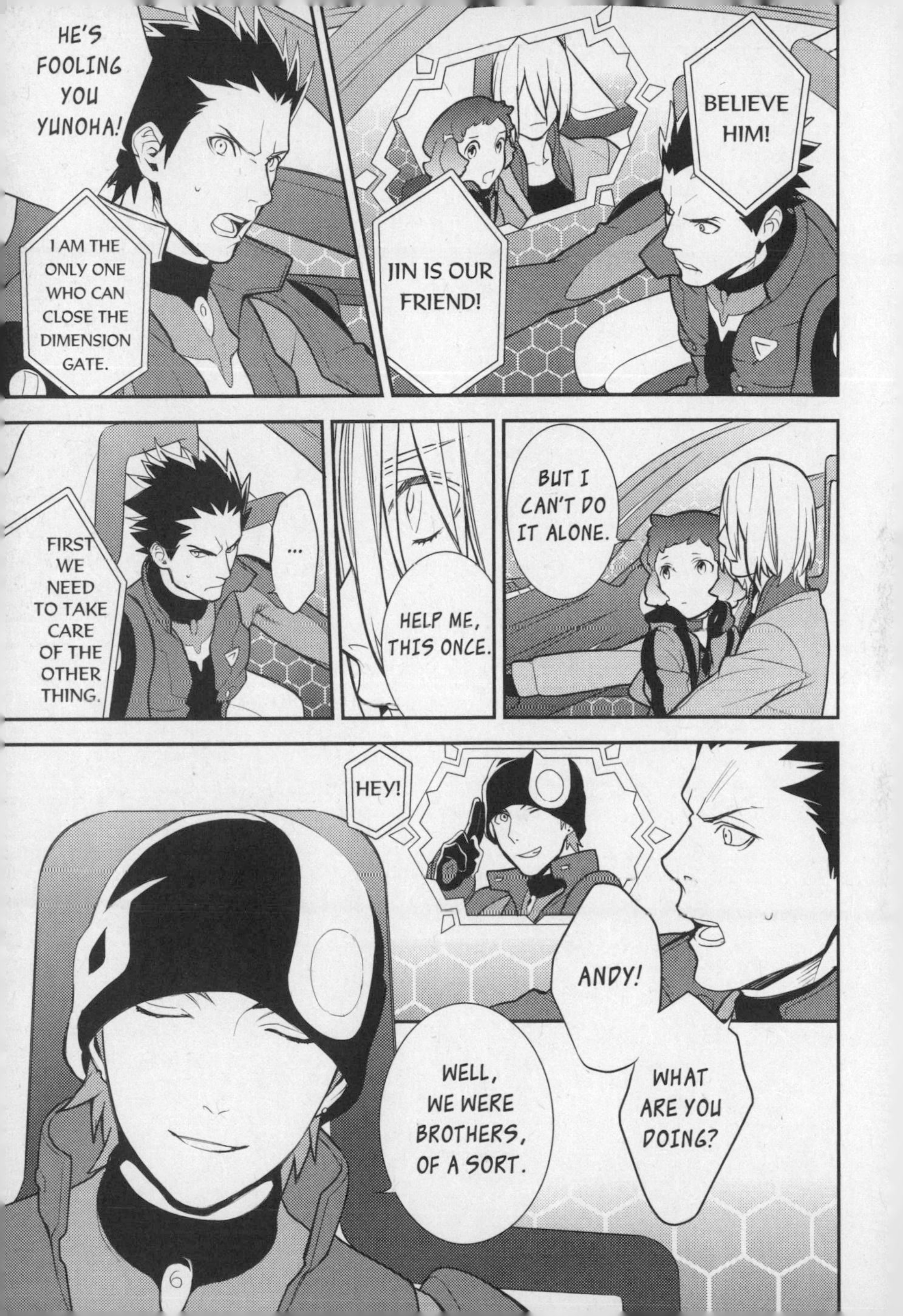
BELIEVE HIM!
JIN IS OUR FRIEND!
HE'S FOOLING YOU YUNOHA!
I AM THE ONLY ONE WHO CAN CLOSE THE DIMENSION GATE.
BUT I CAN'T DO IT ALONE.
HELP ME, THIS ONCE.
...
FIRST WE NEED TO TAKE CARE OF THE OTHER THING.
HEY!
ANDY!
WHAT ARE YOU DOING?
WELL, WE WERE BROTHERS, OF A SORT.

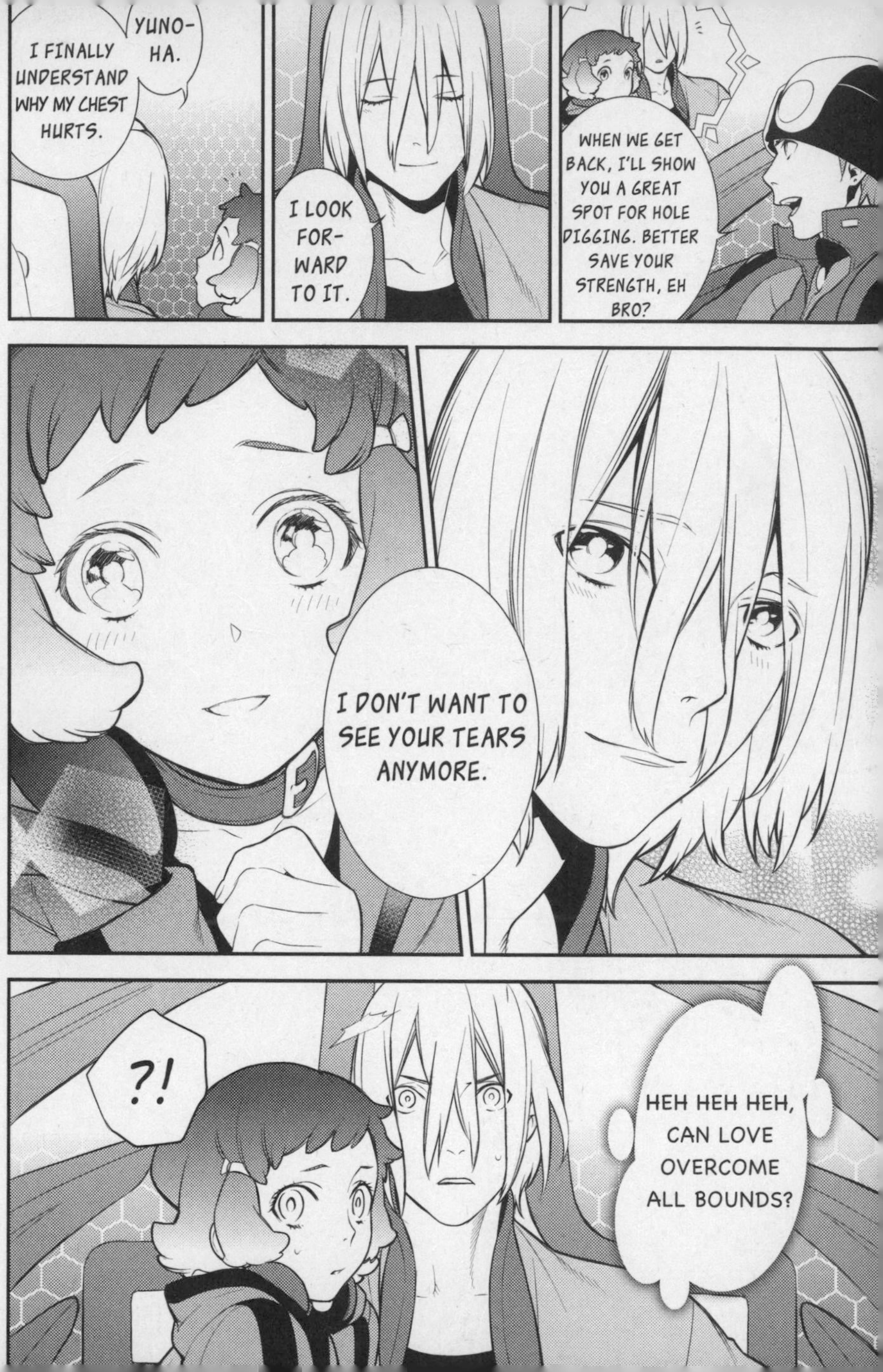
WHEN WE GET BACK, I'LL SHOW YOU A GREAT SPOT FOR HOLE DIGGING. BETTER SAVE YOUR STRENGTH, EH BRO?
I LOOK FOR-WARD TO IT.
YUNO-HA.
I FINALLY UNDERSTAND WHY MY CHEST HURTS.
I DON'T WANT TO SEE YOUR TEARS ANYMORE.
HEH HEH HEH, CAN LOVE OVERCOME ALL BOUNDS?
?!

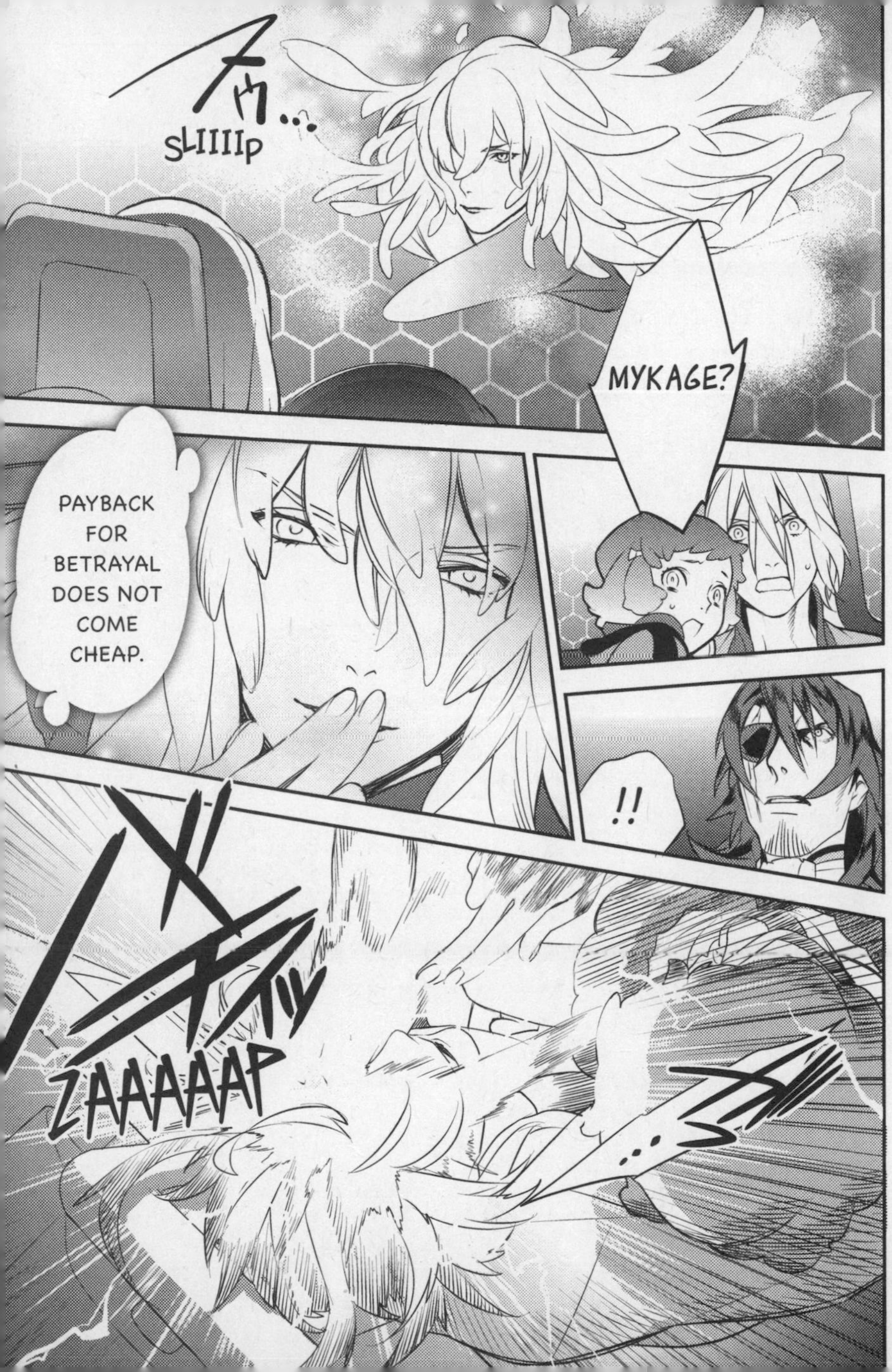
SLIIIIP
MYKAGE?
!!
PAYBACK FOR BETRAYAL DOES NOT COME CHEAP.
ZAAAAAP

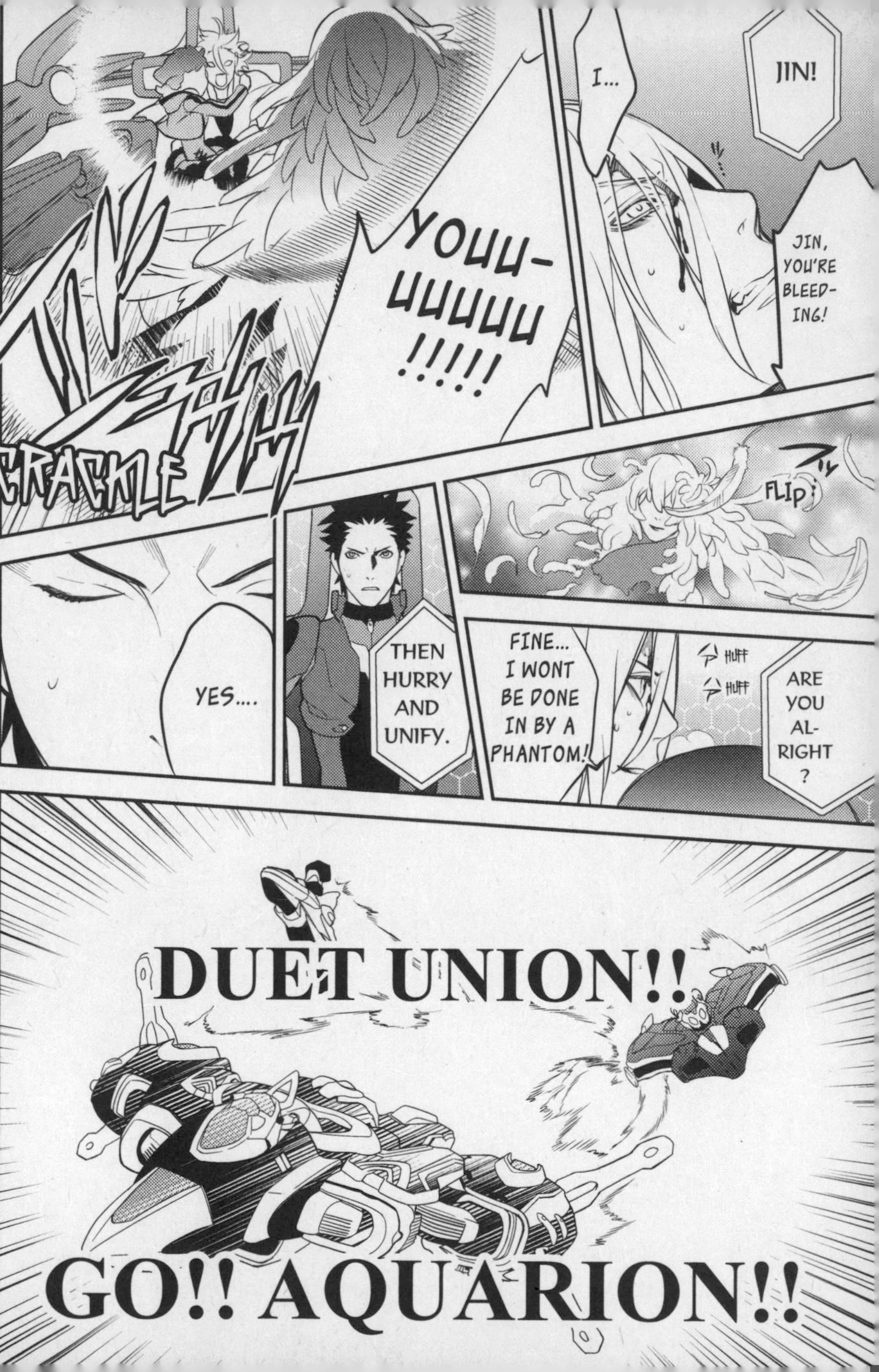
JIN!
I...
JIN, YOU'RE BLEED-ING!
YOUU-UUUUUU!!!!!
CRACKLE
FLIP
ARE YOU AL-RIGHT?
HUFF
HUFF
FINE... I WONT BE DONE IN BY A PHANTOM!
THEN HURRY AND UNIFY.
YES....
DUET UNION!!
GO!! AQUARION!!

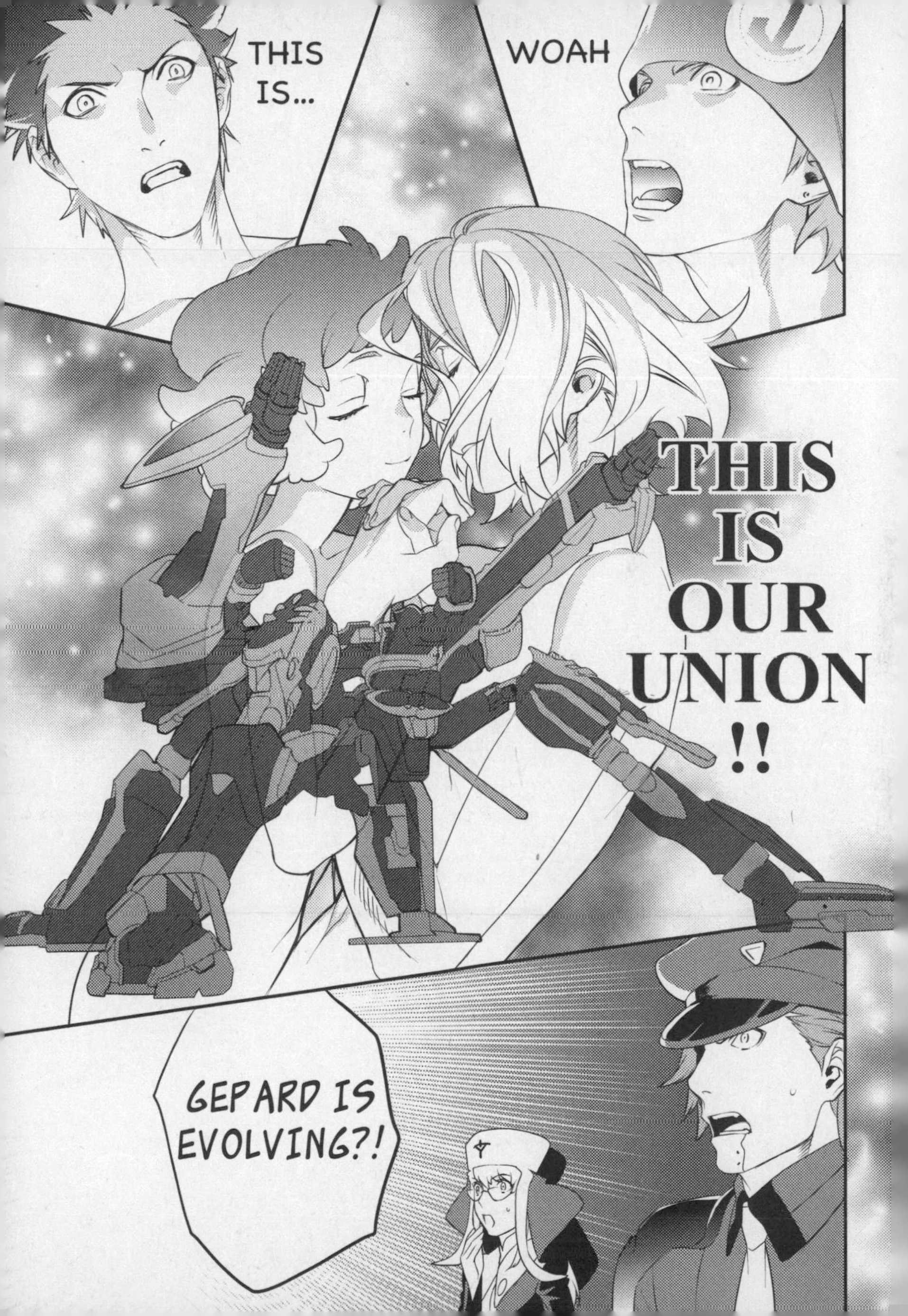
WOAH
THIS IS...
THIS IS OUR UNION!!
GEPARD IS EVOLVING?!

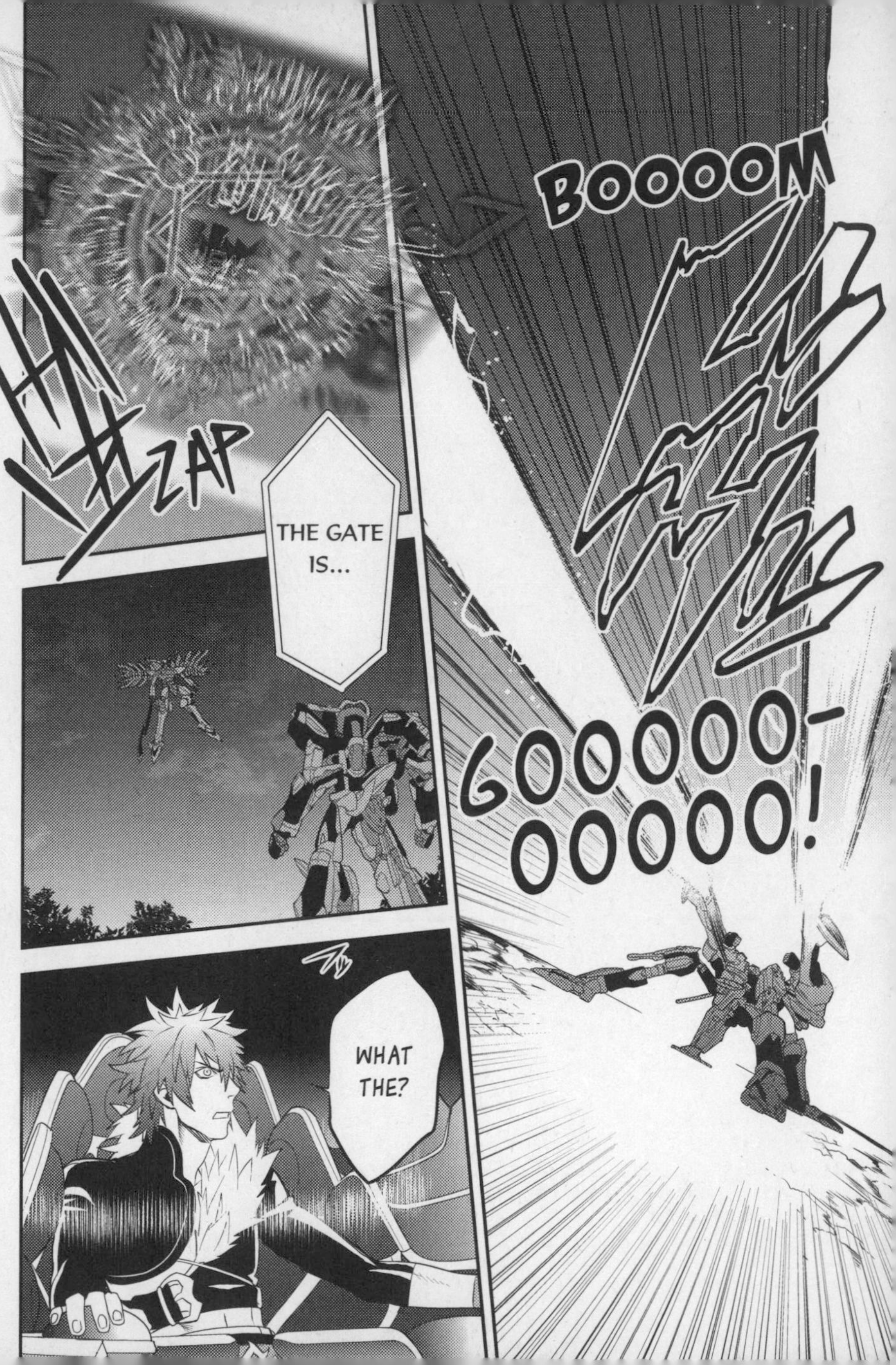
BOOOOM
GOOOOO-OOOOO!
ZAP
THE GATE IS...
WHAT THE?

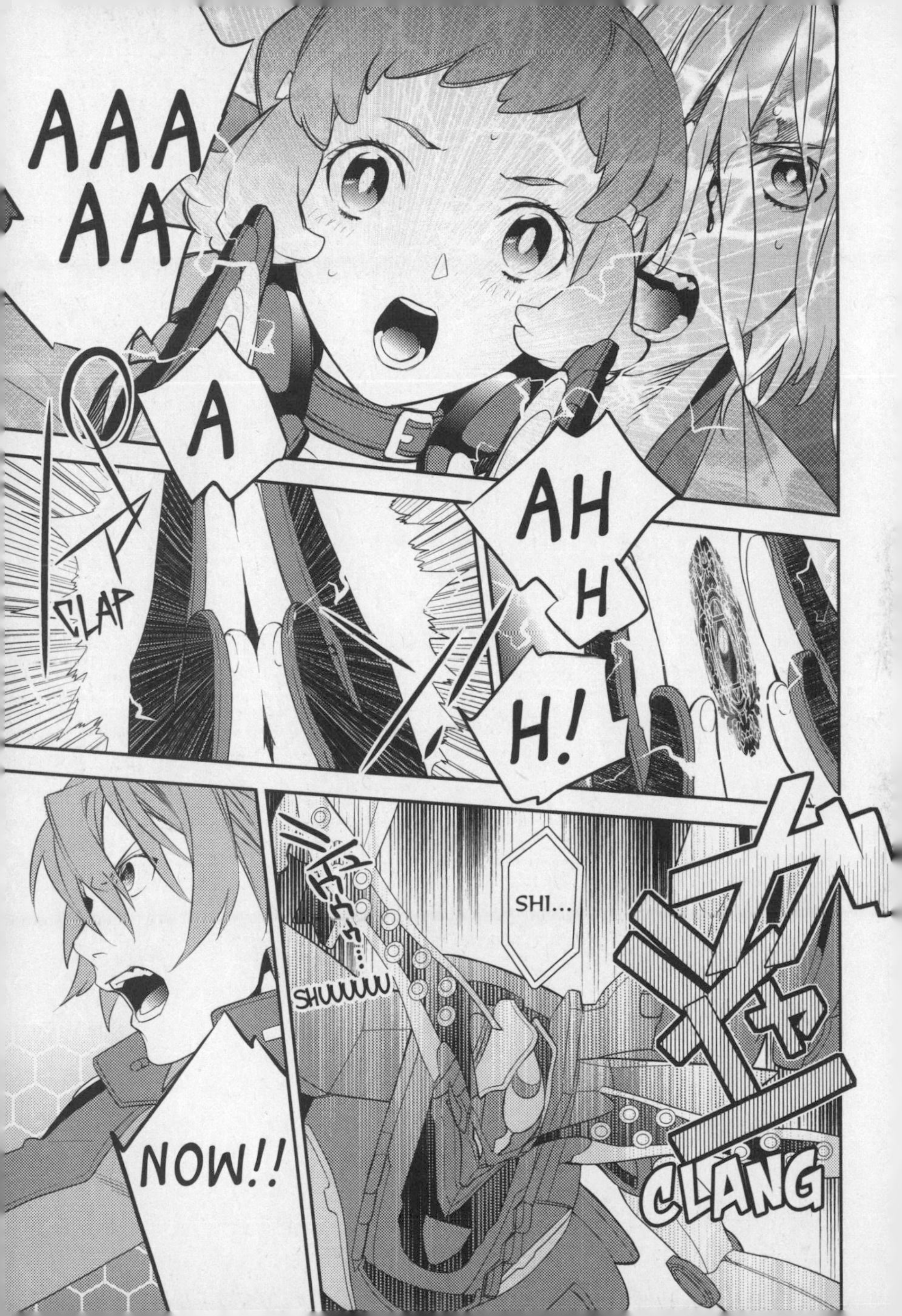
AAA AA
A
AH H H!
CLAP
SHI...
SHUUUU
CLANG
NOW!!

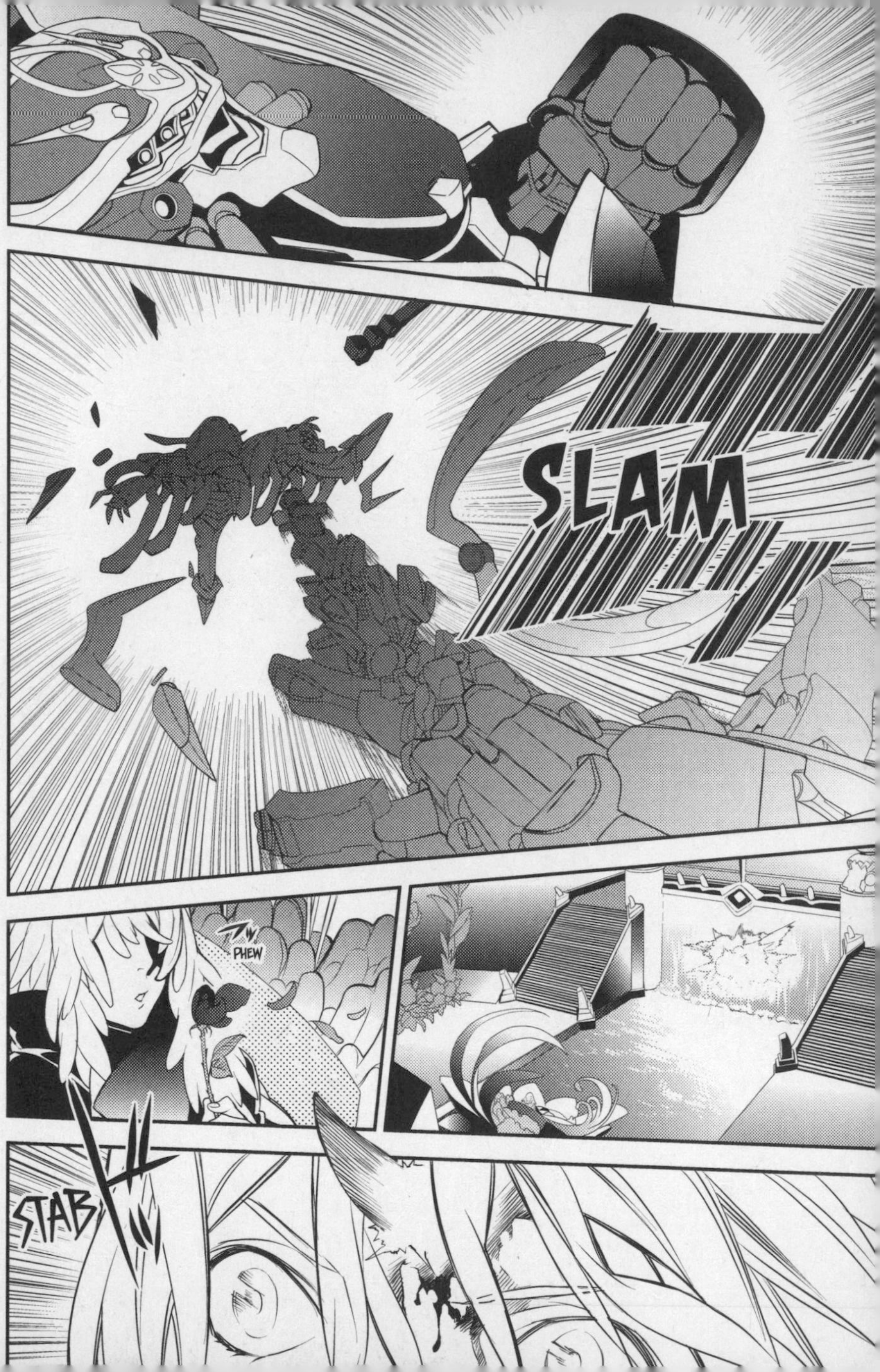
SLAM
PHEW
STAB

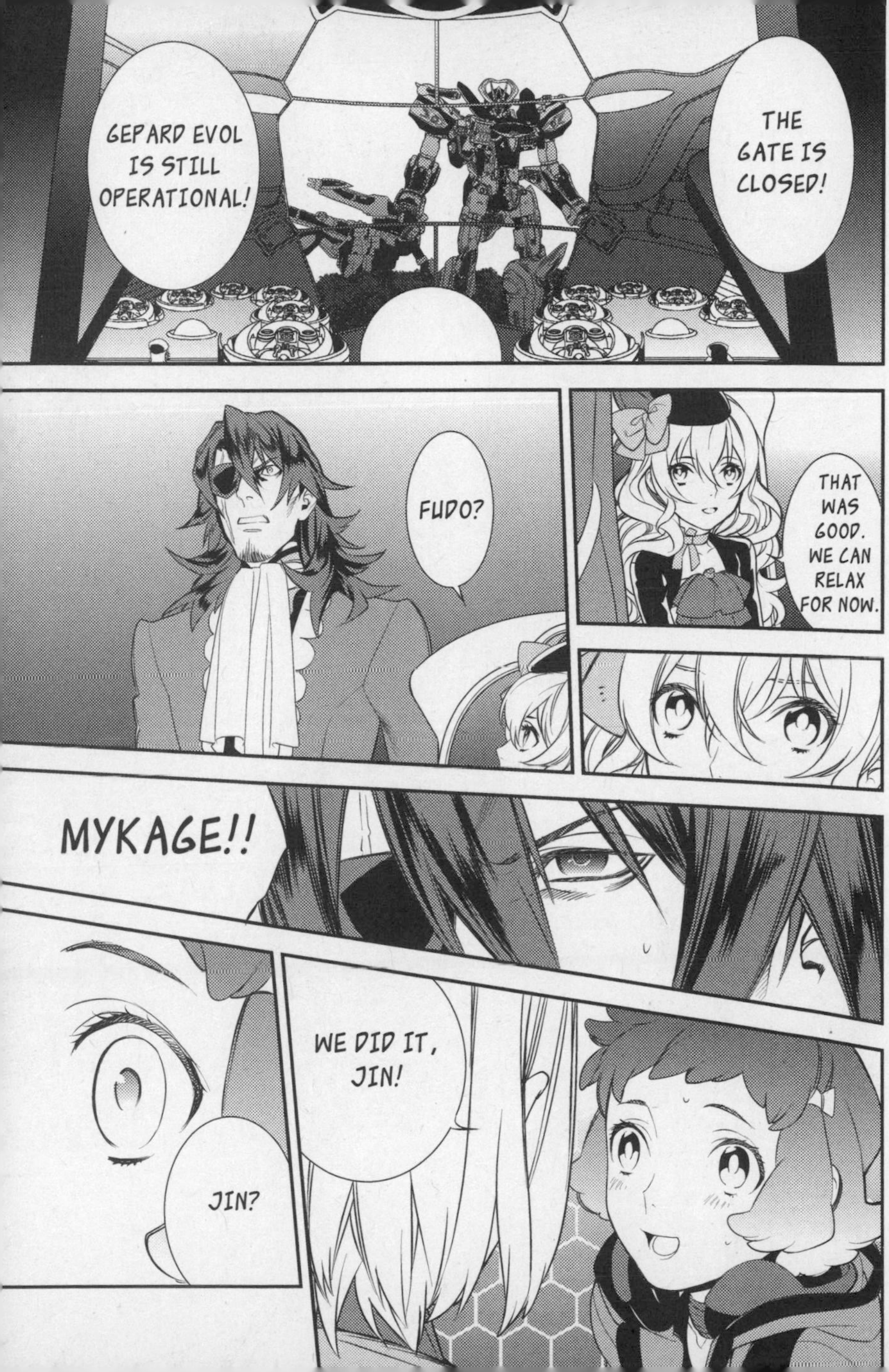
THE GATE IS CLOSED!
GEPARD EVOL IS STILL OPERATIONAL!
THAT WAS GOOD. WE CAN RELAX FOR NOW.
FUDO?
MYKAGE!!
WE DID IT, JIN!
JIN?

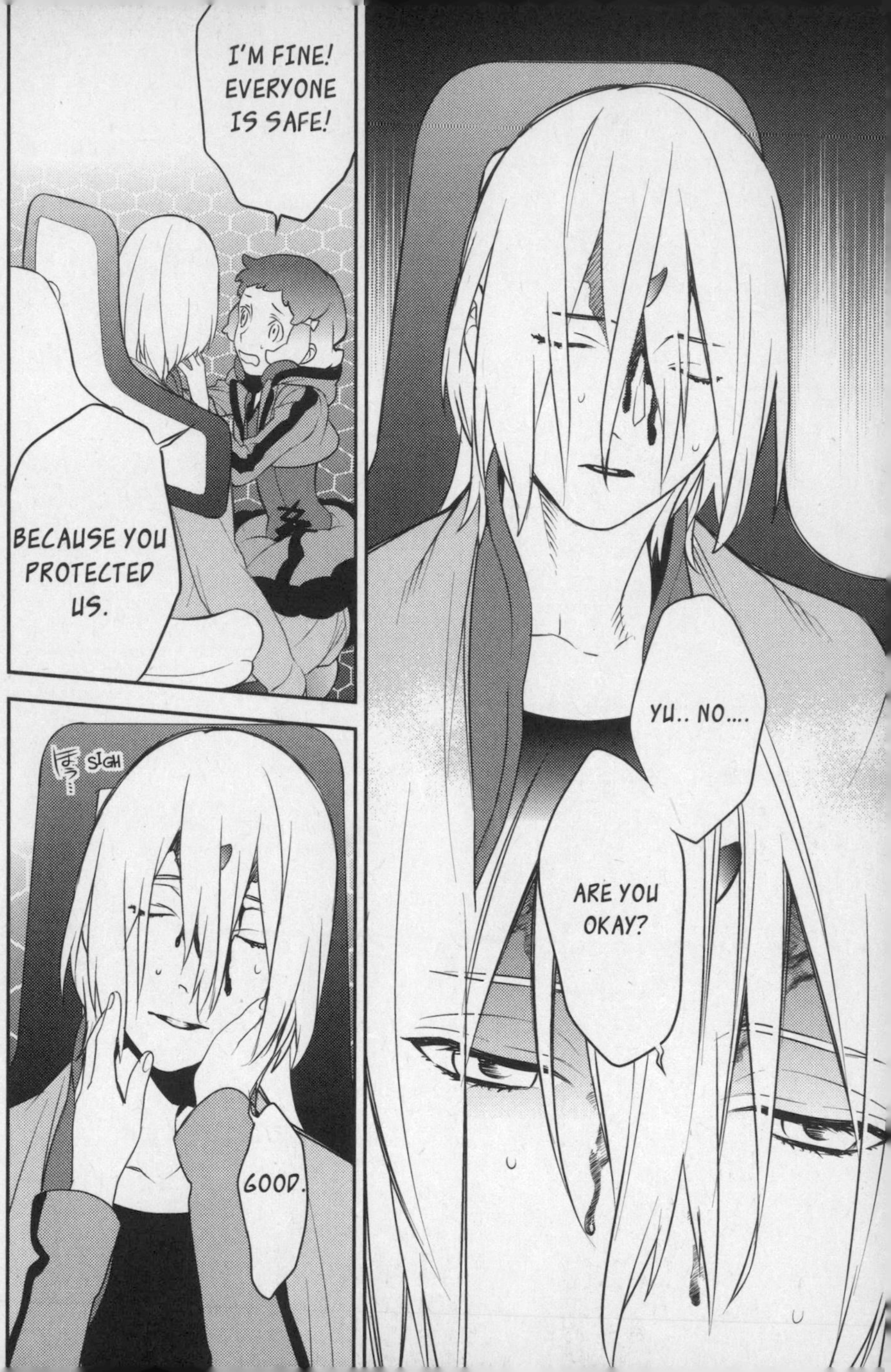
YU.. NO....
ARE YOU OKAY?
I'M FINE! EVERYONE IS SAFE!
BECAUSE YOU PROTECTED US.
SIGH
GOOD.

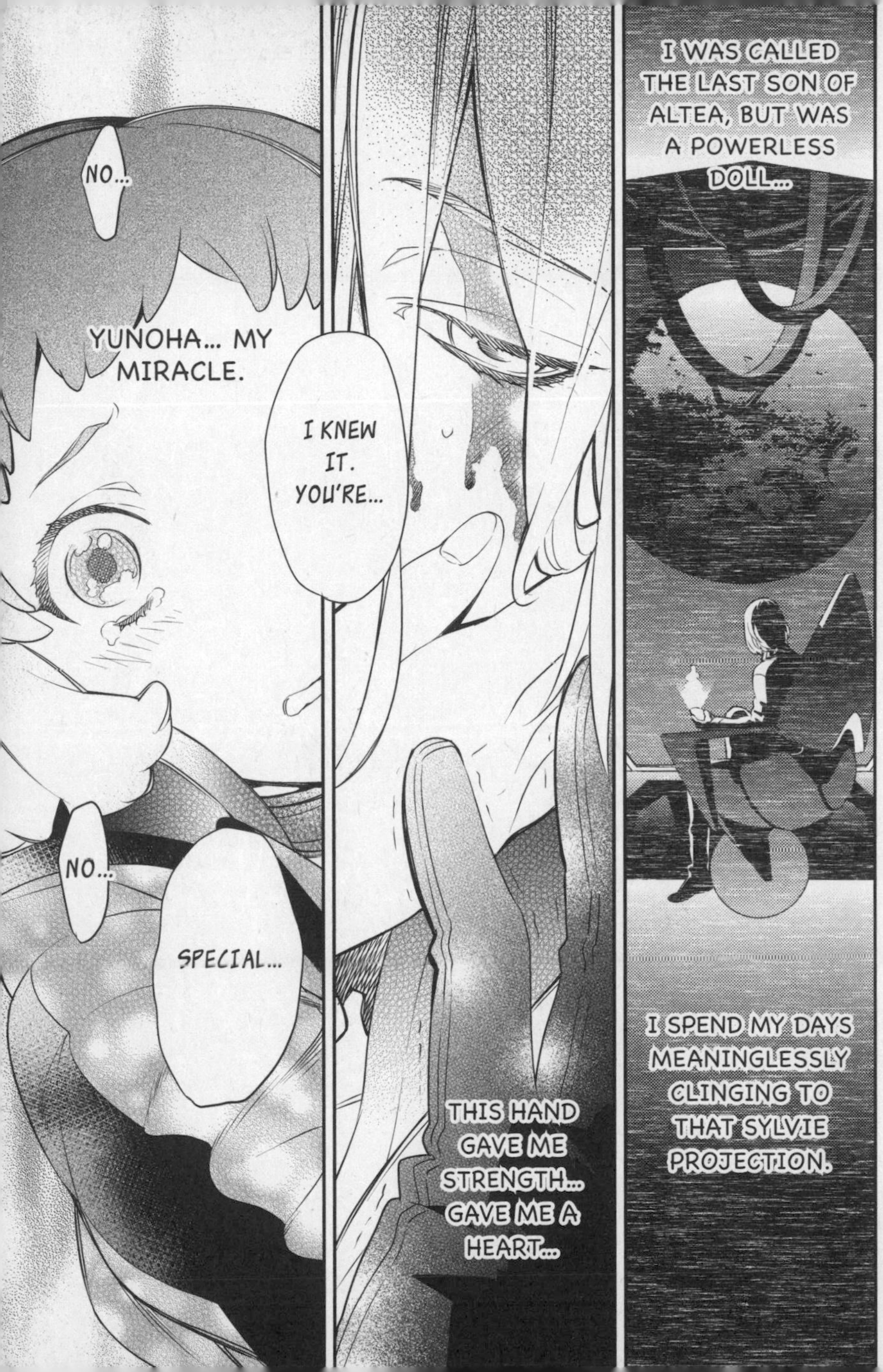
I WAS CALLED THE LAST SON OF ALTEA, BUT WAS A POWERLESS DOLL...
I SPEND MY DAYS MEANINGLESSLY CLINGING TO THAT SYLVIE PROJECTION.
I KNEW IT. YOU'RE...
THIS HAND GAVE ME STRENGTH... GAVE ME A HEART...
NO...
YUNOHA... MY MIRACLE.
NO...
SPECIAL...

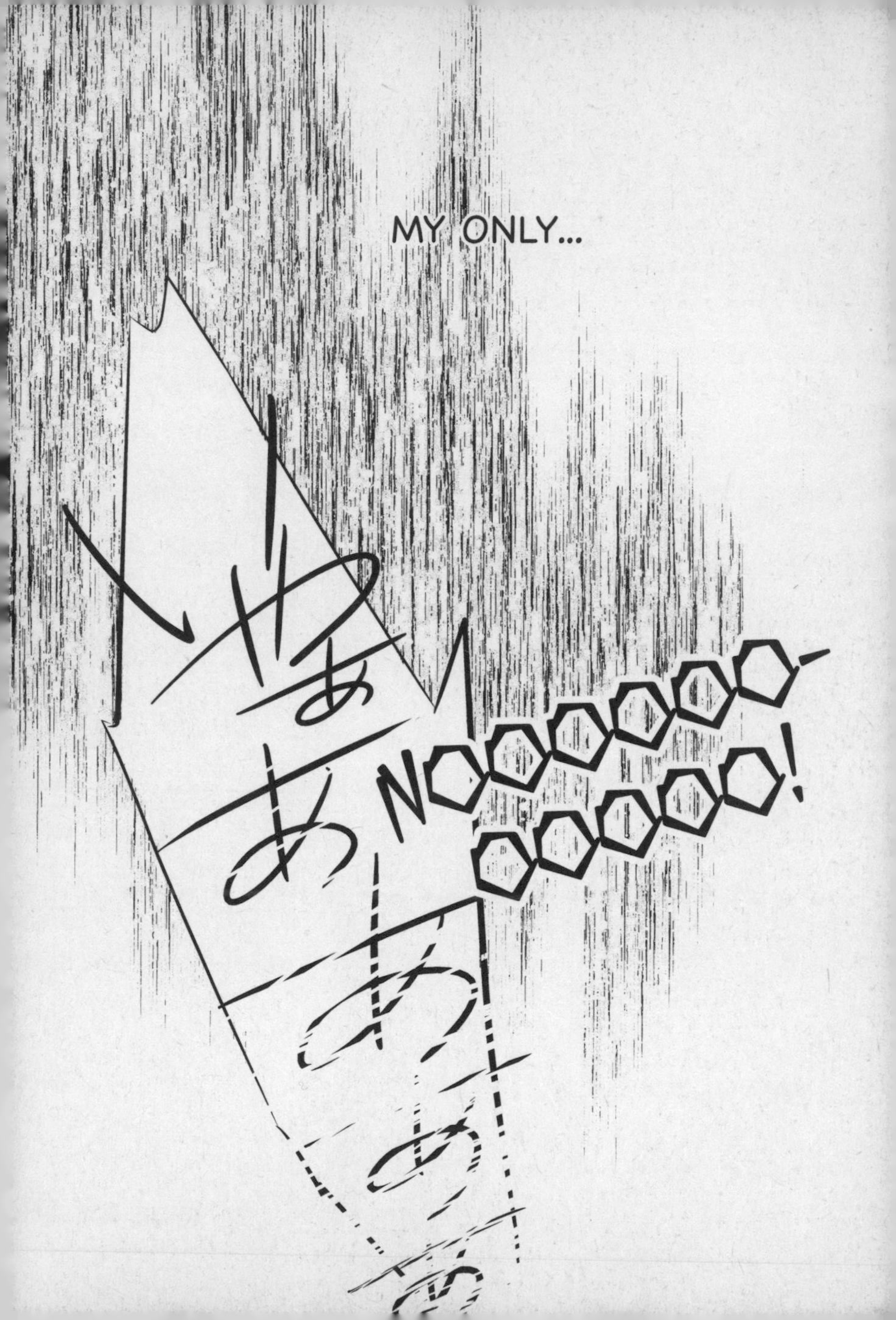
MY ONLY...
NOOOOOOO-
OOOOOO!

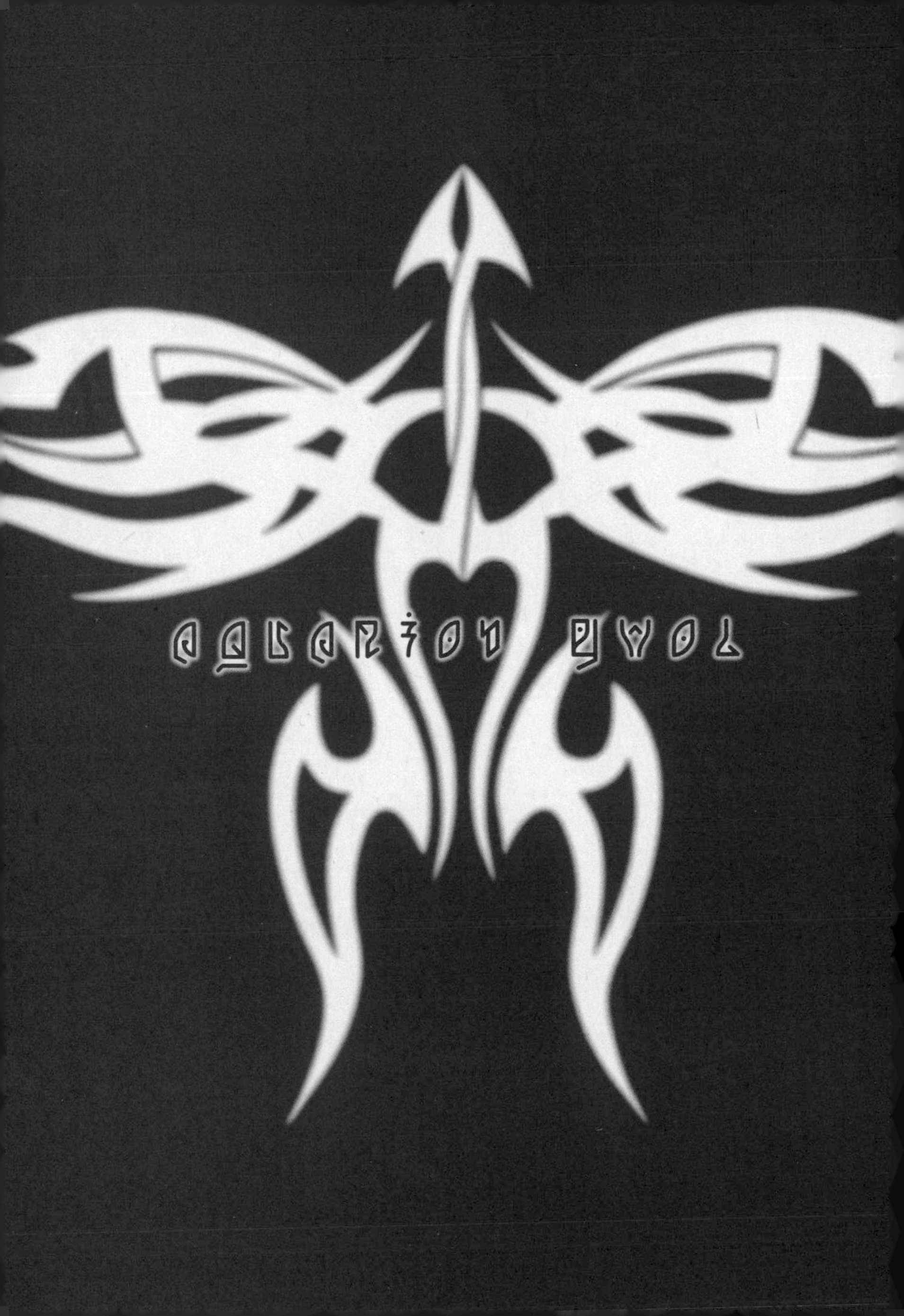

NEXT UNION

The fourth volume...